They Called Me "King Tiger"

They Called Me "King Tiger"

My Struggle for the Land and Our Rights

Reies López Tijerina

Translated from the Spanish and edited by José Angel Gutiérrez
With a Foreword by Henry A. J. Ramos

Arte Público Press
Houston, Texas

This volume is made possible through grants from the Rockefeller Foundation and the Charles Stewart Mott Foundation.

Recovering the past, creating the future

Arte Público Press
University of Houston
Houston, Texas 77204-2174

Cover design by Ken Bullock

Cover photo and eight-page photo insert courtesy of
Reies López Tijerina's personal collection

Tijerina, Reies López.
   [Mi lucha por la tierra. English]
   They called me "King Tiger": my struggle for the land and our rights /
by Reies López Tijerina ; translated from the Spanish and edited by José
Angel Gutiérrez.
      p.   cm. — (The Hispanic civil rights series)
   Includes bibliographical references.
   ISBN 1-55885-302-2 (alk. paper)
   1. Mexican Americans—New Mexico—Social conditions—
20th century. 2. Mexican Americans—New Mexico—Economic
conditions—20th century. 3. Land tenure—New Mexico—History—
20th century. 4. Tijerina, Reies. 5. Civil rights workers—New
Mexico—Biography. 6. Mexican Americans—New Mexico—
Biography. 7. Civil rights movements—New Mexico—History—
20th century. 8. New Mexico—Ethnic relations. I. Gutiérrez,
José Angel. II. Title. III. Series.
F805.M5 T5413 2000
978.9'0046873—dc21   00-059426

0 1 2 3 4 5 6 7 8 9   10 9 8 7 6 5 4 3 2 1

To the Tijerina children between Reies and María Reies Hugh "David" (deceased), Rosa, Daniel (deceased), Raquel, Ira de Ala, and Noe. And to all other *valientes* seldom mentioned in the struggle for *la tierra:* Santiago Anaya, Valentina Valdez, Bobby López, Moisés Morales, Juan Valdez, Félix Martínez, Ventura Chávez, Baltazar Martínez, and the many others still unnamed.

Foreword

They Called Me "King Tiger": My Struggle for the Land and Our Rights is the memoir of one of the Chicano Movement's most significant and forceful personalities. Reies López Tijerina was a New Mexico-based Pentecostal preacher, who for a decade spanning the late 1950s to the late 1960s, organized Spanish-speaking families across the southwestern U.S. to seek repatriation of lands obtained by North American Anglos in violation of the Treaty of Guadalupe Hidalgo (the 1848 treaty that ended the U.S.-Mexico War). Tijerina's movement, which ultimately consisted of efforts to reclaim disputed properties by force and Tijerina's own indictment and arrest by federal authorities following an armed raid on a New Mexico courthouse that he led, defined important elements of the Chicano Movement. In stark contrast to more conventional community leaders of the day (ranging from conservatives like the American G.I. Forum's Dr. Hector P. García to progressives like inspirational United Farm Workers' principal César Chávez—leaders who sought reform through extant U.S. governance processes), Tijerina openly defied federal and state authorities, and advocated radical change in U.S. policy and governance.

In effect, Reies López Tijerina was the Malcolm X of the Chicano community. He both frightened and enraged Anglo Americans, as well as more conservative Mexican Americans. As a youth, I vividly remember my father, a conservative Latino World War II veteran and businessman, commenting on Tijerina. To my father and many others of his generation, Tijerina was someone to be disdained. He was unAmerican. He was an extremist. He was violent.

To be sure, Tijerina was the nation's most controversial Mexican American in an era of controversy. More than any other individual of his times, he stood as an unedited commentator on the Chicano community's plight in U.S. society. Always charismatic, but at times venal and racist, Tijerina was unafraid to think the unthinkable, to say the unspeakable. He challenged the American legal and political system as no Chicano leader before him or since has. He defied all the rules.

Largely for these reasons, Tijerina remains controversial still today among those who remember him. But thirty years following his heyday, in an era marked by political lethargy, Tijerina has been mainly forgotten. Few younger U.S. Latinos born in the years following the 1960s recognize the name Tijerina; and U.S. history books, so inclined to overlook the experiences of Spanish-speaking peoples in American culture, never have found a comfortable way to acknowledge his story.

But Tijerina's story is an important one, however uncomfortable it may be to many, even most contemporary observers. Notwithstanding lingering questions about Tijerina's judgment, his strategies, and even his sanity, it cannot be denied that Reies López Tijerina led one of the most significant movements on behalf of modern Chicano civil rights that our nation has seen. In waging his war for the land, Tijerina inspired countless community and youth leaders of the era to take up the cause of organized resistance. Although the movement's more confrontational elements were appropriately quelled, the engagement and passion of unprecedented numbers of Chicano community members (and especially youth) around Tijerina's struggles played an important role in galvanizing a new consciousness among the Latino people of the U.S. This new consciousness ultimately reinforced the efforts of Latino civil rights leaders and groups of the 1960s to push successfully for the broader recognition and inclusion of Spanish-speaking people and issues in American policy making.

Because of his significant contributions to community organizing and empowerment efforts of Chicano/Latino groups of the 1960s, Arte Público Press offers Tijerina's memoir (ably translated from its original Spanish text and condensed by fellow '60s activist José Angel Gutiérrez) as a seminal entry in its Civil Rights Book Series. This series, supported by leading U.S. funding institutions, such as the Charles Stewart Mott Foundation and The Rockefeller Foundation, seeks to expand national understanding and appreciation of the significant struggles and contributions of post-World War II Latinos in American civic culture. By elevating attention to Latino community issues, leaders, and institutions that have shaped contemporary American realities, the series is intended to enhance popular recognition of the national Latino community's essential place in modern American society and history.

They Called Me "King Tiger": My Struggle for the Land and Our Rights is Reies López Tijerina's personal account of one of Latino America's most dramatic modern claims to recognition, recompense, and self-determination. It stands as an important chronicle of the 1960s Chicano Movement and will inspire, even today, much provocation for thought and debate on the meaning of being American at the outset of the 21st century.

Henry A. J. Ramos
Executive Editor
Latino Civil Rights Book Series Arte Público Press

Introduction

Reies Lopez Tijerina, one of the principal leaders of the Chicano Movement of the 1960s, began keeping a diary of events in 1974. He wanted to write about his twenty-year struggle for the land, from 1956 to 1976. He would turn fifty years of age in 1976 and wanted to leave a memoir of his efforts. He used these diary entries to write his autobiography. According to Tijerina, with the help of Gregorio Casuals, José Antonio, and Verónica Alvarez, he made contact with the publishing house Fondo de Cultura Económica in Mexico, and they expressed an interest in his manuscript.[1] On January 28, 1978, the Fondo de Cultura Económica published Tijerina's 575-page autobiography in Spanish, with a print run of 5,000 copies.

Reies autographed and dedicated book number 1,585 to me on April 8, 1978, with these words, *"Con respeto y memorias hago este regalo a José Angel Gutiérrez—Después de muchos años, nuestra amistad y mutuo respeto ha crecido más y más."* His book was never reviewed in the United States. Consequently, Tijerina's life story, his version of events that catapulted him into a leadership role in the Chicano Movement, his world view, and the identity of others involved with him during the years 1956 to 1976, remained hidden from or ignored by all of us who read only English. Tijerina, rightfully or wrongfully, wanted it this way. He had been approached by Doubleday in 1975 (319)[2] and later by Samuel Stewart of McGraw-Hill (288, 294) to write his autobiography, but he declined their offers. He did not want to write in English. By 1978, several books about Tijerina and the land recovery movement had been written in English.[3] He was critical of these books, and said so, but did not write his version of events or story in English.

xi

I maintained contact with Reies over the years. On August 20, 1994, while I was visiting him in Albuquerque, he asked me to find a way to have his autobiography translated into English.[4] This is that effort. He also gave me another manuscript he had written.[5] I have condensed his book. There are approximately eight pages of photographs in the original edition that are not reproduced here. The twenty-page prologue by Jorge A. Bustamante in the original work is also not reproduced here. I labored with the question of including or omitting Bustamante's lengthy but excellent introduction. President Luis Echeverría Alvarez and Jorge A. Bustamante were concerned with the ignorance of the Mexican reading public about the Chicano Movement and Tijerina's role within it. Their concern was addressed by the prologue in the original work. Perhaps their concern is just as valid today, not only among Spanish-reading Mexicans but also among English-reading Hispanics ignorant of this chapter in the history of our people.

The name of Reies López Tijerina, along with the Chicano Movement, has died in the public arena. There is no contemporary public discussion of that movement or its leaders. The various campuses that once had Chicano Studies programs and courses have declined. "Chicano" as a self-descriptive term has lost out to Hispanic. There are few Chicanos and Chicanas left. Almost everyone is either Hispanic or Latina/Latino. There is very little formal study in any institution of higher learning of the land recovery movement led by Tijerina and of the Chicano Movement. Yet, Reies López Tijerina is very much alive and still active today. On October 19, 1999, for example, he presented the University of New Mexico with his archival material. On November 5, 1999, he was in Austin, Texas, meeting with senior staff of Governor George W. Bush, discussing land titles and land issues in Texas and the Southwest. The man lives but has been relegated to that historical abyss of forgotten heroes.

Jorge A. Bustamante's *Prólogo*

Jorge A. Bustamante's lengthy *Prólogo* in the original work begins with an explanation of Tijerina, the uneducated Chicano leader, in the context of his environment and in the larger context of Chicano history.

Professor Bustamante details the history of persons of Mexican ancestry (Chicanos) that remained in the lands Mexico ceded to the United
States after the war of 1846-48. The Chicano history Dr. Bustamante
presents is one of marginalization and subordination of Mexicans by
Anglos and contains ample documentation with extensive footnotes.
Professor Bustamante discusses the various political stages of resistance and struggle that the Mexican, now American, community
engaged in from 1848 to the present time. In this latter era, Bustamante
places Tijerina as a central figure in the struggle for civil rights by Chicanos in the United States. Bustamante describes the various other
organizations active in political work at the time Tijerina reached his
zenith. He briefly explains the unique struggle of these various organizations, such as the *Movimiento Estudiantil Chicano de Aztlán*
(MEChA), Brown Berets, Raza Unida Party, Mexican American Political Association (MAPA), and United Farm Workers. Bustamante also
provides statistical data to show the socioeconomic disparity between
Chicanos and the rest of the population, as well as the condition of Chicanos in the various states of the Southwest. Bustamante cited the work
of various U.S. academicians and especially recommended such Chicano scholars as Rodolfo Acuña, Carlos Cortez, Juan Gómez Quiñónez,
Octavio Romano, Américo Paredes, and Ernesto Galarza in support of
his interpretation of Chicanos in the United States and their Chicano
Movement.

Note on Methodology

I had many problems with the translation of this work. First, getting someone to volunteer to do this project proved fruitless. Nicolás
Kanellos of Arte Público Press provided support and commitment to
publish a translated and abridged edition of Tijerina's book. Hiring
someone to undertake the work was cost prohibitive. I ended up doing
the bulk of the work. Clarissa Martínez de Castro, Texas Office director for the National Council of La Raza, translated some of the pages.
Second, translating is but one side of the coin; there is still the composition of a new manuscript. Karen Magee and I did all that work. Karen
worked long hours trying to decipher my dictation and tirelessly pro-

duced draft after draft for me to review and edit. I thank Clarissa and Karen for their assistance. Third, there was the immense responsibility of editing some 600 printed pages of Tijerina's words into fewer pages. What to take out? What to leave in? How to summarize the way he wrote it became constant preoccupations with every paragraph and page. I am sure Reies López Tijerina will not be completely pleased. All he originally wrote is not in these pages. Such a book would be too expensive for many interested persons. Fourth, the actual task of translation often met with difficulty. All books contain typographical errors and even some factual errors. I am sure that the editors of the Fondo de Cultura Económica had great difficulty understanding Tijerina's handwriting and the spelling of names. Some name errors in the original text are so obvious that I took the liberty of translating the incorrect word in Spanish into the correct English word. For example, the name of Jerry Noll, an Alianza member and leader, was misspelled as Jerry Roll in the original (171), the Internal Revenue Service (IRS) was incorrectly abbreviated (201) as IPS (Internal Prevenue Service). The name of the Native American tribal chief Mad Bear was misspelled as Bad Bear (209). Beverly Exalrod (221) was corrected to Axelrod; Bob Brawn (217) was corrected to Brown; and Elfidio Baca was corrected to Elfego Baca (401). More substantive and obvious errors were, for example, "*El New York Times había publicado el libro Tijerina and the Court House Raid.*" (354) and "*Hoy leí en el periódico Sear's Catalogue sobre la relación del senador Montoya con la mafia de Arizona.*" (495). In the chapter on events in 1975, several entries were misdated such as *28 de febrero,* and *29 de febrero,* which should be dates in the month of May (518–519).

Tijerina's use of various names for the same organization of land claimants and for the land claimants themselves caused me concern. Tijerina used interchangeably the names *Alianza de Pueblos y Pobladores, Alianza Federal de Mercedes,* and *Alianza de Pueblos Libres* in the manuscript referring to the organization. In this work, I simply use the term *Alianza* to refer to the organization. The membership and his followers were described *en español* as *valientes, pueblo de la tierra,* and *gente de la tierra.* I either used members or followers or supporters and, occasionally, people of the land or Southwest. Similarly, Tijerina uses the word pueblo to mean community, people, and Native American tribes. At times, Tijerina referred to the Treaty of Guadalupe-Hidalgo as simply the Treaty of Guadalupe. It is the same treaty. A more difficult translation issue arose with Tijerina's use of the term *Indohispano*[6] as an ethnic group designation for the ethnic community also known as Chicanos, Mexican Americans, Hispanic, and Mexican. Unfortunately, Tijerina is not clear when he wants the reader to know he is referring to a Mexican from Mexico, a Chicano in the Southwest, and Hispanics in the United States. I did the best I could within the context of the wording to affix an appropriate descriptor. He often used Mexican police or agent, in contrast to Anglo police or agent, to mean a Chicano or as he would say, an Indohispano. He personally prefers the term Indohispano as a self-descriptor and explains his rationale in his work. Fifth, the organization of Tijerina's book is not consistent. There are seven chapters in the original work. He began his book with the events of the year of 1956. Clearly, he spent more time in writing Chapter 2, *Mi vida de fugitivo,* than any other chapter. At 307 pages in length, this is the longest chapter, and a book in itself. Tijerina entitled every chapter in his book by year, except the second and last. The third chapter is about events during the year of 1970 and includes activities of the next three years. In chapter four, he continues with events in the year 1974, followed by the chapters on 1975 and 1976. In these chapters, he literally relied on his diary entries to compose his narrative. Because these chapters probably are the actual diary entries, the composition leaves a lot to be desired. Tijerina wrote these chapters in a choppy and fragmented prose. He not only explains what happened on a given day, but also adds his thoughts and ideas, some related and others unrelated to the happenings, within that daily entry. Many entries in these chapters suffer from a lack of cohesion; the prose or subject matter does not flow. The words seem disjointed, unconnected, and isolated. It just doesn't read well. But that is exactly how diary entries are written, as thought fragments to prompt recall at a later time to their author. I assume that Tijerina, tired of maintaining a diary over so many years, had resorted to shorter and briefer entries toward the end of the book. There are entries in the last chapters consisting of a single sentence. The last chapter on the Central Intelligence

Agency (CIA) is somewhat prophetic. Government surveillance of the Chicano community, as of other groups and leaders, such as the Southern Christian Leadership Conference (SCLC) and Rev. Martin Luther King, Jr., and the American Indian Movement, were just coming to light at the time Tijerina was writing his autobiography. Throughout his book, Tijerina made frequent mention of the government conspiracy to destroy the Chicano movement, his land recovery movement, him, his brothers, and family. He was correct and on target in his paranoia. The CIA and the Federal Bureau of Investigation (FBI) both maintained surveillance of the Alianza and Tijerina for years. I have those files, particularly the FBI file on Tijerina and other Chicano organizations and leaders.[7] Lastly, in his book Tijerina used terms of endearment, at times, for two of his brothers, Margarito and Anselmo, and referred to them as Mague and Chemo, respectively. These are not other family members or supporters. He also used the formal and respectful title given to senior members of the community, Don and Doña, for some individuals. I have kept those references to his brothers and community elders as written.

Reies López Tijerina: The Movement Leader

I admired Reies López Tijerina for his political courage and leadership when I was a beginner in Chicano politics and activism. Reies was truly a revolutionary. He did what Malcolm X and the Black Panthers only talked about. He waged war against the state of New Mexico and the United States government. Armed with the constitutional power of citizen's arrest, he set out after many high-profile individuals in state and federal positions, including the chief justice of the United States Supreme Court. He literally took possession and control of illegally occupied land in New Mexico. He set the stage for Native Americans to press and obtain their land claims. He began early coalition and alliance building with black leaders and organizations. He internationalized Chicano politics and sought relations with the government of Mexico, Spain, and the United Nations. By raising the issue of property rights and land grant claims, he was the first architect of Aztlán. And he was proclaimed the first National Hero of Aztlán (345).

I regret that he went to jail for crimes he did not commit and lost valuable time. Reies and his family paid an extremely high price on our behalf. And, we do not know how to take care of our leaders. Ultimately, Reies lost control of agenda-setting within the Chicano Movement and lost his following. Parole conditions prohibited him from holding office within the Alianza or speaking about land recovery. Today, no Hispanic leader talks about nation building (Aztlán) or raises the issue of land recovery. I regret he was unable to expand his media message about the Alianza and the land recovery movement beyond Albuquerque and most of New Mexico. And I regret that Reies, César, Corky, and I could not find the way to join forces during years we had the attention and support of Chicanas and Chicanos across the country. My hope is that this small effort of translating the autobiography of one of our great leaders during the Chicano Movement will lead to deeper understanding of leadership, social movements, organizational politics, strategy and tactics, power relationships, judicial power, land grants, and history. These are a few topics to be found in Tijerina's work. I also hope that reading this will inspire some to take up the cause of land recovery or at least begin to raise the issue of getting our land back and making one Mexico.

José Angel Gutiérrez

Notes

[1]According to Professor Jorge A. Bustamante, then a professor at the Colegio de México, Reies López Tijerina sought out former president of Mexico Luis Echeverría Alvarez, asking for help in publishing his autobiography. Tijerina tendered his voluminous, handwritten, manuscript to the former president. Echeverría, in turn, called on the publishing house Fondo de Cultura Económica to review the material and also asked Dr. Bustamante to help the publishing project along by writing an introduction about the Chicano Movement and Tijerina's role in that larger struggle. Echeverría thought the Mexican public was largely ignorant of the Chicano Movement and its principal actors and objectives. Tijerina's narrative, without such a prologue placing Tijerina within the context of the larger social protest movement of Chicanos, would not be understood or appreciated by the Mexican public. Tijerina resisted this addition to his lengthy manuscript, but was finally convinced by Echeverría and Bustamante that such an introduction would prepare the Mexican reader to understand more fully and completely the detail in the book. All three, Tijerina, Echeverría, and Bustamante, wanted the book to make an impact and enjoy the merit that it deserved.

[2]This notation, and all others like it, are page references in the original work.

[3]See, for example, Michael Jenkinson, *Tijerina* (Albuquerque: Paisano Press, 1968); Peter Nobokov, *Tijerina and the Courthouse Raid* (Albuquerque: University of New Mexico, 1969); Richard Gardner, *Grito! Reies Tijerina and the New Mexico Land Grant War of 1967* (Indianapolis: Bobbs-Merrill, 1970); and, Patricia Bell Blawis, *Tijerina and the Land Grants: Mexican Americans in Struggle for their Heritage* (New York: International Publishers, 1971).

[4]His authorization to translate and publish his book was witnessed by Rees Lloyd, Patricia Tober, and Fred Reade.

[5]The working title is *My Life, Judaism and the Nuclear Age.*

[6]On October 19, 1999, the University of New Mexico, Zimmerman Library, hosted a reception and ceremony for Reies López Tijerina. The occasion was the presentation of his personal collection of archival material. The program description was entitled "Commemorating El Día del Indio-Hispano." At the bottom of the program sheet was a quote attributed to Reies López Tijerina, circa 1969, *"They won't let us be Americans. We are not Spaniards. We are not Indians. We are Indo-Hispanos. We have found ourselves as a people."* The variations in the spelling of the term are numerous.

[7]See, for example, Ernesto B. Vigil's *The Crusade for Justice: Chicano Militancy and the Government's War on Dissent* (Madison: University of Wisconsin Press, 1999) for such a study on the role the FBI and other police agencies had in damaging the organization and individual members.

Chapter 1

1956

Finally we had found a hundred and sixty acres of land in the desert of Arizona. We paid fourteen hundred dollars for this virgin territory. Here I would take my family and those who accompanied me in this great adventure. They were few but very brave. I considered them brave because they knew, as I did, that we had left behind the cities, with all their vanity and corruption. We had abandoned a form and a style of life that we considered evil and opposed to the road to justice that had been indicated to us by the Man from the Holy Land. The brave ones accompanying me were Manuel Mata, Rodolfo Márez, Juan Reyna, Vicente Martínez, Francisco Flores, Simón Serna, Luis Moreno. All had families. We had pooled our money to buy this piece of land. I would have wanted a place in Texas, where I was born and raised, where my mother was buried, but we could not find such a place. The land was very expensive, and we did not have much money. The brave ones who followed me had worked the summer of 1955 in Fruta, Colorado, on the ranch owned by Bill Byers, and we were only able to save a bit of money. After we bought this land, we had about five hundred dollars left. I had fought with the church (with all religions) during ten long years, trying to get it to take the side of the poor in the struggle against the rich, but I had failed. They told me and I convinced myself that my struggle was futile. I began looking for an alternative. Saving my family and whomever else wanted to separate themselves from the system of the church and corrupt society was my alternative.

Here on the desert of Arizona, my soul would find the peace and security that we all wished for. We decided to call this land, this virgin land, Valley of Peace. Here, neither the church nor the school would be able to condition the minds of our children. We were far from danger, from temptation, from the influences of monopolies, and we would be happy. Like ants, we began to move the dirt. For the time being, each family lived under a tree, while each of us dug a cave from the garbage dumps near the cities of Casa Grande and Eloy, Arizona. We got car hoods to cover our subterranean caves. Quickly, we made friends with persons near the Valley of Peace. By day we picked cotton to earn our food, and by night we continued excavating the dirt to make our homes. Our dreams and convictions quickly expanded throughout the state of Arizona. I went to Phoenix and obtained permission for our colony to construct and erect a school for our kids. Mexicans, Indians, and Blacks from the surrounding areas began to visit us. Many of them would tell us their problems and their grievances. No sooner had I gotten the first one out of jail than I was expected to attend to all the others who came. Mothers, fathers, wives, and other relatives came to see me so that I would get their loved ones out of jail.

Our lives at the Valley of Peace were simple. Our women would make our clothing and our dress for the entire family. They would cook on stoves made from gasoline tanks that we found in the garbage dumps. Everyone educated his or her own children. The food was a common pantry. Between us all, we cleaned up one hundred and sixty acres. We converted this land into what we considered a paradise. We soon were enamored with our paradise. We were very happy. No one spoke of returning to their hometowns, and, meanwhile, the neighbors would come and go.

On the 18th of April of 1956, the first resident of the Valley of Peace was born. I helped my wife with the birth. The girl was born in the subterranean home that I had built with my own hands. I was nearly thirty, and this home was the first home that I had built in my entire life. It cost me sixty days of work, but not one penny. When my wife gave birth, I took the child in my arms and I named her Ire of Allah (Wrath of God). When she was born, I saw a rattlesnake at the head of the bed. I moved my wife and newborn daughter away from that corner and killed that snake. Some ten years earlier, the United States had begun to make atomic bombs day and night without pause. And they continued. I was convinced that the church harmed humanity more than any other organization on earth. I knew that if there was a just God, he had to be angry and unhappy with those that managed our government and religion here on earth, and that is the reason that I gave my daughter the name of Ire of Allah.

I also was very unhappy with the form in which men are managed. From the beginning of the year, various members of the school board for the county of Pima came to visit us. They wanted us to send our kids to the schools in Casa Grande and Eloy. We refused, giving them a legal excuse, but they insisted. We told them about the horrible crimes committed against an eight-year-old girl. She was waiting for a school bus on the road named Sun Land Gin Road. One day she didn't come home. Two days later they found her dead. Later, an Anglo male was accused of having raped her. Our children had to cross three miles of desert to get to where the bus would pick them up. We asked for police protection for them and they denied it. The school board, however, aligned themselves with the state politicians and the police. They all aligned themselves against the Valley of Peace and began to cause us problems. Although the prosecutor and the judges demonstrated disgust toward the inhabitants of the Valley of Peace, our children were able to attend our own private school.

One day a jet, a war plane, crashed on our property. The explosion scared us. We reported it, and they came to remove the remains of the airplane, but they did not ask about any damages or harm suffered by our inhabitants at the Valley of Peace. Neighbors from Toltec and other surrounding communities would bring their children to play with ours. Only the first few months did we enjoy ourselves with the peace and liberty that we sought. It was the Anglos who began to cause us difficulty. The Pima Indians, natives of these lands, never caused us problems, nor did the Blacks, much less the Mexicans.

At the beginning, I did not know what the Anglos had at the base of their hearts and minds. I thought that the small problems that the Anglos spoke of were superficial and that momentarily they would disappear. But I was wrong. One day, a group of young Anglos on horseback, between fifteen and sixteen years of age, came by. Without talking to us, they rode their horses over our subterranean homes. The roofs began to give, and dirt began to fall inside our habitations. They ran their horses over one house after another with pistols in their hands. The first time they did this, we ignored them. We thought that, being children, they would soon tire and leave us alone. But this was not the whole of it. One day we came from working, picking cotton, and we found two of our homes without rooftops. Some of our brave ones had made homes with wood and palm leaves. We had found two burned to the ground with all their belongings. Manuel, Rodolfo, and I went to report it to Sheriff Lawrence White. He listened to us and, at the beginning, indicated an interest in sending two of his agents out, but when we told him the markings on the horses that had been bothering us and told him from which ranch they came—we had followed them—Sheriff White changed his mind. He did not send anyone to investigate. We later related the same story to Don Pelkam, an FBI agent in Casa Grande, but he explained that that was not his jurisdiction. However, when the airplane, the jet plane had landed, had crashed on our property, this same agent had visited our colony. But now, he ignored us completely.

A week after my daughter was born, I was invited to California. Manuel and Rodolfo went with me. We stayed with Cecilia Moreno and her husband. I spoke to the people near the community of Visalia. While in Visalia, I got a phone call from Guadalupe Jáuregui. Guadalupe had remained in charge of the Valley of Peace. His news was bitter. On top of the injuries and damages we had suffered over the years by living there, we had just been flooded. "Your wife is living under a tree," Guadalupe said to me, "because the subterranean home is full of water." The news split my soul. I consulted with Manuel and Rodolfo and left the house. That night I could not sleep. Alone, I retired to meditate. I had recalled ten years earlier being in California. Back then, under similar circumstances, I had left my wife too fast to try to find my way in life. I felt great bitterness . . . "When am I going to find the mission for my life," I thought that night. I anguished knowing that my family lacked a home, food, and money, and I was unable to help them. All night I stayed outside the house. That night I had a vision: A man landed near my subterranean home. Behind him another landed to his right and surveyed the surroundings. Then a third, dressed similarly to the other two, landed nearby. The three sat over something that appeared to be a cloud. They spoke to me. My wife followed me. They told me they came from far away, that they were coming for me, and they would take me to an old ancient regime.

My wife said, "Why my husband? Aren't there others?"

The three responded, "There is no other in the world that can do this job. We have searched the earth and only he can do this."

At that moment, I interrupted and I asked, "What job?"

They responded, "Secretary."

And without saying more, they lifted themselves, and I saw them leaving high up above the ground, so far up that I fell backwards looking at them. I clearly saw their flight, and like a lightning bolt, the transport that they were on took them far, far away, and it seemed they landed in a dark pine woods. Others were around me, but I didn't know who nor how many. Finding myself suddenly in this dark forest, I felt a horrible fear. Never had I felt terror so strange. At that moment, all I thought was how to escape and leave there. I ran as fast as I could, looking for an exit, and soon I ran up against a cemetery full of horses. They all were frozen over the ground. One of these got up and came toward me. Without thinking, I climbed on him, and the horse took me out of that place. One of the beings that had been left there also jumped toward my horse and grabbed my waist. He never could climb on the horse, and the horse never touched the ground. It appeared to be flying.

Like lightning, I got to an ancient regime; a wall encircled that great city. I was received with great applause and greetings. I was carried on shoulders. Thousands and thousands surrounded me. A person was hanging from my waist. They would not let him come in. They told him, "You have no part in this and you cannot enter." I wanted to get down. I wanted them to let me go, but they would not let me. Upon entering in the city, I saw far away and I saw an ancient man dressed in white clothes down to the ground. Intuitively, I felt that this old man was a principal in this ancient regime. I was afraid. I thought all this was a great error. Finally, I obliged the multitude to put me on the ground. As I got closer to the old one, I saw the many wrinkles on his face. Little by little until I got to him, I thought his skin resembled that of a child, although his great age was obvious. Behind this old man were six or seven other persons of authority. They saw me with envy and jealousy.

When I got near the ancient one, he said, "Speak so I can know you."

Simultaneously feeling respect and terror, I said, "Yes, sir. Glad to meet you."

"Enough." He merely pulled out a key made of silver, and with the other hand, he didn't let me speak anymore. With one hand on my mouth, he pointed to a majestic area and said, "You shall reign over all of this." And he added, "And over you, only me." And he gave me the key.

Then he turned and looked at me and said, "Let's walk far over that way so you can see this majestic place and the great throne in the center."

At that moment I opened my eyes. The sun was shining on me. Although the night had been very cold and I had stayed outside the house, my body was very warm. This was completely strange to me, and I felt completely sure that I had witnessed a revelation, a vision, a super dream. I got up and ran to where Manuel and Rodolfo were. They were still in bed. I told them everything and felt that my heart was satisfied and sure. From that day on, I began to see things in a different way and to understand things that I did not understand before. I felt blessed in the weight of this mission that had just been given to me. Now my life would have a direction, and I would have the security that I was not alone. I believed in what I saw and planned on obeying, fulfilling the mission of those three persons whom I considered interplanetary messengers or angels.

"Let's go to the Valley of Peace," I told my brave ones.

The next day, we made arrangements and left for Arizona. I had a car. Simón Cerna, a new brave one, joined us with his family. In the Valley of Peace I brought all the families together, and I told them of the mission I had received at the hands of these three angels. We did not have any money, and, momentarily, it was important that we find food for our families. María and I had David, the oldest, Rosita, Danielito, Raquel, and Ire of Allah. We left in a caravan headed toward the state of Colorado. In the city of Fruta, Colorado, Rodolfo and Celia had their parents, and we already knew the rancher, Bill Byers, that harvested sugar beets during the month of May. There, all the families lived in a great excavation surrounded by trees. During the time that we worked there, we saw a clear signal against the blue sky. We saw a rainbow. I saved in my heart what that signified to me. From the day that I had that vision, I began to talk to my faithful companions about the new direction that we would seek. "Little by little," I said, "it will be revealed to us what we must do."

During those days I reviewed my life. I remembered that the people of Tierra Amarilla had invited me to their land in the years 1945, 1951, and 1952. I proposed a trip to New Mexico to the brave ones. "Whatever you say, Reies" was their response. I explained the details of this trip very carefully to the women. They all approved and were very satisfied. We decided to leave in the car belonging to Luis Moreno. We left behind the families while five of the brave ones went with me to Tierra Amarilla. We left a few brave ones and some of the older ones. Coming with me were Manuel, Rodolfo, Luis, Juan, and Simón, "The Cyclone." It was June 1956, when we left for New Mexico.

We got to the home of Zebedeo Martínez in Monero, New Mexico. We had dinner and conferred with Zebedeo Martínez, Zebedeo Valdez, and others. I asked them to relate to us the story of the land grant of Tierra Amarilla. They told me what they knew and offered to take me to Chama, Tierra Amarilla, and Ensenada. The next day we spoke with the older men from the surrounding areas. At the home of Cristino Lovato, they came to hear what I had to say. They all were members of the Society of Jesus: old Indian-looking Mestizos, truth and sincerity shining from their faces. Beginning with the oldest, everyone gave us a long, sordid, violent history of what had happened to them in New Mexico since the loss of their properties, their communal lands, *ejidos*. Over the centuries, they had depended on these lands to make their living. "Sweat, blood, and tears was all these men gave us."

I felt in my heart a stab: these ancient humble people had a just and sacred cause. I felt in my body and my soul and my spirit that these people were worthy of justice.

"Do you want justice?" I asked.

They all answered me, "For more than a hundred years we have asked Washington and heaven, but no one does us justice."

I told them that I had preached for ten years from the Bible and that, although I did not know anything about the land that they fought for, I was willing to study the documents, the history, and the law behind these land grants. I had but one condition: we had to unite. We had to re-gather the strength that the Anglos had taken from us.

I spoke to them for more than two hours. Although they did not notice, I noticed that they were conditioned by the education of the Anglos, and they were fearful. My first job would be to remove that fear. They were intimidated, and this was not going to be easy.

When I asked for the titles to their lands, they answered, "We don't have them."

The same lawyers that represented us and the Treaty of Guadalupe Hidalgo had stolen them.

They responded, "We don't know that treaty. We thought that Guadalupe Hidalgo was a man that had been president of Mexico."

I told them that I would have to go to Mexico to look for all of the things that we would need in this struggle. Graciously, they offered me help for this trip to Mexico, but I refused. We returned to Fruta, Colorado, and bought a bus for those going to the Valley of Peace. I took my family to Texas and left them at my brother Ramón's farm. I was thirty years old when I left for Mexico. I did not know anyone in the Mexican capital city. I stayed in Mexico for three months.

Before anything else, though, I visited the Villa de Guadalupe, where the Treaty of Guadalupe Hidalgo was signed. Then, I visited the castle at Chapultepec, where the young soldiers told me the story of the six hero children. When the United States waged war against Mexico to steal their land in 1847, those cadets, rather than surrender to the Anglos, fought to the end. The last one of the cadets, wrapped in the flag of Mexico, flung himself to the ground from the castle heights. From there I went to the General National Archives and began to study the archives. I learned to read sixteenth-, seventeenth-, and eighteenth-century Spanish. I made friends in the colleges, at the National University of Mexico, and also with members of the government, lawyers, and members of the Catholic Church. I related the story to the press of the forgotten Mexico in the United States. Again, I went to the Villa de Guadalupe, forty-five days later. I knew the beginnings of the history of the Aztecs, Mayas, Incas, Chichimecas, and the Meshicas. But these trips oriented me better about the history of Mexico.

For the first time, I had a book in my hands, *las leyes de las Indias* (The Laws of the Indies), nine books in three volumes: 6,500 laws. I knew and felt that I had to study "The Laws of the Indies" very well to help my oppressed brothers in the United States. Here was the law that gave form and character to the Mexicans. These laws had governed the Indies [Americas] for more than three hundred years. One day, I went with some students to the famous Tepito. "Here," they told me, "you can find the old books on the Treaty of Guadalupe Hidalgo." For an hour I looked and found nothing. Then, they took me to Lagunilla second-hand market. There, I found a book on international law by attorney Pedro Zanabria, published in 1954. In this book was the Treaty of Guadalupe Hidalgo. I paid twenty-five cents for it and took it straight home. I began to study it, letter by letter, with careful attention. Again, I went to Teotihuacan, where the great pyramids of the Sun and the Moon are located. I visited the city of San Juan Teotihuacan. I spoke with the people there and made friends among the older residents. They gave me different stories of the origin of the place. "Place of the Gods." "Where the Gods and humans meet." My faith believed everything, saved everything. A doctor and attorney, Mr. Nieves, director of the Restorers of Anahuac, gave me a lot of information on Mexico (Tenochtitlan) and its history.

I went for the third time to the great pyramids. One time I climbed to the summit of each. And I stayed there a long time, thinking about the sad history of my people in New Mexico, Texas, and California. I meditated over the vision of the three angels and of that ancient regime. I felt like a stranger on this great planet. It was old, and I did not know the history of my own people, much less that of the world. Something intuitively told me that I had to study and learn many things so that I could understand the rights of my people and how I could help them. But like fire and a surge of lightning, I felt in me the strength and determination running in my veins like a consuming fire. I felt that it was getting late for me to return to the old men in New Mexico and unite them into a strong force with the goal of removing the fear the Anglo had placed in their hearts through their foreign education. That day, I returned to the home of Mr. Santana Vergara, who graciously boarded me. My soul was completely tranquil and pacific. That night I had such a real dream that for many days I was still absorbed and pen-etrated by it. In that dream, I found myself amidst the magnates of Mexico and the continent. But I treated them with a confidence that only exists between brothers of the same family.

Christmas and the New Year arrived and I was still in Mexico. From the first two weeks since I had arrived in Mexico, the memory of my children and my wife accompanied me. Now, after ninety days, I felt a drowning sensation to be with them. But the longer I stayed in Mexico, the more I discovered great surprises. I decided to return to my family and to the Valley of Peace with my brave ones. I gave thanks to the Vergara family. During my stay in Mexico, although my mission was one and strict, the forces of the world were also active against me. A niece of Mr. Vergara, who had been assigned to show me the princi-pal places of interest, behaved like a sister toward me at the beginning. At the end she was in love with me without me knowing. She was twenty and I was thirty years old. The great respect that I had for her doubled, knowing that she joined in my visions and dreams that had brought me to Mexico. The more I told her of my passion for the oppressed people in New Mexico, of the tears of my people that were being shed in search of justice for the last hundred years, the more she took a liking to me. And the more serious and irrational her love for me became. My struggle against the oppressors of my community was as large as the internal struggle in my heart for this *mestiza, indohispana.* She filled all the characteristics of beauty and loveliness that I had seen of Indian women depicted on calendars in Mexico. I did not find the wisdom to comfort her nor the intelligence to quiet her. Finally, with my promise that I would return, she became tranquil. But in my heart, there was no room for competitors in the struggle for the liberty and justice of my community. I knew that only time would cure this young woman of her false illusions. My heart had already decided everything.

I returned from Mexico confident in my mission. I had consulted with many lawyers about the rights of the original settlers, the owners of land grants and of the communal lands. Before having gone to Mexico, I had talked with my brothers Anselmo and Margarito. I told them the news that I would no longer preach religion. "From today on," I told them, "I am going to fight for the lands of my people. I am going to confront the Anglos that stole them from my people." When I returned from Mexico, I went again to see Margarito. He told me he was tired of living in San Antonio. Before I left for Mexico, he had promised me that he would return with me to the Valley of Peace. I came to get him. He was ready.

We left the for the Valley of Peace the first days in January 1957. Margarito had been on parole since 1950. He was tired of having to report. Rodolfo Mares came from the Valley of Peace for my family and me. Margarito understood that we would have to fight physically against those who would oppress us. That is why he left without notice or reporting to his parole officer. I did not know anything about this. On the contrary, I would have told him to notify his parole officer.

In the Valley of Peace, many of the people were waiting for me to help get their people out of jail. They waited to consult with me over many of the affronts that they suffered at the hands of the police, the schools, the ranchers that didn't want to pay them their wages, etc. I did not know what to do with so many problems and so many grievances. I did not even know what the Anglos would do with the Valley of Peace.

One January morning, directors from the Department of Education arrived at the Valley of Peace. This time they did not speak much. They only threatened us with jail unless every parent sent their kids to the Anglo schools. The brave ones and I understood that these people were angry and that they would put us in jail. We gathered all the families. We discussed the threats by the Anglos for more than six hours.

"Where is freedom in this free world?" asked Juan Reyna.

"Are they going to expel us from our homes and our own property?" asked the wife of Manuel Mata.

I had obtained a permit from the State Department of Education in Phoenix to educate our own kids. For three months, the brave ones and I had labored building a school. We had constructed a large, one-room school. But the Anglo students who lived near the Valley of Peace burned it to the ground. The paradise of peace had been converted into a concentration camp. The families felt fear and terror. It had been worthless to speak to the prosecutor. We sought relief and sympathy everywhere, but no Anglo felt sympathy or had consideration. I spoke to the magnates of education about the right the Supreme Court of the United States conferred on the Mennonites, the Amish of Pennsylvania, the Quakers in Ohio and other states in the eastern United States, granting people the right to educate their own kids. But no right, justice, or reason convinced those magnates. I could not believe it. We had left our states. We had sacrificed. As parents, we had separated ourselves from the world to find peace, and now they were taking our right to educate our kids away from us. With the threat of jail and with guns they obligated us to accept a foreign education that perverts the honor of the sexes.

"Don't these directors respect their own constitution that they have written?" asked Rodolfo.

At that time, I did not know that Rockefeller money was planning to build a model city about a mile from the Valley of Peace. For the moment, all I knew was that the Anglos did not want us to educate our own kids. All the doors were closed to us. I had asked for advice from the invisible forces, but there was no solution to the threats of violence from the Anglos. I asked myself, "Why don't they want us? Where does this great hate come from that manifests itself through these magnates?" They did not bother us because of our religion. They never invited us to their churches nor tried to take us to their reunions. But they did want our children in their schools. And by force, they decided to educate them.

The people of the Valley of Peace felt sorrow and bitterness. Manuel, Juan, and I went to Phoenix. As a last recourse, I went to the press. We described our case to the two great newspapers of Phoenix, but nothing was ever published about the history of the people of the Valley of Peace. What most pushed us to relocate to the desert were our children. We wanted to liberate them from the bad influence that was eroding family and spiritual unity. This influence, I was convinced, came directly from Anglo education. The Anglo believed that it was possible to discipline everything, except the family. Discipline the police, discipline the military, but they did not believe in disciplining the family. The brave ones that followed and I did not want that kind of education. Another thing that repulsed us about Anglo education was the perversion of the sexes. What they called "sexual education." The Anglos got lost going in that direction. We did not want to lose. So, after all we had worked for in the desert, and as far as we had gotten from civilization to save our children, we found ourselves lost and anguished.

After having asked heaven and earth to witness, we decided to leave. We left the state of Arizona and headed to New Mexico. The older ones that did not have children stayed behind in the Valley of Peace. Those of us with children went in the big bus that we had bought in Fruta, Colorado. Other families followed us in their own cars. We arrived in a town called Gobernador in New Mexico, the first days of February 1957. All dirt roads and the land were covered with snow. That is as far as we were able to go. Gobernador was an old city, completely abandoned. There was not a single soul. The cold and the snow obliged us to seek refuge in an abandoned church. After a few days, we ran out of food. The last thing we ate was rice without salt. The children began to cry and the women got very sad. On foot, my brother Margarito and I took to the road. Rodolfo and Simón went into the woods in search of animals to kill. By the second day, they found a frozen, dead deer. They built a fire and began to cook the deer meat. Then, they took it to the church and gave the deer meat to the women, as if they had killed it. They lied to save their families from hunger. Later, after time went by, Simón and Rodolfo confessed that they had not killed the deer, but had found it dead. Margarito and I arrived at the ranch of Manuel Trujillo, who gave us fifteen dollars so we could buy food for our families. He also loaned us a car with tire chains so that we could get our families out of that abandoned city.

Trujillo and his son, Maximiliano, cared for this ranch and its cows, but they lived in Lumberton, New Mexico. They told us the same story that the others had told us about Tierra Amarilla. They told us the same story of how the Anglos, through abuse and treachery of the laws, had stolen the land from the colonizers that were Hispanic. That was the way of life, they said. I would stay up late, talking and questioning

Don Manuel. Don Manuel offered us a ranch to live on, with our families. This man opened his heart to us. He showed us nothing but love and appreciation. He was our guardian angel who liberated us from the cold, from hunger, and from death.

Rodolfo and Simón were put in jail. A forest ranger had found them eating deer meat and arrested them. They did not want to tell him that the deer was dead when found. Later, they did tell the police the true story, but there was no room in the forest ranger's heart for justice or mercy. Don Manuel asked me, "Why are you, your women and children, out in this place during this cold and snow?" I explained to him our history and how I, at the beginning, had thought of coming to New Mexico with two of my brave ones, while our families remained at the Valley of Peace in Arizona. However, the directors of the board of education had forced us to send our children to their schools by a certain date or face jail. I told him this was the reason we had to leave with our families. Don Manuel showed us great consideration after listening to our story. He was eighty-five years old and knew the story of New Mexico. He was a wealthy man and had educated his children well. I considered having found him by accident a good sign. This man gave me the names of all the politicians who were powerful and managed New Mexico, as well as the name and history of each judge that controlled "justice" in New Mexico. Don Manuel Trujillo was my first and best teacher on the question of the land grants in New Mexico. I would tire him, asking questions day and night. He loved me a lot and took me into his confidence. Mountains and valleys surrounded his ranch. This place was full of paintings and writings in caves done by the Indians who had lived there hundreds of years earlier. I loved that place. There were a lot of deer and water in this hidden ranch.

Don Manuel, personally, took me to Tierra Amarilla, where he gathered all the members of the Brotherhood of Jesus, the Penitents, he knew. I again saw Cristino Lovato, Enetro Velásquez, José María Martínez (also known as Marion), and all those that I had visited in June 1956. I showed them the Treaty of Guadalupe Hidalgo and several legal opinions that I had obtained from attorneys in Mexico about the land grants (the *mercedes*) and the rights of the original settlers. Don Manuel left me in the home of Cristino Lovato. By day and by night, he would give me details of how the Anglos had taken the land of Tierra Amarilla. The names of Sargeant, T. D. Burn, Catron, Mundy, and others rang repeatedly. At a great meeting, I told them that the Anglos were on top because they built corporations and associations. I alluded, for example, to the American Bar Association and the American Medical Association, labor unions, unions of teachers, of police, of carpenters. In other words, everything was organized around an interest. I concluded, "You and I have many interests in common, but we are not united. We have to unite all of the heirs of the land grants in Tierra Amarilla. You live amid the great corporations of the Anglos, like dwarves among giants. If we unite all the land grants, we too can be giants along with the lawyers and the judges."

I returned to Don Manuel's hidden ranch. We gathered all the brave ones. Each group had gone to different communities in the area. Zebedeo Martínez and the other Zebedeo were present. We discussed the necessity of food for our people. We agreed that some would stay on Don Manuel's ranch, while others would go to the Valley of Peace and work the first harvest to make a little money so that we could return with our families. Rodolfo, Simón, and José stayed. Margarito, Zebedeo, and I would go to the Valley of Peace.

Arriving at the Valley of Peace, we were visited by Sheriff Lawrence White, gun in hand, with his deputies. One of the ranchers whose children had burned our school, had made false accusations against us. We were put in jail in Florence, Arizona, for ninety days. At the end of the ninety days, they dismissed the charges and released Zebedeo and me, but not Margarito, because he had a parole violation. This hurt my soul. I knew that the Anglos didn't want us in Arizona because we were "stirring up" the Mexicans. In reality, we were opening the eyes of the poor people. We were allowing "Wetback" Mexican workers, who had crossed the border illegally, into the Valley of Peace. A group of Mexican workers had given us a lot of information about the criminal tactics that several of the ranchers used against them when they were *braceros* (legal contract workers). They would make them work while withholding their wages until the *braceros* would rebel. Then, they would assassinate them. I had already made several protests without a positive result. Rumors along those lines, about a rancher who lived near Elgin, Arizona, were heard.

I was opening my eyes more and more with respect to the mentality of the Anglos. One day I visited my brother in jail and he told me, "I want you to do an urgent favor for this Anglo. He is in prison for robbery and his wife has a child. She doesn't know anyone and is there somewhere in Eloy, Arizona. Furthermore, she doesn't have any food or milk for the baby."

With a clean heart, my wife and I went to visit this young girl, about twenty years old. We took her home. We bought milk for the child, and my wife gave her a couple of dresses because this young woman didn't have but what she wore. I worked a lot for this Anglo. The wife's name was Terry. Finally, I got her husband out of prison. After two days, I was arrested and jailed. They accused me of trying to free my brother. I was released on a $1,000 bond and they accused Juan Reyna of assisting me. My appointed lawyer, someone named Sult, told me that the local politicians did not want me around. He advised me to leave the state of Arizona; otherwise, they would kill me. He also told me that the Anglo that I had helped get released from jail and his wife, Terry, would testify against me. "Leave while you are still alive," my lawyer told me. This hit me like a bolt of lighting. Leave? Make me a fugitive in the entire nation? And my family? And my brave ones?

In September, I gathered everyone at the Valley of Peace. I presented the case to the community. I would do what the majority wanted me to do. But if I became a fugitive, this would be what our adversaries wanted. Lose the Valley of Peace? Nobody wanted that. If I jumped bail and forfeited the money, we would also lose the one hundred sixty acres of the Valley of Peace.

Chapter 2

My Life As A Fugitive

The residents of the Valley of Peace voted to lose the land and save my life. From that day in October, I became a fugitive. I entered a new world. Now, I was a citizen of the night. My instinct became that of an animal. I would be fleeing hunters. I quickly discovered why deer and rabbits listen in all directions while they eat in the field. I felt the heavy weight that the judges had placed on me. At the time, I did not imagine all the implications of a fugitive's life. Little by little, I discovered the world of fugitives. Again, I picked up my family and left Arizona. By the next day, we were at Don Manuel's hidden ranch. I explained to them that I was a fugitive. My family began to feel the results of fugitive life. I would no longer be able to work as before. During the first few months, nobody bothered me. A state police officer, Freddie Martínez, knew that I was a fugitive, but because of his respect for Don Manuel, he never bothered me. Freddie would come often to Don Manuel's ranch to hunt deer. At other times, he did not bother with having to kill deer because his friends would do that for him. In December 1957, police surrounded Don Manuel's ranch. They arrested Manuel, Rodolfo, Zebedeo, and Jorge Carrillo. I managed to escape into the foothills. They charged them with having taken milk, sugar, lard, and beans from an abandoned camp. None of them pled guilty to these charges. These brave men had never been in jail, much less violated a law of the United States. They all had wives and families.

This winter was very cruel and crude. All the land was covered with snow. Freddie Martínez, the policeman, told Don Manuel that the FBI and the local Sheriff of San Juan County were looking for me.

Don Manuel posted bond for these brave men, who were accused of a break-in. I knew that Manuel and Rodolfo were totally innocent. We lived together, and they had not left the house the night of the alleged robbery. I could not affirm the innocence of Jorge and Zebedeo, because they did not live in that same ranch area. The sheriff threatened Maximiliano, Don Manuel's son, for having me at the ranch. I spoke with Don Manuel and the other brave ones about the need for me to leave that area so that the police would leave them in peace. Zebedeo Valdez offered me his car because I did not have one. I had left my car behind at the Valley of Peace. At midnight I left the ranch with my family. Simón Serna and his nine sons accompanied me on the road toward Texas. As we got to San Antonio, we burned the car that Zebedeo had loaned us.

Zebedeo Valdez was one of my first brave recruits. He had followed me since he had heard me speak at Salt Lake City in Utah. His heart was just and free from any evil. That made him a very distinguished man among all the brave men that followed me. I shall never forget his valor and his compassion in the pursuit of justice.

In Texas, Simón worked to feed both families. During this time, my older brother, Anselmo, decided to leave his life of "slavery" and joined our effort to liberate the lands and to seek liberty. I had finally convinced him about the Anglo-American not having a room for us in their anti-Mexican government. He had always argued with me about these points. "What are you going to be able to do against this powerful giant?" he would ask. He would tell me, "You are crazy, Reies." But, finally he decided to join me and went back to New Mexico with us. Before leaving, my wife had our sixth son. We did not have money for the hospital, much less for a midwife. So, I had to attend to the childbirth myself. A little boy was born and we baptized him Noé, in memory of what Jesus Christ had said in the last days before the destruction, that the world was going to be like in the "days of Noé."

I left my wife, after she gave birth, with the six children. Anselmo and I left for New Mexico. The car that I had obtained was an old 1928 car. On the way, I stopped in Austin to visit Alvino Mendoza, one of my first brave ones who had helped me in 1950. He offered me his car and I left him mine. That same day, we left for New Mexico. During

May 1958, I traveled the other counties and land grants in New Mexico that I had known before. The more I learned about this area, the more histories I heard from the ranchers, the more I detected and understood the terror and fear that the Anglo had put in the hearts of our oppressed community. This community was intimidated. What was I going to do for them to help them in their own struggle? I asked myself that repeatedly. My first task, I decided, was to remove the fear and disintimidate them. Alone, I was going to battle the giant Anglo corporations. The old suffering people in New Mexico had faith and love for their land. They still felt in their skin and bones the abuses and the injustice that the army of lawyers had perpetrated against them. The new generation of youth, educated by Anglo teachers, had already been tamed and conditioned in their mentality. They were losing our culture and adopting Anglo styles and pride, as if they were Anglos. The youth were at the point of losing the last roots and fibers of their culture and love for their own families.

I had to investigate much to document the cause of our settlers. The Anglos had more than a hundred years' advantage over me. They had sown the seed and had conditioned the mind of my community for more than a century. I did not even have money to buy the books I needed, much less to support my family. Without knowing the history of the United States and without any political influence, I took this on. And worst of all, I was a fugitive from justice. The FBI was pursuing me. The state police of New Mexico were looking for me. On the other hand, the religious leaders considered me a rebel from the Church. My community, I found, was full of complaints, tears, sorrows, and agony, but without valor, without determination. Many times, the heirs with their complaints almost made me lose my energy, my valor, and my spirit. Their pessimism was incredible.

One day in May, some of the heirs to the land grant of Tierra Amarilla got together. The president had taken me into his confidence and invited me to speak at the reunion. I had just begun to speak to the assembly when one of the principals whispered something to the sergeant-at-arms. The sergeant-at-arms immediately told me to stop speaking. I responded to him that the president, Ubaldo Martínez, had given me permission. The sergeant-at-arms hit me over the head with his club and cut my scalp. Anselmo immediately jumped on the sergeant-at-arms and took the club from him, beating him with it. Rodolfo beat on the man that had incited the sergent-at-arms. Everything stopped. More than a hundred people were involved in the melee, but most of them showed me great respect and moved me out of the arena. One of them later told me that the one who had provoked the fight, an Anglo, was a friend of the sergeant-at-arms. That day, I discovered the fear the people had and how the Anglo was going to impede my progress. There were jealousies and envy between land grant heirs who were poor but honest. And there had always been puppets among them that had helped the Anglos steal their lands back in 1846 through 1904.

As a fugitive, I could not approach or visit the centers of archival material. I could not visit libraries. So, during these first years, I had to get my information from the people. The older ones were my teachers. With their information, I confirmed my faith, my strength, and my determination to pursue the land grant issue. In Canjilon, Coyote, Española, Las Vegas, El Tecolote, and in Taos, the story, as related through the voice of my people, was the same.

Anselmo was jailed in the Tierra Amarilla courthouse. And I hid in one ranch or another. The sheriff, Daniel Rivera, had taken the car that Alvino had loaned us in Austin. The prosecutor accused Anselmo of "assault" against the sergeant-at-arms during that reunion in Chama. Anselmo was sick in jail and asked for medicine. The jailer, Eulogio Salazar, told Anselmo that he had orders from the sheriff not to give him a thing. After eleven days in jail, Eulogio was moved by my brother's poor condition and opened the door to the jailhouse so that he could escape. Now, Anselmo was a fugitive also. He walked more than fifteen miles to the ranch of Pablo Zamora. From there, they took him to Don Manuel Trujillo's ranch.

One morning at 3 a.m., before Anselmo had arrived at the Manuel ranch, sheriff's deputies surrounded us. Everyone was asleep. As I heard a sound at the door, I woke up and alerted my brother-in-law, Efraín Escobar. I took my shotgun loaded with buckshot. Efraín took his 30-30 Winchester. We saw through the window that there were agents out in front. All of them were armed. I climbed to the second floor with Efraín behind me. There, as we went through the back door of the house, an agent saw that the door was half opened and took aim. I felt as if I was encircled. I woke Manuel and his wife, Alicia, and Manuel's father. I told them that police surrounded us. I told Alicia not to dress so that Sheriff Crane would not come into the last room where Efraín and I were hiding. Sure enough, the sheriff's deputies entered the home, arrested Manuel and his father. Behind the door, I waited to see if any of the agents entered. Through the door crack, I saw Sheriff Crane, pistol in one hand and a flashlight in the other. I sweated while he decided what he was going to do. Instinctively, I took the safety off of my shotgun. Efraín was at the other corner of the room with his rifle. They never approached that last bedroom. Thank God. Because we would have had to shed blood. They took Manuel while Efraín and I went out the back door and climbed to my favorite location, the high rocks above the ranch. Within five minutes they came back and surrounded the ranch again. But this time they did not get off. They only released Manuel, whom later met with us and told me that after five minutes of having arrested him, they told him that they were looking for Reies Tijerina. Crane, supposedly, had said, "I know he is in there." But they did not dare to come back into the house. This was the last time that I was surprised. Never would they catch me asleep.

They returned three times that summer. Anselmo and I would sleep in the rocks high above the ranch house. The dog at the ranch was named Napoleón. He used to sleep with us, and I taught him not to bark. He would imitate us hiding from the police when the cars would arrive and would just look, as we did, at the goings on below. There was a small little house near the ranch, Hidden Ranch. One dawn, this little house was surrounded. Maximiliano was sleeping inside. They surrounded this little house and flashed their headlights at once. This time they had FBI agents with them from the city of Aztec in San Juan County. Maximiliano told us the agents were all very afraid. On another occasion they surrounded the house of Don Manuel at two in the morning, but they never were able to accomplish their goal, which was to arrest me. I knew that if they had caught me, they would have used any excuse to kill me. A Mexican agent from Blanca, New Mexico, in the same county of San Juan, discreetly would send us word about what the Anglos said: "We have to capture this Communist because, left free, he will infect all the other Mexicans with Communism."

All the Anglos in Arizona knew that I was not a Communist, that I had not even read Marxist literature. Anglos had preached this anti-Communist gospel for more than the last twenty years. They had the community conditioned and regimented against "Communism." To say that someone is a Communist is the easiest way to kill or destroy that person. I understood how serious their conspiracy to kill me was. Who, in this conditioned community, was going to be angry if they killed a Communist while escaping? I had no hate towards Communism. The land and the culture of my people were and are my ideology. The tactics of scaring a community with Communism to hide and mask the practices of discrimination and injustices done against those early settlers weren't going to work on me. This was and is my hardest job: to clean up and awaken the consciousness of my brothers; to rescue them from their inferiority complex; to remove their fear.

As a fugitive I had many disadvantages. But on the other hand, I also had more time to read and study the books and documents that the brave ones brought me. I was shown a cave that only Don Manuel Trujillo and Maximiliano, his son, knew about. It was two miles from Don Manuel's hidden ranch. They loaned me an old mattress, blankets, and a very tame black horse. I spent many days in this cave. Frequently, I was accompanied by many of the faithful brave ones. I read a lot about the history of the United States and the Constitution of the United States. I learned the weaknesses in the Constitution of the United States. I found that the Constitution does not offer a single provision or safeguard to the family. Moreover, it does not deal specifically with corruption and the degeneration of the sexes that was destroying society. Specific rights for the family, a keystone of society, are not found in the Constitution of the United States. This Constitution, in my view, is unable to withstand the pressures of the modern technological world. It reflects the mentality of those that wrote and signed it two centuries earlier.

By June 1958, I had escaped the police six times. The states of Arizona and New Mexico considered me a fugitive and had joined forces in trying to apprehend me. The pressure by these organized police forces against me mounted every day. The more that my people hid and protected me, the more the agents of the government became irritated. When I left for Mexico in 1956, I did not imagine myself being an international fugitive. I also ignored the seven years that waited for me. I was also a fugitive in terms of education and learning. I decided to leave New Mexico again and go work in Texas to avoid the escalating danger for Don Manuel Trujillo and the brave ones. Anselmo accompanied me and Rodolfo loaned me his car. Behind the back seat, we put a fifty-gallon drum of gasoline. During the first days of July, we left for San Antonio. I picked up my family at night because they told me that the FBI had been asking around there for Anselmo. They asked for Anselmo in order to not alarm the people, when in reality they were looking for me.

The next day we arrived at a ranch of a friend of mine. When I had been a pastor of a small Mexican church in Eden, Texas, I had met Torres. He invited me to help pick potatoes in Plainview, Texas, and we picked potatoes for about two weeks. I spent the fourteenth of July, the anniversary of my marriage, there with him. One day, without explanation, about midday, the police surrounded the house. We had just returned from picking potatoes because the crop had just about been exhausted for that day. As we finished eating, I laid on a cot facing the window and the only door that that little two-room house had. Rosita, my nine-year-old, was taking a bath. I was just dozing off when I heard the arrival of the first car. I felt that it stopped at the front of the door. I raised my head to see, always with suspicion and being ever vigilant for the police. I realized that I did not recognize the faces or the car. Instead of speaking, I made signs, hand signs, to Anselmo, pointing toward the door. Fortunately, the two agents went around the back of the house. We crawled on the floor toward the windows leading to the door. My wife was in the other room toward the back of the house and my son, David, eleven years old, was playing outside. We managed to crawl over to the bathroom, where Rosita was bathing. My wife already had experience with the police. When she saw us crawling toward the bathroom, she realized that something was wrong. Rosita was alarmed as we entered the bathroom. She opened her mouth to protest because she was nude in the water. I made signs telling her to be quiet and not put on her clothes. Quickly, I heard the police enter the door without knocking, threatening the other people in the room. They threatened my wife to tell them the truth. We heard them searching throughout the house and under the beds. My wife told them that Anselmo and I had gone to the post office. They went out the door without coming into the bathroom, but four cars of police agents stayed out front, including a Texas Ranger, city police, and the county sheriff. My wife came to the bathroom and told me that two police were still outside the door and the others were gone. I asked for my Spanish gun, a 385 Llama, and my steel dagger that Don Manuel had given me. The police covered three sides of the house, but they could not cover the back part. We opened the window of the bathroom, and I cut the screen with my dagger. We jumped out into the next lot. I ran like a deer without looking back. I did not even check to see if Anselmo was coming with me or not. Some friends of mine lived about a block from my house. And two young people, by coincidence, were just finishing changing the oil in their car and saw me. I saw that Anselmo was catching up to me. We explained to these youth what was happening, and they took us to Lubbock and left us at the home of Rubén Torres, a nephew of minister Torres. We stayed there about six hours until nightfall. Then that night, a friend of Rubén's took us back to Plainview. I wanted to leave my wife a message and find money for bus fare. Rubén's friend took me to the home of Evaristo Torres and his wife, Guadalupe. They hid me there, and Guadalupe took the message to my wife. That night I slept between the garbage cans in the back. The next day my wife got paid, and she sent money for Anselmo and me to take the bus, enough to get to Bloomington, New Mexico. From there we walked back to the ranch of Don Manuel Trujillo. My wife moved to Canyon City in Texas to pick cotton. Later, she called me that she was in Lumberton, New Mexico. Zebedeo Valdez took me to where my wife and six children were. Anselmo, meanwhile, was living in the caves by the hidden ranch of Don Manuel Trujillo. My brother Margarito was in jail. They had taken him to Michigan City, Indiana, from Florence, Arizona, to complete his five years of punishment. Manuel, Rodolfo, Zebedeo, and the others were also jailed. Now, Anselmo was also a fugitive and was separated from me.

I decided to take my family to Quanah, Texas. We all picked cotton there, but I would not sleep inside a house anymore. I would sleep among the weeds and trees far away from the house. Every car that approached the house would oblige me to seek further cover. While we were eating one day after a couple of weeks of this kind of living, my daughter Rosita said, "Daddy, the police." I jumped through the window headfirst. I always had an exit prepared in the event that police would come. I made sure that I could escape at any moment. My family and I decided that it was best for me to go to Mexico. My wife did not want the police to apprehend me. Upon saying good-bye to my family, my heart broke. My son David was just eleven years old. How much could he help his mother? He was the oldest. Esteban Noé was five months old. Lita (Ire of Allah) was two years old. Raquel was five, Daniel was six, and Rosita was nine years old. I found strength in the hope that one day my children would be proud of what their father had done for the millions of Mexicans that suffered in the United States.

My whole family went to say goodbye at the train station. While they cried quietly, the train began to pull away, further and further away. Never had my heart felt such a hurtful departure.

It was the first day of September 1958 when I got to Mexico for the second time. Without money or clothes, other than what I had on, I went again to the home of Santana Vergara. I made application for political asylum with the Secretary of Foreign Relations in Mexico, but I was told that the United States was not pursuing me and therefore I was denied. I continued to make friends in Mexico and studied the laws governing the land, the water, land grant rights, *pueblo* rights, communal land rights, as they were called in New Mexico. I had meetings with lawyers and judges.

While in Mexico, I waited for my family. Mr. Santana Vergara built a small three-room house for me and said, "Bring your family. Here you have a home that isn't going to cost you a thing." I had told him and others the story of the Mexicans in the United States and my struggle for the land and liberty of our people. Don Santana had a lot of sympathy for our cause.

Reporters from *La Prensa, Excelsior, Novedades,* and *El Universal* were beginning to know me better. From time to time, these newspapers would carry a story about "the forgotten community." That was how they referred to Mexicans in the United States. Some of them that began to sympathize with our cause and understand what we were struggling for took me to visit communities, cities, and ranches in rural Mexico. I noticed that the moral values and respect for the rights of others were stronger in the rural areas than in the capital of Mexico.

My family arrived just before Christmas. For me, this was a great day. At least I was together with my family. Shortly after New Year's, Anselmo arrived. Within days, I received two hundred dollars from the community of Tierra Amarilla for the first time. I had been in touch by mail with them about my experiences, but I did not expect the money. Several times they had called me by telephone and I had sent them copies of articles that had been published in the newspapers about our struggle. I sent them copies of the Treaty of Guadalupe Hidalgo. I sent them professional opinions on our legal claim to the land. I sent what I could that would be of benefit. When my wife arrived, she had a hundred pesos. Anselmo had a hundred and twenty dollars. With the two hundred dollars that we had received, we had enough money to last for three months.

In May, Anselmo returned to the United States. While crossing the border at Juárez into El Paso, federal agents arrested him, and he was imprisoned in New Mexico for the next two and a half years. Simón Serna was to meet Anselmo at the bus station; he sent me a telegram telling me of Anselmo's arrest. My family also left Mexico once again. Cotton harvest was to begin. Meanwhile, the Mexican government would not protest any of these injustices or the problems that the Mexican people had in the United States, much less reclaim its interest in the land. On the other hand, the poor people of Mexico were very interested. The press and various reporters were interested in our problems. At the beginning, they called me a "pocho." But I countered that accusation by accusing them of being too British. They used many words in English like "water closet, sweater, orange" for soda drinks, and many others. I accused them of being the true *pochos* for giving into the customs and traditions of the British and the Anglos.

While I was in Mexico, frequently I would be consumed with rage and misery when I would see advertisements in English, Anglo fashion styles, foreign corporations selling products from the United States. It did not bother me so much that they were from a foreign country as much as what the products and companies falsely represented to the Mexican people. In time, they would ruin the Mexican people.

Finally, the month of September 1959 arrived. I did not have any money. I was living a life without a purpose. I decided to return to my land and my people. I arrived in San Antonio during the last days of September. I crossed the border at Laredo, Texas, with a borrowed name. My brother told me where I could find my wife, and he took me to where she was picking cotton. Once again, I was reunited with my wonderful family and wife. From mid-September to the last days of November, we picked cotton in various places around Shamrock, Texas. On one occasion, I organized a strike because the rancher would give preference to other workers to pick in areas of the cotton patch that were better, and he would keep the Mexicans in the area where it was poor picking. There were at least fifty of us picking cotton. I organized a protest and went to confront the rancher, who succumbed to our pressure quickly. This was a victory, but it was very small, but the satisfaction obtained from this was very large.

With the money, I returned to Tierra Amarilla. This part of New Mexico is very cold. Snow had already begun to fall, and the land was covered with snow. The most faithful to our cause found me a house near La Ensenada. At least half the houses were vacant, undoubtedly as a result of the land robbery of earlier years. I fixed my home so that I would be able to escape. I dug two secret caves—one below the floor of the house and the other below the pantry. If they would find the first one, they would not find the second. While there, I met Eulogio Salazar. Eulogio had been the jailer in Tierra Amarilla. He was the one that had freed Anselmo. Anselmo told me that before Eulogio released him, he had mentioned that we had many charges against us and that they would surely charge him also. Eulogio Salazar came to my house Christmas night. He brought "Christmas" or presents to my children. He also brought a 50-pound box full of clothes and shoes for my children. I shall never forget this act of charity toward my children, my wife, and me. He became most loyal toward our work. If he hadn't done these deeds, I would never have trusted him. He came in uniform with his pistol in his holster. Eulogio became our best contact. Thanks to him, we knew of the FBI inquiries and those made by other state agents who followed us. He would send word with our loyal ones. Although I trusted Eulogio, I never told him about my secret caves or my other plans. Only my family knew these secrets. And on two occasions, I saved myself by hiding in these caves.

I missed seeing my brother Chemo and decided to go visit him at the state penitentiary in Santa Fe. A few days after the New Year of 1960, my wife and I went to see him. Cristino Lovato took us. By ten-thirty in the morning, we were knocking on the door. We were asked, "Whom do you come to see?" I responded, "I am Pablo De Anda and this is my wife." He wrote our names down. I told him, "I have come to see my brother-in-law, Anselmo Tijerina." Within thirty minutes, we were let in, and when Anselmo finally was brought to the visitors' area, he was shocked to see me. I extended my hand before he could say anything and said, "I am your brother-in-law, Pablo De Anda, and this is my wife. We came to visit you." He caught on quickly, recuperated his demeanor, and soothed his nerves, and we began to talk a little bit. For over an hour. I told him what I had done in Mexico. I told him that Pepe Puebla was the one who had alerted the police to arrest him at the border. I also told him that Dr. Benjamín Laureano Luna had given to Milton Eisenhower, when he visited Mexico City, the memorandum I had written. The memorandum was about our rights under the Treaty of Guadalupe Hidalgo and the violations of it by the United States government. On the twelfth of December 1959, we had sent a letter to the President of the United States, Milton's brother, with eighty-plus signatures of families, including that of Eulogio Salazar. Anselmo was shocked at the name that I had given him, but I told him that things were changing very rapidly. We were gaining a lot of followers, including members of the police.

Cristino Lovato was a senior brother of the Morada (the temple of worship for my Penitent Brotherhood) in Ensenada. He introduced me to many brothers in other Moradas. I began to learn the history of the Penitents and discovered a great deal. They were the few who saved the little culture and history of the settlers of New Mexico that remained. They also were the few who had the strength to resist Anglo influence. They still lived with the dream of recovering their land in New Mexico. Through them, I learned of the criminal element of the Santa Fe Ring headed by Thomas B. Catron. Catron had legally stolen the land of many Mexican families through his lawyers and Anglo politicians. Just like the English pirates legalized by England, the U. S. authorities legalized this Ring. Thomas B. Catron knew that the Penitents were the *Gorras Blancas (White Caps)*. The *Gorras Blancas* were the force that sought to unify all the heirs of the land grants in New Mexico to continue resisting and struggling against the encroaching whites. There also existed a religious barrier between the whites and the settlers. The whites were Protestants and the settlers were Catholics. And this led me to study the role of the Protestants in the theft of our land. I found that the great organizations and principal religious orders of the Protestant denominations never lifted a finger against the illegal activity of Thomas B. Catron and his gang. When Governor William A. Pile ordered his secretary, or more accurately, his librarian for the New Mexico territory, Ira M. Bond, to destroy all the Spanish archives in New Mexico, no one spoke up, much less the church. How were they going to protest? William A. Pile was an ordained Methodist minister. This happened in March of 1870. Little by little, I reconstructed what had happened in New Mexico more than 110 years ago at the hands of the Anglos.

The Eisenhower Letter

Some two months after the December 12th letter to President Eisenhower, we received a response. The few lines were cold and without any flavor. The letter from the president got me to thinking. I did not know anything about politics. I knew church politics after more than ten years of struggle with the church. I knew its hypocrisy. I began to understand and detect a similar hypocrisy in the government of the United States. This letter was just another little fragment in the great historical map of the Anglo. I continued to pursue the contact I had with a few Anglos and politicians because Eisenhower's letter had given me singular spirit. The content of our letter was: Tears and petition from an oppressed people in their own land, in their own home. Instead of giving up the struggle, I decided and became even stronger in the pursuit of justice in New Mexico. All around me were lands and cities and places, rivers and mountains with the names in Spanish of our antecedents.

Before the snow had receded, a friend of mine from Lumberton, Lino Gómez, gave me an old car. From there I went to Cortez, Colorado, to organize a few settlers in that area. About ten miles outside of Farmington, a car rear-ended me. The drivers and passengers were young, intoxicated Anglos, in a new car. At first, I thought this was a trick and that I would be apprehended. But Cristino Lavato, who was accompanying me, decided that he should be the one to say that he was driving. So, when the police came, I was not questioned. The police took us to Farmington and left us with a sister of Zebedeo Valdez. From there we called Lino Gómez and, within two hours, we were in my house in Ensenada. A week later, two agents came to my house and I disappeared immediately. My wife attended to them. After they had left, my wife told me that they were from an insurance company, and they were coming to investigate the property damage done to us. My wife had asked them for two hundred dollars, which they paid very happily. But I thought it was too little. I went and spoke with Crucito Manuel and asked him to write to the insurance company that the damage to my car was at least another seven hundred and fifty dollars. Within two weeks, they sent me seven hundred and fifty dollars.

My family really needed this money. Picking cotton, we had earned a little more than a thousand dollars, but all this money went to further the cause of my oppressed community. All my own money, and that which I was able to get from others, went into the purse of the community. My heart hurt greatly every time my children asked me for new socks or shoes and I had to deny them. I frequently would take them to second-hand stores to buy used clothing. This way we could use the money to fund the struggle for the lands. During cotton-picking season, we would spend twenty-five dollars on groceries for the eight of us in the family. I would give Daniel and Raquel each ten cents, and to David and Rosita I would give a quarter so they would spend it on whatever they wanted. David was a growing young man, as was Rosita a growing young woman. David would pick close to five hundred pounds daily and Rosita about four hundred to four hundred and fifty. It broke my heart not to be able to give them any more money or buy them a new dress or a toy or a doll or a shirt, much less a pair of socks. Every year during the cotton-picking season, the rich Anglos would sell their used clothing to us. They would clean out their drawers and closets and give us their old clothing. These were the clothes that I gave to my children, but it was a small price to pay. I was the only man who understood how the Anglo had stolen over one million acres of our land belonging to 1,700 land grant heirs. This consciousness and truth is what burned me most when I denied new things to my children.

During this time, Bill Mundy's ranch was burned. According to the local rumors, Mundy, a real redneck, had burned it himself to collect the insurance money. Mundy had been helped by other Anglos to take over the Tierra Amarilla land grant. According to some of the Mexican workers, Mundy and his son, after the burning, began to wear pistols around their waists every day. They would practice like old cowboys, shooting at targets as if someone were going to attack them at any time. Later, the ranch of Raymond Spill also burned. Many of his cows and fine bulls were found dead or had disappeared. During this time, I found the need to return to Mexico and attempt to interest the government of Mexico in the Treaty of Guadalupe Hidalgo. I had plenty of proof of violations of the treaty and the destruction of the archives on our properties by William A. Pile, as well as the criminal gang activity of the Santa Fe Ring. I also had with me copies of the letter we had sent to President Dwight D. Eisenhower and his cold response. As I made my preparations to leave, the local police obligated all people in the area living near the Mundy ranch to take a lie detector test. Even my wife was being made to take the test. I told her that she did not have to submit, that it was her right to refuse, and it was best if she not take it. Everyone passed the test except for Bill Mundy. When they asked him about the many horses that had disappeared from Hush, New Mexico, he got very nervous. This showed up on the machine. The community was exonerated.

With borrowed identification from Tito Salazar, I crossed the border at Ciudad Juárez, Chihuahua. From there I took the bus and within two days I was in Mexico City. I carried a document with five hundred signatures addressed to the president of Mexico, Adolfo López Mateos. In addition, I took with me a speech by Anthony Joseph, delivered in the House of Representatives in 1888. I took many documents to prove that the U.S. was not honoring the terms of the Treaty of Guadalupe Hidalgo. I could show that our land was stolen. The treaty was signed on February 2, 1848, but it was not until 1891 that the Congress of the United States established the Court of Claims to adjudicate the land grant claims. During these forty-three years, the Santa Fe Ring stole all the land grants. In 1891, when the Court of Claims began its process, they insisted on proof of title to the land. Each land heir was to present his deed. But how could he or she? The families had already delivered to Governor Pile and his librarian the original deeds that were then destroyed? In Socorro, New Mexico, eight hundred families had claim to the land grants in that area. Governor Manuel Armijo had signed the proclamation acknowledging the existence of this land grant, but his signature was deemed to be false. The last secretary to the governor of New Mexico, Donaciano Vigil, testified that that was the signature of Governor Manuel Armijo, but all was in vain. On the other hand, the Court of Claims gave to Thomas B. Catron and many of his cohorts the land grants that they claimed. With colored proof, the court gave Catron half of La Miranda land grant, previously known as the land grant of Sangre de Cristo, comprising one million and a half acres. One of the defenders of this land grant was the priest, Antonio José Martínez. Since 1826, the Mexican governor of New Mexico had told Father Martínez to beware of the Anglos. When these came into New Mexico in 1846, Father Martínez was ready. The Anglo politicians and the Catholic Archbishop, Jean Lamy, hated Father Martínez. Lamy connived to remove Martínez from his post and discredit him before the community.

Upon my arrival in Mexico City, I made many new friends, including the famous Lombardo Toledano. I knew that he was a socialist and member of the Communist Party of Mexico, but thought that he would be able to help us if he understood the conditions of our people and the violations of the Treaty of Guadalupe Hidalgo. I told him the story. At the end of our interview, he thanked me very much and promised to use his influence to see what he could do so that the government of Mexico would take responsibility for people in the United States of Mexican ancestry. And he would try to see what Mexico could do to obligate the United States to fulfill its obligations under the Treaty of Guadalupe Hidalgo. But he asked me for twenty-five thousand dollars for his services and expenses. I left his office shamed. The interview turned out to be a request for money. I realized that it was not going to be easy to touch the heart of Mexico. I had many friends in Mexico, but their influence was limited. All whom I showed the documents that I had brought from the United States expressed shock and dismay. I wanted to get to the president of Mexico, Adolfo López Mateos. So I tried to make contacts with the foreign secretary, with the attorney general, and the people at the General National Archive. Meanwhile, I spent time visiting colleges and universities, trying to find a contact to get to the president.

In the United States, I knew of the grave danger that I was facing, but I thought in Mexico that the Anglos could not reach me, so I became careless. One day as I visited the main post office in Mexico City to buy stamps and mail letters, I placed my portfolio next to me. In an instant it disappeared. In it went all the documents that I had gathered and the petitions that I had from the people in New Mexico. I felt horrible. I did not know what to do. For days, I would wake up at night not believing what had happened. I did not want to accept the reality of such a thing. This tragedy caused me to return to the United States as soon as possible. I called friends in Juárez to call Tierra Amarilla so they would come for me. On this occasion, Pepe Puebla loaned me ten dollars for food and the bus trip. But I knew about him already. He had fingered Anselmo to the police. I did not trust him. I gave him wrong information about my trip. I made plans to meet with those coming from Tierra Amarilla at another hotel in Juárez. We met at the Hotel Río Bravo in a few days. From there, close to midnight, we attempted to cross into Juárez. As we reached the United States side, the border agents examined our luggage and found five copies of the magazine *Política*. They searched more and found a box of bullets. They called the central headquarters in El Paso to come and interview us. In the meantime, I pinched Lita, who was then four years old, hard enough to make her cry.

Using that pretext, I convinced the agents to hurry up with their search and not wait for the response from downtown. I knew that if the agents from El Paso came with my photograph, it would not match the identification I had borrowed from Tito Salazar. For some unexplained reason, such as divine intervention, the people from El Paso did not arrive. The local agents returned my magazine copies and bullets, and said, "Go. You can go." I had never been scared for such a long period of time. I felt good being able to get away from there. Once in El Paso, we separated, each of the three cars in our caravan going in a different direction. I got back to Tierra Amarilla within a day.

My Apache Friends, July 4, 1960

The Liberty Bell cracked three times as if it was God's will. My people were in no mood to celebrate the 4th of July in 1960. The U.S. government had placed a radar station with two hundred soldiers on Tierra Amarilla land. At a prearranged time, the people of Tierra Amarilla had their own bonfire to celebrate independence. They burned the radar station. Hundreds of agents came to investigate the arson. The press never reported the incident, fearing that people would be stirred up, according to a coyote source we had within the press. After the 4th, I left to visit Rodolfo and Zebedeo and then went to Lumberton.

In 1957 and '58 I had made friends with the Apache Indians of Dulce. They had invited me to several of their festivals. Anglos are not permitted at any of their events. I remember reading a book by David C. Cooke, *Fighting Indians of the West.* I learned how the Mexicans and the Apaches lived in peace until 1836. The Apaches confirmed these stories to me. At that time, the government of the United States sent James Johnson and fifteen other Anglo males from Missouri to provoke a war between the Mexicans and the Apaches. In the town of Santa Rita del Cobre in 1836, some fifteen years after the independence of Mexico, the Mexican community invited the Apaches to come for a fiesta. More than four hundred Apaches, without arms, arrived headed by their chief, Juan José. He spoke Spanish perfectly well. The Anglos arrived at the fiesta with two cannons. When everyone was having a good time, they began firing their cannons and weapons toward the area where the Indians were, without pity. Johnson personally killed Juan José with a bullet to the back. This massacre began the fifty years of war between Apaches and Anglos up to 1886, when the great chief, Gerónimo, quit the fight. But all the Mexicans in the area of Santa Rita del Cobre had to pay for this massacre for having allowed these assassins from the White House into their midst. Mangas Coloradas rose from this massacre to become the warrior who fought against Anglos and Mexicans for that treachery.

From there I visited the hidden ranch of Don Manuel Trujillo once again and spent a long night talking with him and his son, Maximiliano. Max was very preoccupied with the conflict between Communism and capitalism and asked me my opinion. I told him that I was not involved in those issues, that my ideology was the land, the culture, and the liberty of my community. My weapons were courage, my heart, and rage at the injustices. "I do not believe in importing religions or ideologies," I told him. "This land belongs to us and we must defend it ourselves because we were the heirs to it. We belong here and we have been born here. This is our homeland." I told Max that the Mestizo did not come from Europe or from the East. The Mestizo was born when the East and the West were joined. *Las Leyes de los Reinos de las Indias,* Law 2, Title 1 of Book 6, legitimized matrimony between Spaniards and Indians, the East and the West. That law created a new people, a new race, and the Anglo since then has been preoccupied with the potential of this new race. Therefore, the Anglo has pursued the killing of Indians and Mexicans with aplomb.

About two in the morning we saw some car lights coming. Although Zebedeo and Rodolfo were not fugitives, they went into the hills with me. Sheriff Crane routinely ordered his deputies to check on the house. The next day, we left to Monero and later on to La Puente, some five miles from Tierra Amarilla. The Anglos in the area had used the 4th of July fire at the Mundy ranch to obligate the politicians and force the police to capture Reies López Tijerina. Tierra Amarilla was full of police. The military had put up a radar station, a large army base there in Tierra Amarilla. But the local people would not identify or denounce me. In Tierra Amarilla, there are no Anglos, only natives and children of the original settlers. That is why they can only send Mexican police into the area. But the Mexican police, some of them, were our friends. They had joined our side. That night, I had to sleep in the chicken coop of Cristino Lavato. Cristino is the best symbol of the Mestizo people I have seen. He understands that he is the heir to the land, which the Aztecs used to call Aztlán. Cristino, like Don Manuel, had opened the doors to his home and his heart to me. Many a time, he fed, clothed, and hid us from the police. That night, however, I slept in the chicken coop. My family was still not with me, since I had fled a few days earlier. After two nights in the chicken coop, Tito Salazar brought my wife to me.

About that time, my brother Ramón and his wife visited me from San Antonio. Ramón had not joined our cause, but had left the religious ministry like I had. Together, we went to visit Poth, Texas, land near where I was born and of my early childhood. My mother is buried there. And we went to visit my brother, Cristóbal. We spent two or three days there at home. He was set to join the cause, as soon as he could sell his house and pay some of his debts. So we went to San Antonio and to pick cotton. We picked cotton in West Texas all the way to Tucumcari, New Mexico. There, the old car my wife had bought burned up. My wife had to stay there until they finished the cotton picking and we were able to buy another car. Meanwhile, I arrived in Albuquerque on my birthday, September 21, 1960. I looked for a house to rent in Albuquerque and finally found one on Rosemont Street: two rooms for thirty dollars a month.

This was the largest city in New Mexico. Within days, I received word that John Keeling of Eloy, Arizona, wanted to buy the Valley of Peace land in Arizona. He had offered thirty-five dollars an acre for the 160 acres there. I was surprised that the land was still in our name and that no one had taken it from us. I suggested to Rodolfo that we immediately go and pay the back taxes on the property. On this occasion, I had to dress like a woman. In Mexico I had bought a woman's wig for eight hundred and fifty pesos. With the wig and dressed in women's clothing, I passed as a woman and escaped several times when my life was in danger. So, I went to visit the courthouse and the jail in Florence. We paid the taxes, and then I went to visit some of my old friends in Casa Grande, and finally we went to Eloy. We found out that they were constructing a model city near the Valley of Peace. Millionaires from New York were buying the land some three miles from our place. The price there was five hundred dollars an acre, so we decided not to sell anything to Mr. Keeling. Instead, we decided to see if we could get a better price for the land.

My brother Margarito had been released from prison in Michigan City and was now living with my sister Joséfina in Chicago, Illinois. He had written asking me to visit him, but I did not have enough money to make such a trip. In 1959, during the cotton-picking season, I read about the Black Muslims in *U. S. News and World Report.* The reporter tried to hide his disgust of Elijah Mohammed. I admired the strength of this man and his people. And I thought that maybe I could combine the trip to Chicago with an interview of Elijah Mohammed. When I went to see Margarito in Chicago, I was given an appointment. I knew why the whites hated the Nation of Islam and I also knew why they hated us. Elijah Mohammed, like me, had been in prison and was a fugitive for awhile. I knew he could tell me a lot of the secrets of his cause that I would benefit from. Within two days of being in Chicago, Elijah Mohammed sent a limousine for us. We were taken to the mansion of the Nation of Islam at 4748 Woodlawn. He received me like a prince would receive another. He explained to me, "The reason I made you wait longer than necessary was because I wanted all my assistants to be present. I have asked Allah to guide me in creating unity between the Arabs and Africans and Latin peoples of the Americas. This is the day that we can begin that work. And I know that if you could not speak for all the Mexicans, you would not be here." We ate lunch at two o'clock in the afternoon, and then we met privately. He did not let any of his lieutenants attend the meeting. He told me what I wanted to hear. He spoke of the local issues and then about some of the global issues. "This," he told me, "is only from my ear to yours." I told him briefly of my struggle for the land, and how the government had stolen our land. The U.S. Supreme Court had stolen the land from us with illegal findings and conclusions of law contrary to all the terms and stipulations of the Treaty of Guadalupe Hidalgo. The day ended very well for me.

We returned to my sister's house. The next day, according to our agreement, the Honorable Messenger Elijah Mohammed sent a limousine to take us to a special apartment with all the necessities, telephone, food, etc. He hosted us for seven days. Every afternoon the limousine would take me to the mansion to continue our important discussions. After seven days, I fully knew the secrets and the values of this man who was so brave in his struggle for the rights of his people.

I returned to Albuquerque to continue the great task of awakening our community and removing the complex created by the Anglo's education and conditioning. I believed my job was to awaken them and remove the fear in order to free our lands. My worst enemies were not the Anglos, but the Hispanics who opted for the "American way of life." The Anglo has used our own brothers to lead the way toward the "American way of life." These are the ones who commit treason against their own culture in order to avoid hunger. I always guard myself against them, all the time. My life as a fugitive had taught me many things that are not learned in school or at West Point. I gathered my few friends in Albuquerque and told them about my trip to Chicago. When I had left New Mexico the last time, the police had been looking for me. Now that I had returned, everything was quiet. We had dinner at the home of Juan and Fernanda Martínez, Félix's parents. Félix's mother had twelve sons and two daughters. This woman's valor reminded me of my own mother. Nobody or nothing caused her fear. Her sons got that electric spark of valor from her. She and her husband educated all her children on our history and the rights to our land. This woman assisted me daily, weekends, and throughout the months. We sent word out in the area and gathered the community people together one evening. For two hours I talked to them about my work in the other communities, my trip to Chicago, and the necessity of forming a union of *pueblos* and heirs. I told them, "All the Anglos are united. We, as we are today, are like dwarfs in the land of giants. The judges have a union, the lawyers have a bar association, and that's why they have been able to defeat us. They are without any rights whatsoever, and yet, we have all the titles to our property and the law on our side. If we want the respect of the judges and lawyers, we have to unite the descendants of those early settlers. Not only those from Tierra Amarilla, but also those from Albuquerque and Las Vegas, Santa Fe, etc. This fight is not of one or ten or twenty years because the Anglo took a hundred and twenty years. We can't undo this in only ten years, but I assure you of one thing: I plan to see, with my own eyes, the completion of the prophecy by Isaías: 'Each will flee to his own land.' The Jews are fleeing to their land since 1947. And if the Anglo helps us, one day he'll have to do the same, because we have roots here, and the Anglo doesn't. We have roots of blood and land. The Anglo has none—no blood root nor land."

After my talk, I saw that many pulled out their handkerchiefs to dry their tears. I told them many other things that night. I sensed a harmonious environment and my soul was well served. I also told them that I planned to live in Albuquerque for quite a while. The next day, we went to Monero and I visited Rodolfo and Zebedeo. Both were out on bond and they could not visit me. I told them about my adventures. They were pleased that I had been able to free myself from the Anglo prisons. I asked them all kinds of questions about being in prison.

"Are there rich people in prison doing time just like the poor?"

They told me, "Only the poor are in prison."

"Are there more Anglos than Mexicans or about equal?"

They said, "No, there's more Raza than Anglos."

"Are there prisoners there because of political corruption or a corporate corruption?"

"No," they answered me.

So then, I said, "We've got to wage war against the white-collar criminals. Those are the ones that are destroying justice and the confidence of the people. There's the secret of the rich and of the politicians. The police do what the powerful want. That's why they chase common criminals, but forgive and tolerate the rich and powerful."

The next day I went toward Chama. That was the place where I had been beaten at the meeting, but I loved that old plaza. I was there on August 6th in 1945, when the Anglos dropped the bomb on Hiroshima. This was a repeat of what the Anglos did in Santa Rita del Cobre in 1836. In Chama I first learned of the problem the people who owned the land had with the European strangers that came from east of the Mississippi. Near that plaza lived Iginio Martínez, who only spoke about the land theft. His sons also burned with fervor over the loss of land. They could not believe that land could now be held in the name of one person. One person cannot hold communal lands. The communal land system exists in the Orient and the Western world, but only the Anglo has violated that. Outside of the Anglo, all the races of the world practiced and respected communal land holdings. It is not possible for the Anglo to escape a violation of such magnitude and with such serious consequences. If the Anglo doesn't change, he's going to lose everything, like Hitler.

In Albuquerque during the first days I arrived there, I went to the library at the University of New Mexico. In the Coronado Room I found the Laws of the Indies. I spent several days and nights there with this book. In another room, smaller than the Coronado, I found the papers of that famous lawyer, senator, and attorney general of the New Mexico territory, Thomas B. Catron, head of the famous Santa Fe Ring. I began to uncover this man's footprints and criminal maneuvers. Later, I learned that Catron was sent to New Mexico, like James Johnson had been sent to Santa Rita, to terrorize the people, except in different ways. New Mexico had more than 100,000 residents, while Santa Rita del Cobre was small and isolated. The criminal deed of Catron would not have succeeded without the help of the White House, without the help of the Protestant religions. When William A. Pile was governor of the New Mexico Territory in the 1870s, Thomas B. Catron was the attorney general. The people in Canjilón, Coyote, and Gallina told me the incredible history of how the Presbyterian Church had taken possession of the land grant of Piedra Lumbre, originally settled by Pedro Martínez in 1760. The people had not forgotten their lands.

Many descendants of all the land grant communities in New Mexico lived in Albuquerque. Through them I learned about the general sentiment of the people. And Albuquerque is centrally located. From there I could travel to the Four Corners of the state. I already had plans to form a union or an alliance of all the land grant communities that would make the politicians crumble. But I was a fugitive and I did not know about the statute of limitations regarding the accusations made by the authorities in Arizona and the FBI. I did not know the law. All of this was new to me, so I began to study a bit of law. In Albuquerque I could also observe Anglo racism and the discrimination practiced on my brothers. And in Albuquerque I could escape the police and federal agents with more ease. The arrival of my bother Cristóbal helped me a great deal with my plans. He became a beer distributor and helped me to support my family, while I dedicated all my time to organizing the struggle for the land. During this time in Albuquerque, I repeatedly dreamed that the U.S. Army was chasing me. I was not caught because they did not recognize me.

Toward the later months of 1961, we made plans to go to Mexico. I gathered my documents and arranged my papers to present our case before the public and the authorities of the government of Mexico. This time my daughter, Rosita, and Cristóbal went with me in his car.

Prior to departure, I explained to the people why it was necessary to go to Mexico again. "If we do not open our mouths, the Anglo is going to eat us up. Our legacy that we leave to our children will be food stamps and fear. The United States is too busy with the nations of the world to attend to us. Besides, the letter we sent to President Eisenhower on December 12, 1959, had a cold response. They told us there was no justice. That's why Mexico is our only hope . . . if they listen, investigate our case and then present it to the United Nations."

The trip was without incident, and we went directly to the home of Mrs. Dolores Díaz de Rebeles. By now, Santana and Carmela Vergara had died. We tried to meet with General Lázaro Cárdenas, who was in Iguala, Guerrero, directing a project on the Balsas River. Carmela Aguilar and her son, Gilberto, made contact with the general. We presented ourselves and spoke with him for more than thirty minutes about the history of the Mexican community in the Untied States, the Treaty of Guadalupe Hidalgo, and the violations of this treaty by the United States. After he listened to us, he spoke for a few minutes. He told us to go see him in Mexico City toward the end of the week.

At the following meeting, I explained to him how the United States called itself a democratic republic and the leader of the free world, but not for us. Our culture does not fit in with their liberty. I told him the history of our struggle for the land. I told him the story of Governor William A. Pile, the Santa Fe Ring, Thomas B. Catron, and the history of the Court of Claims. The leader of the free world did not provide us with protection for forty-three years. I told him the story of Santa Rita del Cobre.

The general had great patience with us. He listened to us. He finally asked, "And how can I help you? What do you want me to do to help these millions that had the bad luck of remaining under Anglo justice?"

"First, we would like for you to go to the president and tell him our story. Seek an audience with the president, Adolfo López Mateos, for us. Second, do what your heart feels you must do for this forgotten community."

The general said, "Well, I do not promise I can do everything, but I promise to do the best I can. Independent of that, I should tell you one thing. That is, if you are not willing to see blood spilt, forget about all this."

I responded, "My general, your advice comes as a military person. I think that's your experience. I do not doubt that your advice is well founded, but we have to seek our solution through the world of peace and justice. Now, if after we exhaust peaceful means and our oppressor insists on his tyranny and continues abusing us, our lands, and our lives, then we have no other road but to choose between death and slavery. The people know the land is something to die for, but the Anglo has no such concept."

Before we said goodbye, I gave him a copy of the memorandum that I had given to the press and to the foreign secretary. I had written a five-page memorandum on January 17, 1959, while in Mexico with my family and Anselmo in the home of Santana Vergara. I could not deliver it to President López Mateos then, so I left it with Carmen Aguilar Pacheco to give to the president's private secretary, Hubert Romero. Mr. Romero, in turn, forwarded it on September 28, 1959, to Manuel Tell, the foreign secretary.

I have a copy of that memorandum in my archives. I save it as if it were a treasure. The memorandum was sent on behalf of the seven states of the Southwest that once belonged to Spain, and later to Mexico. After I gave the memorandum to the general, we said goodbye with a strong hug. Cristóbal and I left his home very happy. In the six years that I had come to know Mexico, I became aware of the reason why Mexico did not recognize our history in the United States. The Anglo terror that has been put into us has also been put into Mexico and all of Latin America. This terror has penetrated the highest professional circles and press in Mexico. The Mexican press dares not investigate or publish the savage atrocities the Anglo commits against the people in Texas, New Mexico, Arizona, and California. To my surprise, I found a humiliated Mexico without courage to launch a campaign against the bloody history of the United States. But I was not dissuaded, just like I'm not dissuaded when I see the poor people in New Mexico.

Press Conference of 1961

I finally got my friends to arrange a press conference at the National Press Club in Mexico City. The one who helped me was Dr. Benjamín Lauriano Luna, president of the International Front for Human Rights. We had known each other since September 1958, when I first went to Mexico. Dr. Lauriano was the one who gave a copy of my memorandum to Milton Eisenhower on September 8, 1959. Copies of my memorandum appeared in the United States through the United Press International wire service. An article appeared in the *Albuquerque Journal* and the *Tribune* on September 9, 1959. At the press club I spoke about the Treaty of Guadalupe Hidalgo and the stipulations and requirements for the United States and Mexico. I told them about the 125 years of Anglo occupation of Texas and the secret tactics that were used to steal the land. I spoke of the various crimes. Recently, archaeologists had found remains of people who were massacred by Anglos. I explained, in detail, the role of the Anglo judges and their complicity in the theft of our lands. I also explained the 115 years of oppression by the Anglo in the state of New Mexico. I gave them the evidence and documentation gathered by Hubert Bancroft and Ralph Twitchell on how the Santa Fe Ring, under the leadership of Thomas Catron, had been organized. I explained the Supreme Court decision in *Sandoval v. United States*, which ruled that Mexican communal lands did not belong to people because Spain and Mexico had never given these communal lands to the people, only lent them while those governments existed. The protection of communal lands also passed to the United States, "insomuch as these lands now belong to the United States, now that the United States has substituted its sovereignty for that of Spain and Mexico."

I posed this question to the newspapermen: "If the Supreme Court of the United States is correct, why did not Mexico confiscate the communal lands from Spain like the United States has? And, doesn't the United States claim to be more just and democratic than all other governments?"

I explained the process of Anglo education in the United States. There is no opportunity for a Mexican child to know the deeds and history of his past. For example, they teach that the Anglo pacified and civilized the Southwest, but they do not teach that our parents were the Spanish and Mexicans that settled from St. Augustin, Florida, to San Francisco, California. They do not teach that all the rivers, mountains, and cities of the Southwest have names in Spanish, names chosen by our ancestors. These facts that could give a child pride in being Mexican is frozen, hidden, and denied. The children learn only what the Anglo wants them to learn. Our children do not learn that George Washington, the father of the United States and the first one to sign the Constitution of the United States, had many slaves. Our children never learn about the history of the Treaty of Guadalupe Hidalgo or the history of the loss of our lands. They only know Anglo history and how the Anglo wants it to be known.

I concluded with this: "So now, my friends, we not only find ourselves in the need to fight for our lands, but also to fight to save our children from the perverse education of the Anglos. But the worst of it all is that the Anglo, more than anybody, is so well conditioned in his own style of life and mentality that he does not believe he's made a mistake. According to his fanatic mentality, I am the bad element. They do not say that I am doing wrong in trying to awaken my community. No, they say I am full of hate, that I am a fugitive Communist. They do not remember that their parents were pirates and that their inheritance is that spirit and mentality of pirates."

That night I received a lot of applause from the newspapermen. I made a lot of friends. I gave each newspaperman a copy of the memorandum that I had given to Milton Eisenhower. Then, I gave them a copy of the article from *The New Mexican* of May 10, 1960, about the four Anglo ranches that had been burned: those of Raymond Spill, Bill

Mundy, Jack Cowan, and Albert Spill. The article said these burnings were a wave of terror that had been unleashed in New Mexico. Our people, the descendants of the original settlers, had been made to take lie detector tests to prove their innocence of these burnings. They all passed. Only Mundy and his henchmen failed. I wanted the press club to believe me, and that's why I made my presentation and circulated these articles. Fortunately, the newspapermen told me, "Now, we understand the problem of the Mexicans in the Southwest." And they added, "Rest assured that the secret kept by the United States about this region will be known throughout Mexico in a few days."

Albuquerque, 1961

Reflecting on my prior life as a fugitive, I'd go over my experiences and the impact that they had had on my life. I had no doubt that all this had affected me profoundly, as well as my family. My senses had fully developed. The danger that others could not see I could feel. The wariness of the animal in the jungle, I felt all over my being. Truthfully, without knowing, I was going through a singular education, an extraordinary education that very few had. At the beginning, it had only been a test of nerves and a great discipline for my heart. Gradually, I overcame terror and fear. If I could win my first encounter with the judicial system, everything else would become easier. I was going to go to jail ultimately, but I would choose the day and the reasons. If I had gone to jail, like my brother Margarito in 1957 or 1958, the Anglo would have rejoiced because the people who have lost their lands would not have had someone to speak for them. I was not going to give them the satisfaction of taking our land and our culture, nor was I going to let them interrupt my mission. I would fight to the death for justice for my community. We had been waiting for 115 years. This is why I did not develop a psychopathic complex during these years as a fugitive. The Judge of Judges was my judge. If He would not turn me into the Anglo judges, why should I fear them then? While I was a fugitive, all I could do was document the injustices, educate and teach my people what the Anglo had done. I sought to unite them in a clandestine fashion.

Manifest Destiny in Reserve

During 1962, I would go in and out of Albuquerque. Cristóbal and his family returned to Texas. The economic difficulties for my family got worse. My wife suffered and struggled for many years. She was tired of all of this. I always told her, "One day all of these things will change. Be patient." But that day would not arrive. She, like me, was getting up in age and was thinking of life at age forty and fifty. When she began studying how to be a secretary, our difficulties multiplied. She mentioned divorce for the first time, and it seemed to me like I had been hit by a car. The difficulties between us began the first days of 1962. Because I had been a fugitive, any time there was a knock on the door, I'd run out the back. One time, some men drove up and I disappeared. It turned out to be a pastor and his assistants from a church who were dispensing gifts to people in need.

In 1962, we moved again. This was when things came to a head between the United States and Russia over nuclear warheads in Cuba. The Manifest Destiny of the United States again was coming to pass since it was involved in the internal affairs of fifty other nations. Many people across the world were championing their causes for homeland: the Philippines, India, Africa, and the Arab world. The United States forced the Arabs to leave their lands, which they had occupied for two thousand years to make room for Israel. These are some of the explanations that I gave my community about our struggle for the land and what the United States faced around the world.

On August 3, 1962, I wrote the first plan to create the Alianza Federal de Mercedes (Federal Land Grant Alliance). It was a two-page letter, and I did not sign it because I thought one of the copies might fall into the hands of those who were hunting me. A copy is still in my archive. While the United States and Russia were reaching their climax over the nuclear crisis in Cuba, on October 22, 1962, my wife and I made plans to move farther north. I circulated a second letter to create the Alianza de los Pueblos y Pobladores (Alliance of Towns and Settlers). This second was not dated. I moved my family again to 600 S. Broadway. The Alianza Federal de Mercedes was already functioning but not incorporated.

I returned to Mexico in 1962. This time it wasn't to make contacts or talk to the president; rather, it was to study law, only that law that had to do with the land, with the Treaty of Guadalupe Hidalgo. I went through Texas and invited Cristóbal to join my daughter Rosita and me. Once again, we visited General Lázaro Cárdenas and had a long discussion with him about communal land rights. When he was president of Mexico, General Cárdenas had returned many of these lands to the people. He knew a lot about this issue. He also gave us his opinion about the legal rights of communal lands. According to him, although he was not an expert on property law, communal lands are perpetual property of that community or that city. Other lawyers and friends of General Cárdenas and Dr. Ben Lauriano Luna gave us their opinions about communal lands. Cristóbal and I were short of money, so we returned within a month. I felt very secure about the right of our people to the lands. I felt sure that the people of the world would continue to claim their lands, just like the Indians were doing in the United States. I was also sure that my quest, the land recovery movement, was my mission in life. I was sure that the judicial power of the United States had failed to make me a marked man and even possibly assassinate me. All this, to me, signaled a good future.

As 1963 entered, my wife and I discussed divorce as a solution to our problems. Over the previous eighteen months I had reconciled myself to that reality more and more. I knew I loved her very much and that she loved me. I knew that we had both been faithful to each other. But the toll that my life as a fugitive had taken on our relationship was too great. My children were going hungry and doing without the necessities of life because of my life. Many times my wife saw me abandon the cause of the struggle for the land to attend to the needs of my family. I tried working at ranches. I tried getting odd jobs, but within days my wife would see my spirit decline, as if I were a prisoner. My wife would tell me, "Your heart is not in this. It's better that you continue your mission." Finally, my wife went before Judge Paul Larrazolo and obtained a divorce. I did not appear. I still feared the power of the judges over my liberty. My wife took custody of the six children, our three boys and three girls. My wife continued helping a lot in the Alianza, and my sons and daughters did not go far away from me.

The Incorporation of the Alianza

During the month of January, we notified people that on February 2, 1963, we would come together to incorporate officially the Alianza Federal de Mercedes. I chose this day because that was the same day the Treaty of Guadalupe Hidalgo was signed. It was also the birthday of my daughter, Rosita. On this day people from fourteen land grants or communities came together.

I spoke about unity. "We live in a world of corporations. Those who are incorporated are respected. Those who are not are standing alone and are ignored." I told the people gathered there how the Anglos had used their tactics against us in court. I also told them of the criminal action by Governor William A. Pile. If the Anglos do not respect the rights of others, I told them, "we're going to have to struggle for many years. We're going to have to go before the United Nations. We're going to have to create public opinion so that it embarrasses the oppressor. The strong ones will continue with me and the weak ones will stand away from us."

That day was the beginning of our future generations' success. This Alianza of communities and land grantees would become the terror of those who had stolen our land and destroyed our culture. Every one of the existing corporations had been built around money, law, education, political power, medicine, religion, etc., but our Alianza was organized around the 1700 land grantees of our ancestors. What united us were the rivers and the mountains that our parents baptized. We were united by 100 million acres of land, property of the children of those settlers. For this reason, the Anglos were going to hate me with a hate that has never been seen in the southwestern United States. They would accuse me of having awakened and united the people of the land. But the Just Judge of Judges will look after me. At the end, He will say who had justice and reason and those who did not. I did not ignore the power of this country or its mentality.

At the Alianza meeting, I was chosen as director general and Eduardo Chávez was elected vice-president. The first office of the Alianza was in my own home at 1010 Third Street. We began publishing a regular newspaper. I bought this building from Edwin Stanton, who used to publish *The News Chieftain*. As part of the purchase deal for the Alianza offices, I also got to publish regular weekly articles in his newspaper. For more than two years I wrote for *The News Chieftain*. We gave the Valley of Peace, the 160 acres that we had in Arizona, as down payment to Stanton. We made arrangements to pay on the $25,000 debt. The building had more than 10,000 square feet. On June 13, 1963, we sent letters to the two governments that had signed the Treaty of Guadalupe Hidalgo. We reminded them of their commitments under the treaty and we reminded them that millions of Mexicans depended on the treaty and its guarantees to live without violations and prejudice. We never received a response. We asked the U.S. president for a meeting to discuss the issue. We asked the Mexican president to ask the U.S. president to meet with us.

The press began calling me "Don Quixote," to ridicule my intent to recover the lands lost by our people. The press name of Don Quixote and the arrogance of the United States president, by ignoring our letter, only meant one thing: The Anglo knew that we had prior rights to the land. Their lack of response did not disillusion me in the least. I knew that the Alianza was what the Anglo had feared since 1846. The Anglo feared that the natives would unite and form an extraordinary force. The usurping Anglo knew that his day had come.

During 1963, we visited many communities. We talked to people in these communities about their rights and how strangers had come, stolen our land, and denied us our basic rights. There were many days during that time when we went from village to village and ranch to ranch, organizing the heirs to these lands. On August 19, I wrote a letter to Attorney General Robert F. Kennedy. I asked him to consider the problem of the ten million citizens that depended on the international Treaty of Guadalupe Hidalgo. I did not get a response. We thought the Kennedys would be different from the other politicians. On August 23, I went to Chicago to see Robert Kennedy in person. He had not invited me, but we knew that he was going to speak to a group there. I decided to deliver my letter personally, which I did. I never received a response, either.

Shortly after we formed the Alianza, Rosita and I went to Mexico again, and we stayed there three months, explaining to the Mexican community why we had formed the Alianza and what the goals of our organization were. Now, I was freer to do those things I wanted to do. My time as a fugitive had already passed. During this time in Mexico, I thought of a plan to bring a caravan of automobiles to protest the violations of the Treaty of Guadalupe Hidalgo. The Mexicans liked that idea. Neither the Mexicans nor the world knew about the *Indohispanos* in the southwestern United States. My responsibility was to seek public opinion and create consciousness about our community, which had been ignored and lay dormant for more than 120 years.

Once I returned to Albuquerque, I began talking to our members about this automobile caravan and began to make plans to prepare for such a trip the following year. We had to prepare because our community had never raised its voice in the international arena. We also made preparations to have the first convention of the Alianza on September 21, 1963. We rented the auditorium of the Rio Grande School because our membership did not fit into the Alianza building anymore. Approximately 385 persons registered for this convention. The Anglo press, radio, and television gave us very little publicity.

Mexico: January 1964

After the beginning of the year, I went to Mexico again with Rosita. On January 9, we presented a memorandum to the National Confederation of Farm Workers in Mexico. I personally delivered this memorandum to the secretary general of the confederation, Javier Rojo Gómez. He was very attentive and gave me plenty of time to explain the details of our history. He promised that he would do whatever he could within Mexico and his government to see that they would back us in our petitions to the government of the United States. I considered this meeting a great success. On January 14, I presented myself to the secretary to the Secretariat of Foreign Affairs, at a meeting that I had solicited for several weeks. I presented a copy of the memorandum that I had presented earlier to President Adolfo López Mateos. I always asked for file stamps from the offices of the secretaries that I delivered these documents to, so that I would have proof of delivery for our archive. On January 29, I received a telegram from Donato Miranda Fonseca, the president's secretary, asking me to come to a meeting. I was very happy to have gotten this response. On February 4, I presented myself at the offices of Donato Miranda Fonseca at the appointed time. He was very courteous and respectful and gave me his complete attention. I told him briefly what our problem was. I spoke of the theft of our lands by the aggressors in the United States and the violations that our community had suffered under the Treaty of Guadalupe Hidalgo. I felt that the government of Mexico had begun to listen to us, and this gave me great comfort.

I returned to Albuquerque a few days later and then returned to Mexico again. Rosita was going to be fifteen years old and was celebrating her birthday at the home of Lolita Rebeles. I thought all was well and that we were marching along according to plan. The FBI, the embassy of the United States in Mexico, and the White House, however, all were moving against me. They were in a panic, and I did not know it. My good friend Ed Stanton was in the Department of Intelligence during World War II. He called me from his office to tell me of FBI visits to his office in Albuquerque. The FBI had bought a subscription to *The News Chieftain* and was reading my columns, week after week. According to Stanton, the FBI wanted to suspend the Alianza and to prevent the automobile caravan from going into Mexico in September 1964. An agent had told him that the White House did not want this caravan to take place because it would cause problems for the United States.

"This agent asked me to speak with you and to dissuade you from going forth with this caravan."

I asked Stanton, "And what did you say?"

"Well, I told him that he should come and speak with you in person. And that the government should do justice to the people whose lands have been stolen, and then you all would cancel the caravan."

Another thing that Ed told me was, "Reies, an agent is going to come and see me on a certain day to get my response. I suggest that you come to my office that day and listen to him and meet him. I can place you near our meeting area so that you can see and hear him without him seeing you."

I liked this idea very much, and that's what I did. The name of the FBI agent that showed up was Gordon Jackson. Among other things, he accused us of being a bad element and that the caravan would be a criminal act. The agent tried really hard to poison Ed's mind.

Ed said, "I know the history of these people. I know that they have had their land stolen. Don't they have a right to fight and struggle for their rights, especially here in their own country?"

The agent answered, "Well, there's courts for that."

But Ed told him, "According to the record, the judges and the courts were exactly the ones who stole the lands."

The agent did not have time to listen to these things, much less Stanton's story of how he had fought for the land grant in Socorro. His group had been defeated in that effort and run out of town in a gunfight with the Anglo landowners.

The agent interrupted Stanton and said, "Then you believe these people are right? Are you with them?"

Ed answered, "No, I'm not with anybody. I am on the side of justice. And if we have no justice for the people and have promised certain guarantees under the Treaty of Guadalupe Hidalgo, then they have no other choice but to go to Mexico to obtain justice and seek redress from the other government that signed the treaty."

The agent told him that I was a fugitive from justice in Arizona and that I had a bad record.

Ed said, "Well, why don't you arrest him?"

"Because the statute of limitations has run," said the agent.

I heard everything, but the agent did not know that I was listening. This was a very important lesson to me. I found out that the government would do everything in its power to stop me from bringing the land theft to the public's attention. Here we hadn't even begun to fight, and the FBI was already trying to stop us from the pursuit of our rights. I never forgot the conversation between this agent and Ed Stanton.

In the first few days of July, I made my last trip to Mexico. Rosita accompanied me again because they loved her a lot in Mexico. Lolita was sixty-five years of age with married children. Her husband worked at Petróleos Mexicanos (PEMEX). They were a wonderful couple. "Bring Rosita with you," is what she would tell me every time I went to Mexico. So I always took my daughter with me every time I did go to Mexico. If it hadn't been for this family, and their great love for me, I would not have been able to do the work that I did in Mexico.

During one of the trips in Mexico this year, I went to visit a friend of mine, Judith, in Chihuahua City. She introduced me to university students. The students invited me to speak at one of their public meetings. I attended and began to explain the purpose and goal for the automobile caravan into Mexico. I did not know that the governor of the state had his offices across from the park where I spoke to the students. The next day, when I went to a newspaper office for an interview, police agents came and arrested me. While I was not mistreated nor denied my right to speak freely, I was interrogated for over an hour and detained in prison. While in the prison, I spoke to people that I had met in Mexico City back in 1958. I spent the night in that prison. Rosita called Cristóbal and many others. Dr. Lauriano began looking for me. They called the Foreign Relations Secretariat and the United States Embassy in Mexico until they found me.

The next day, upon my release, we returned to Mexico City. I went to visit Luis Echeverría Alvarez, attorney general of Mexico at the time. I delivered a letter to him dated July 20. In this letter I referred to the memorandums that I had delivered to President López Mateos in 1959 and in 1964. I explained to him what the Alianza Federales de Mercedes was and its purposes, as well as the plans for the automobile caravan. I did everything that I thought was necessary to make sure that we would have no difficulty in bringing our automobile caravan into Mexico. I got the distinct impression that his government would allow this caravan into Mexico. So I proceeded to explain to the press that I thought the caravan was going to be a great success and that we would be able to educate the Mexican people about the forgotten community in the United States. A few days later I met with representatives of different groups and political parties to discuss the activities for the automobile caravan. I placed great emphasis on the educational goals of the caravan to educate the Mexican public and the care we were taking for it not to be used for the political ends of groups in Mexico. I declared that the Indohispano in the United States only was looking for support so that the government of the United States would be made to comply with the obligations of the Treaty of Guadalupe Hidalgo and return the lands that were stolen from us. Every one of the representatives of the various groups and political parties I spoke to gave his commitment to an adequate reception for the automobile caravan.

One evening, I had dinner with some of the friendly journalists to discuss the latest news that appeared in *La Prensa* and *El Universal* covering details of the caravan. That was the last night that I spent in Mexico. The next morning at seven, after washing my face and before completely clothing myself, I went to say good morning to Lolita. I just happened to look out the front door and saw a strange car with three individuals inside. When they saw me, they got out of the car and headed in my direction. I thought of closing the door, but I felt that since I was in Mexico, there was nothing to be fearful of. All the years that I had been a fugitive flashed before my mind at that moment. What could this be? The eyes of the individuals that came toward me were not normal. Their looks were not friendly. I called Lolita to come and witness what was about to happen.

The agents identified themselves and proceeded to take me to their car. They took me to their office. I was able to call Rosita but only allowed to tell her to give them my identification. I could not tell her anything else. I was very concerned about Rosita. She was only fifteen and I was responsible for her. I spent two hours being interrogated by them. I took the opportunity to explain our struggle for the land, the contents of the Treaty of Guadalupe Hidalgo, how our land was stolen, and the reason for this caravan that I was proposing to bring to Mexico. They put something in writing and asked me to sign it. There weren't any secrets that I was trying to hide. I basically told them the sad history of those of us of Mexican ancestry who had been abandoned in the United States. After two hours, an individual came in and told me they were going to deport me. He read a code section for about fifteen minutes. I asked him his name, and he gave me a business card that said Santiago Ibáñez Llamas. I thanked him and asked if I could get some clothes. All this time, I was shirtless. I thought this was very unjust.

While all this was happening, I thought again of Gordon Jackson and the interview he had had with Ed Stanton. I became convinced that the Anglos were behind all of this, even in Mexico. This was their conspiracy to deport me as a criminal. They took me to the airport at neck-breaking speed and never told me they were going to deport me right then. I just knew they were going to, but thought they would take me to the U.S. Embassy. I recognized the airport. And I did not have a shirt on. The agents put me on an airplane. I spoke to the pilot and told him that I was a persona non grata in Mexico. I felt embarrassed in front of all the tourists and other people who were well dressed. The pilot gave me a shirt, which I put on and thanked him for that.

For years I had spoken about how well Mexico had been receiving our news. All the people had great expectations that Mexico one day would present our cause before the United Nations. Can you imagine my horror in thinking of the shame and ridicule that the Anglo press would now have about us? This was of great sorrow to me. The problem with the bad press we were going to get was that it would never tell the truth. The government of the United States was behind my deportation. I was deported on August 8, 1964, from Mexico City to San Antonio. Once there, I called my brother Ramón, who took me to his house, and then, we called Albuquerque. I told the Alianza, "The caravan is suspended." My brother Cristóbal could not understand. He wanted to know what had happened. I told him, "I was deported from Mexico because of the Anglos in the White House. I'm at Ramón's house here in San Antonio and am all right."

I finally got back to New Mexico with a sad face and my heart in mourning. I was in mourning because of my community. I had uplifted their spirits so much by talking about Mexico, our mother country. I felt great shame now in having to explain to my people what had happened to me at the hands of the government of Mexico. I could tell them about Gordon Jackson, but how could I tell them about Mexico? That Saturday, we got together, and I finally gave them the negative information of what had happened in Mexico. I told the people, "I was not deported. They deported the entire community." I kept saying, "We're not going to let the Anglo divide Mexico and make Mexico be against us. We're going to come out ahead. In the future, we're going to change things. The Anglo will one day pay for what he has done to me and to us on the 8th of August."

During all this time, Rosita stayed by herself in Mexico. I sent my son David to get her, and within a week, they both arrived. Within a few days, the news finally broke in the United States with headlines "Mexico Deports Reies López Tijerina—The Man That Fights for the Land Once Taken by the Conquistadors." The newspapers, radio, and television said, "Nobody wants Tijerina, not even Mexico wanted Tijerina." The Anglo ranchers were happy with this news. We were in mourning as if we had been condemned to permanent slavery. Toward the end of August 1964, we celebrated the second convention of the Alianza in Santa Fe, the state capital. The Mexican professor Agustín Che Cánova spoke to the assembly to the U.S. invasion of Mexico and the the Treaty of Guadalupe Hidalgo. The convention delegates appreciated the words of professor Che Cánova, and through his illumination and education we all felt that a piece of Mexico had been left with us. My people then took the professor to Ciudad Juárez so he could catch an airplane back to Mexico City.

There were many groups in Mexico and the United States that protested my deportation. They sent letters to the authorities and copies of those letters to me, which I have, for the archive. The White House had won this round, but the struggle had not ended. The end of the struggle was coming, and I believed I would win it. In spite of these setbacks, the Alianza continued to grow rapidly. By now, we had affiliates in Texas, California, Arizona, Colorado, and many other states.

The Community of San Luis and Taylor

San Luis, Colorado, became an Alianza affiliate because of the battle between the local community and an Anglo, Jack Taylor. He had come from Virginia and taken title to some of the communal lands. These people had been calling me since 1962, and I had been with them from time to time. This time Taylor had beaten up a couple of young people. With the help of his workers, Taylor had tied them up and then beaten them with green branches until he broke their arms, hands, and heads. He beat them almost to death. According to some witnesses, Taylor was taking them in a pickup to bury them up in the mountains, and he passed through San Pablo, Colorado. One of the beaten young men was able to raise himself from the bed of the pickup and people saw him. They followed Taylor and made him return to San Luis. He turned over the beaten young men to the sheriff, who was a Mexican. The sheriff arrested Taylor and his workers and put them in jail. This was an opportunity to talk to the people about the great need for all of us who were heirs to this land to come together.

The Letter of 153 Land Grant Communities

We spent all of 1964 trying to unite the various communities. Meanwhile, we began gathering signatures from the representatives of the land grant communities, members of the Alianza, on a letter to be delivered requesting an audience with President Lyndon B. Johnson. As many as 153 representatives of the various land grant communities signed this letter. I wanted this letter to be a historic piece. The letter was ready by January 12, 1965.

The community in New Mexico is Catholic and of good moral principles by tradition. I was divorced, and the people did not want me to be single. Parents and spouses preferred that I have a companion so that they could trust me. Even though I knew that my conduct was righteous, my being single led to jealousy and speculation. I could not visit homes if a husband was at work, or even outside the home for fear of causing suspicion. I would be creating problems for the harmony within the Alianza membership. I began to think that it was preferable for me to marry. Months after my divorce, I had spoken with my ex-wife and with our children, telling them that the divorce was causing me problems. I thought that maybe we ought to get together again. I was not successful. The years had created greater distance between us. On the other hand, the community increased pressure on me not to remain single. That did not breed good confidence between those closer to me and the valiant ones of the Alianza. What I wanted to do least was to hurt the Alianza, the work product of my heart.

The Voice of Justice through the Radio

The slogan of the Alianza became "Justice is Our Creed and the Land is Our Heritage." That slogan became the keywords to the Alianza. The logo became the rainbow. On April 1, 1965, I began a radio program in Spanish on KABQ. We bought fifteen minutes of air time for fifteen dollars a day. Seven days a week, week after week, I transmitted a program, "The Voice of Justice," which could be heard as far north as Santa Fe, south as Socorro, west as Grants, and east almost as far as Santa Rosa. It was a station of 5,000 watts. Every morning at 10 a.m. I would speak to our community. This was the best medium to reach the community about the issue of the land. Soon, word began to spread about the radio program. Hundreds upon hundreds of heirs who had not heard of the Alianza began calling and writing to join the Alianza. This daily radio program resulted in the greatest weapon that I had ever used. Our community had never before felt that power in New Mexico.

The politicians and judges began looking for ways to get me off the air. It became clear to me that the power of the judges lies in their ability to interpret the law, which they interpreted to their liking and their mentality, in order to discriminate against the original settlers, Indians and Mestizos. They are behind all the "decisions" in the judicial system that have resulted in the stealing of our land. I spent well over ten years studying the world of the judges. I understood how they interpreted justice. The judges are the ones who legalized terror. They are the ones who robbed us of our culture and abused us. They opened the door to Thomas B. Catron and his allies. The judges are the ones who took the utility and value out of the Treaty of Guadalupe Hidalgo. I explained all this through the radio program. I explained the vitality of the Laws of the Indies. I knew that Article 6, Section 2, of the United States Constitution obligated this country to observe the commitments made to other nations, such as through treaties. It clearly states that the treaties entered into by the United States with other countries are the supreme law of the land. The community was learning more and more through my radio program and losing its fear of the unknown and of these judges.

The Alianza was growing in numbers and strength. Finally, I also began to air a program on Channel 4 television. Through those transmissions I was able to get to the states of Colorado, Arizona, Texas, and Oklahoma. We began transmitting on television five minutes at a time each Saturday, beginning on August 17, 1965. By the middle of the year we had fifteen minutes daily on the radio and five minutes each Saturday on television. We gathered so many members that we did not fit in the Alianza building anymore. We had to buy additional chairs and tables to be able to seat people that came to meetings.

The FBI would tape my radio and TV programs and, of course, clip my regular column in *The News Chieftain*. The puppet Mexicans followed the Anglo lead and would criticize me. They would say such things as, "Reies is an agent of Russia" or "Reies is a Communist." I answered my critics on radio, television, and in the newspaper. Radio and television were my best weapons for reeducating my people.

On August 8, 1965, I met Patricia at a Coney Island Restaurant in Albuquerque. Margarito and Félix Martínez were with me. I told her who I was and about my work. She had listened to the radio program and knew who I was. The next day I began to eat at her house. I did not have a way to cook. I would go from house to house and restaurant to restaurant to eat, so I took advantage of the invitation to eat with her. It took awhile to prepare our marriage. Patricia's uncles accepted me well. Margarito, my brother, had spoken to Patricia's uncles and asked for her hand in marriage. They agreed. We married on September 25. We celebrated the marriage in the Grand Ballroom of the Alianza because I did not have money. And all the people were very happy that I had now begun a new family. I did not have a home to take Patricia to. So, I decided to live in the Alianza's basement that did not have heating or a kitchen or water or a bath. But Patricia knew all of this. I did not hide my mission or how I lived or anything else from her. She had visited the "hole" where I lived. She said, "Happiness and love do not come from pretty things." Patricia's father, however, was saddened when he saw where his daughter, the eldest of the family, would live. But that's how we began our marriage.

Margarito in Prison

On October 2, two strangers were assaulted in Tierra Amarilla. These two Anglos accused my brother, Anselmo, of being the one who had beaten them up. Anselmo had been in the Tierra Amarilla jail previously. So the police showed these two Anglos Anselmo's photograph and they proceeded to identify him. They swore that my brother had assaulted them with a weapon, and Anselmo was put in jail again. Anselmo was not even in Tierra Amarilla when this happened. He was in Chicago. The police, after an investigation, finally believed that Anselmo was telling the truth. They then began looking for another Tijerina, Margarito. At the time of the assault, Margarito had been working at the Alianza. He had no money. We got a lawyer we could afford. On the day of trial, his lawyer did not bring any strong witnesses for the defense. The two Anglos lied again and swore that it was Margarito, not Anselmo, that had assaulted them. My brother was tried, convicted, and sentenced to fifty years in prison.

My Trip to Spain in 1966

I prepared to go to Spain at the beginning of 1966. I wanted to learn from Spanish lawyers what the people's rights to the land were. Furthermore, I wanted to learn more about the General Archive of the Indies. I wanted to buy the books, the Laws of the Indies. For many years I had wanted to go to Spain because Spain had administered this area for three hundred years. Their laws had been the institution that guided communities on ownership of the land. Spain was the mother of our civilization. I wanted to gather the evidence and documents necessary to protect the rights of the land grant heirs. That's why, to me, it was urgent that I go to Spain and learn firsthand about the Law of the Indies and the Spanish judges' interpretations. We could apply these rights to the lands that we had lost. I left Albuquerque on April 12, 1966, and headed to New York. From New York I left for Madrid and I arrived at Barajas Airport. The first few days in Spain, I could not do anything due to jetlag. I had several bad dreams those two days and nights. I stayed at the Grand Mogol bed-and-breakfast during those days. Finally, on the third day, I got over my jetlag and was able to move around.

At the bed-and-breakfast I met a young lawyer, Félix Carbo, who showed me Madrid. He treated me with the highest respect. I told Félix the story of the Southwest, of the people who had lost their lands, and gave him a brief history of our 120 years of struggle under Anglo oppression. Félix was a great help to me in Madrid. He showed me where things were and introduced me to people. One of the things that impressed me the most as I walked the streets in Madrid and other cities in Spain was the absence of police. I asked Félix why there were hardly any police around. He said, "There isn't sufficient crime. It is unnecessary to have police." After seven days there in Madrid, I took the train to Sevilla. I went directly to the General Archive of the Indies. As I traveled between Madrid and Sevilla and other points in Spain, I noticed the absence of barbwire fences. I visited La Mancha, where Don Miguel de Cervantes lived and wrote *The Adventures of Don Quixote.* At the General Archive I found mountains of documents. I made friends with the administrators and asked them to help me locate documents and become familiar with the abundant archive.

The Archives in Guadalajara

I remember having gone to the archive in Guadalajara, Jalisco, Mexico, and having gotten there late. An Anglo was commissioned by the government of Mexico to microfilm the ancient archives. He was in conspiracy with a woman from Albuquerque. When he finished his job at the archive in Guadalajara, he told the Anglo woman where to find the documents relating to the land in New Mexico. She went to this archive and stole the documents. When I got to Guadalajara in 1959, the director of the archive had not discovered that these Anglos had stolen documents from the archive. It was only after I asked him for certain papers having to do with the land in New Mexico that this crime was discovered. The day I arrived at the archive in Guadalajara, I presented myself to the director and told him my mission and who I was in terms of the struggle for land recovery. I knew that Albuquerque had been under the jurisdiction of the administrator from Guadalajara. Within thirty minutes he was able to tell me, "Yes, we have the archives of the settlers in New Mexico." He sent some young people to locate that section of the archive. Within five or ten minutes they came back and said, "We can't find them. They are not in their place." He rushed over and made the same discovery. That's how the crime was discovered. "The last persons who had been with those documents had been this Anglo woman and the photographer hired by the Mexican government."

The Archives in Sevilla

I feared that the same thing could have happened in Sevilla at the hands of other Anglos. The administrators at the Archive of the Indies told me that there had been a fire and some documents had been destroyed. They recommended that I speak to professor Juan Mansano y Mansano, a member of the law faculty, and professor José Llavador

Mira in Hispanic American Studies, both there at the University of Seville. Once I registered as a researcher at the General Archive of the Indies, I was given a pass. Another professor by the last name of Muro also gave me a detailed explanation of landholder rights in the New World. I believed that only Mexico and Spain could open the doors to our claim because Mexico and Spain, for sure, were the origin of these laws. They had conferred titles to these lands and had sent settlers, the heirs to these lands in question. The various administrators and workers there at the archive told me that there had been many Anglos from the United States coming to investigate and research the archives. I became suspicious. I had to learn how to read the ancient Spanish language and wording to understand the documents. All of these lands were ceded under Philip II in Ordinance 99.

In Sevilla, I had the good fortune to find and purchase a copy of the four volumes of *Las Siete Partidas*. These laws govern everything having to do with property rights. I searched for a copy of *The Laws of the Indies*. Unfortunately, I never could find a copy to purchase. Upon return to Madrid, I kept looking in every bookstore to obtain a copy of these ancient codes.

Finally on May 12, I returned to New Mexico via New York. Patricia was expecting our first child. She and I had only spoken once by telephone, but I had written to her daily while I was in Spain. All the people awaited me with great anxiety. Like me, they wanted to know if the cause we were promoting had any kind of support in the interpretation that Spain gave its laws governing the Indies. What the United States believed did not matter to us anymore because the historic process of crimes against us and our rights to the land had destroyed U.S. credibility. The day that I arrived, the community and the membership of the Alianza had prepared a great fiesta and celebration.

The March of July 4, 1966

Now that I had better proof in my hand, and having learned a great deal while in Spain, I decided to have a march from Albuquerque to Santa Fe. This march, I thought, would be a first step so that our children would begin to see how we struggled for our rights. Second, this would be a chance for the world to learn of our grievances. Third, the government would have to listen to us. And if not, we would leave a record that we had tried peacefully to obtain justice for our people.

The entire membership voted for this march. They knew that we were dealing with a giant enemy, the same one who had fabricated atomic bombs and hydrogen bombs since 1945. Their nuclear power had converted them into a gigantic monster on a global scale. They would not be bothered by little incidents involving Blacks or Indians or Indohispanos. But regardless, we had to demonstrate our commitment and show our children the way to protest. The Anglo and his press had hidden the truth from our community, the very ones who had given names to all the rivers, mountains, and cities in the Southwest. The world ignored completely what the United States government had done to the millions of Indohispanos who lived in the Southwest. That's why the coming together of all these communities of the land took the Anglo and his allies by surprise. We made the preparations; we used the radio and the television to inform the people of this march. I still would speak on the radio and television regularly and tell them about my Spain trip and what I had learned there. The people who wrote and called asked me hundreds of questions. At the reception, I showed them the clippings of publicity, of articles that I had given to the press in Spain.

On July 2, 1966, three hundred and thirty persons began that march of sixty-six miles. This was a significant day for me, as it was for all of us. Young and old, men and women began that historic journey with great enthusiasm and expectation. Some of the Anglos who passed us by in their cars would yell at us, "Wetbacks, go back to Mexico." These epithets revealed the mentality of the North American. The first night that we stopped, a car full of Anglos came by and fired gunshots at us. But other than that incident and the epithets, everything went well. We took three days to arrive in Santa Fe. I called friends in Mexico and asked them if any news of our march had been reported in Mexico, and sadly they told me, no. Upon arrival in Santa Fe, the governor made his way to receive us. The governor gave us a brief audience out of courtesy, and we gave him a copy of the memorandum that we had given to others in the past. In addition, in our memorandum to him, we asked that he convene a task force to investigate the theft of our land. This is well documented, and no one can say that we did not ask for justice in a peaceful way.

The governor asked for the opinion of Myra Jenkins, the director of the general archives of the state, and she wrote me a letter later, but she also gave a copy to the press. In short, she said, "The land question has been settled many years back. This Alianza of Reies is seeking money and has no merit." Myra Jenkins' opinion simply promoted stereotypes and repeated the accusations that I had been falsely accused of in the past. In essence, what this lady, supposedly the expert on archives, was telling us was that we should accept the abuse, the theft that the Anglo has committed for the last hundred and twenty years. We shouldn't defend ourselves, much less join the Alianza. She said that the Alianza members were a group of racketeers. The press became Myra Jenkins' mouthpiece, for I was not given an opportunity to respond. The editor of the *Albuquerque Journal* and Myra Jenkins belonged to the same church, and that church owned communal land taken from our ancestors. The community and I were fighting against a political structure and a religious structure that were well supported by the powers that be in New Mexico.

I continued expressing my opinion on the radio and on television, and I kept asking who created this problem? Ever since Spain and Mexico began to settle this part of the Southwest over the course of three hundred years, those people and those communities had protection and respect from both Mexico and Spain. Those governments never stole the land from their people. It was with the arrival of the United States, "the democratic government of the United States, the leader of the free world," that we began to have problems and violations of our land rights. Spain and Mexico have valiantly guarded the archives that document the ownership rights, but people such as members of the Santa Fe Ring have destroyed those records. So I would ask, "Who has caused this problem with the land, Reies or the Anglos?" And every day I would hit on that theme as best I could.

The Taking of San Joaquín, October 1966

That the government would question the right of the people to their land was a cruel and unjust violation of the Treaty of Guadalupe Hidalgo. I now sought to open a new door to the halls of justice. When Ed Stanton fought for the grant in Socorro, he got good publicity in the state, and *Life* magazine published an ample report on his effort on June 29, 1953. In my case, the *Denver Post* was the only newspaper that gave me good publicity, and, on January 3, 1966, *Newsweek* gave me a brief report; it was informative but nicknamed me, appropriately, "Don Quixote." It is notable that when an Anglo sought to reclaim land, the other Anglos thought favorably of him, but when a Mexican attempted the same, they did not like it at all.

The march of July 4 did not have a good result, even though it lifted the spirits of the Alianza. But the Anglo and his allies thought we were crazy. Now our next step, given the cruelty of the government, obligated us to take the land by force at San Joaquín del Río de Chama. This land belonged to more than three hundred and fifty families who had never left their land. The title to this land grant is in perfect condition. The U.S. House of Representatives created a committee on public lands and named as surveyor general, Thomas B. Profit, on July 22, 1854, and Profit confirmed the rights of these families to the San Joaquín grant and made that recommendation to the committee on February 14, 1873. By this time, the Congress had already approved a land grant to Thomas B. Catron and other Anglos who had taken possession of one million, seven hundred fourteen thousand, seven hundred sixty-four point ninety-three acres of land. The people were indignant over this illegal act. Because of the furor that the people raised over this "Maxwell" grant over the ownership rights of Guadalupe Miranda and the other people, the committee stalled other applications. But Catron got his nearly two million acres of land and the people of San Joaquín did not. In 1891, Congress established the U.S. Court of Claims, but the people of San Joaquín never presented their demand. An English corporation, however, bought a few lots from some of the residents and asked the Court of Claims to confirm their right to 472,000 acres. Surveyor General James K. Profit had recommended those lands be given to the people who were the heirs to the San Joaquín grant. Naturally, the Court of Claims refused this British claim with the explanation that the land belonged to the original settlers and their heirs, who then numbered four hundred or more. King Charles IV of Spain had given this San Joaquín del Río de Chama land grant, on August 1, 1806, through the New Mexican governor of the time, Joaquín Alencaster. The principal settler and impresario for this grant was Francisco Salazar, who had settled there with thirty-one other families at least forty years prior to the arrival of the first white man.

In Book 5, Title 7, Law 1, of the *New Recompilation of the Laws of Spain,* it clearly states that a city or pueblo can obtain title even against the crown if they can hold the land peacefully for at least forty years. The same thing is said in the *Law of Prescriptions* in Book 4, Title 15, and Law 1. So even if the title to the land grant in San Joaquín had not been to the letter of the law—but it was—the people had title because of possession for forty years.

On May 12, 1945, the congressman from the northern part of New Mexico, Antonio Fernández, presented the claim of the people from San Joaquín to the 78th Congress. In his presentation, Congressman Fernández repeated the commitments under the Treaty of Guadalupe Hidalgo, the history of the people of San Joaquín, the legal history behind the struggles of the 47th Congress beginning in 1870, and its subsequently leaving everything in limbo. He clearly outlined that the people of San Joaquín had never had their day in court. The only ones who had gotten their day in court and been approved, illegally, were the two Anglos who got title to the "Maxwell" grant of nearly two million acres. The Congress ignored the plea of Antonio Fernández, as it had done in prior years to the people of San Joaquín. The same year that Congress ignored one of its own members, Antonio Fernández, the United States was involved in World War II. This was supposedly in the name of democracy and for justice. Many youths from northern New Mexico were involved as soldiers in this war, defending the rights of England and other European countries. Many of them were in Japan as prisoners of war, and still the Anglo ignored us.

It was now a hundred and twenty years of injustice and oppression that our people had suffered, just as I had said in the letter of December 12, 1959 to President Eisenhower. The people were ready. I only led them. The people of San Joaquín had elected officers. A direct descendant of the original settler, Francisco Salazar, was elected mayor: José Lorenzo Salazar. Samuel Córdoba was elected marshall. We chose October 15, 1966, as the day to take the land of San Joaquín. According to the original settlers and their descendants, the land grant consisted of six hundred thousand square acres, and we thought that the best site to provoke the confrontation with the federal government would be to take the area within the designated grant now called "Echo Amphitheater Park." We took that park by force and held it over the weekend. Their press immediately began their campaign against us, describing it as violent aggression. The newly elected officials of the Pueblo of San Joaquín sent letters to all other residents, asking them to recognize this new government. The letters were also sent to the federal authorities, particularly to the Department of Agriculture, to evacuate these lands.

On October 22, 1966, more than one hundred fifty cars and vans took part in the official takeover. The entrance to the park was full of police agents under the direction of James Evans. The federal government had sent this agent to New Mexico after his having done service in the southern states. According to confidential sources, he was famous for having used his gun to intimidate many Blacks. According to this source of information, he was allegedly responsible for several deaths (but we did not know for sure). I thought that the choice of James Evans was because the White House thought this Anglo supremacist was mentally conditioned to strike fear into the hearts of the settlers of San Joaquín with the hope that they would not follow Reies López Tijerina. This Anglo was the one that spoke the most while we took the lands of San Joaquín. He showed his credentials and showed great courage, but the people questioned him and moved him aside and, at the same time, arrested other forestry agents. The judge of the Pueblo of San Joaquín sentenced these individuals to thirty days in jail and levied a five-hundred-dollar fine, but suspended that sentence and fine on the condition that they not continue to trespass on the lands of San Joaquín and not bother the residents.

The Anglos had a plan to destroy our movement. Basically, the plan was not to arrest or charge any individual member of the founding families of San Joaquín and to target only Tijerina and the officials of the Alianza. They were thus admitting that they respected the rights of the land heirs. The government also recalled the other federal agents stationed in San Joaquín and reassigned them to the state of Arizona. Only James Evans remained. They left him, I think, because they needed a brave man to confront Tijerina. Locally, the Anglo judges won this round. But the community won in the eyes of the world. Moreover, the people of the land began to lose the terror that they had for the Anglo over the past 120 years. The Albuquerque press, loyal to the spirit of the Santa Fe Ring, immediately began a campaign of lies and confusion against us. But this Anglo press would not say anything against the individuals or people. Their target was the founder of the Alianza. The reporters conducting this campaign were not born in New Mexico and only reported emphatically the government's version and the Anglo side. They never reported the legal history of the Pueblo of San Joaquín, and my declarations on the subject were regularly thrown into the trashcan. The truth is that the Anglo and his government are afraid to open the doors to justice, because then everything will come to light, including the crimes, fraud, and conspiracies of the Santa Fe Ring, and the destruction of the archives in Santa Fe by the Anglo governor and Methodist minister William A. Pile. They know full well that their investigation will bring to light the history the likes of which Alexander Solzyenitzin, the Russian exile, would be amazed.

Judge Howard Bratton

After five days of holding the land, we surrendered to the Anglo judge Howard Bratton. That was his day. I was ready to confront him and pay the price necessary for the salvation of my people. I had thought about this for many years. From among the more than 300 participants in the takeover of San Joaquín, only five people were charged. Of these 300 people, there were some 150 actual heirs to the land of San Joaquín. The government did not bother a single one of them. This signified to me that hidden deep in their conscience was the recognition that these people were the rightful heirs to the land. The taking of San Joaquín was the beginning of a large conflict between the Anglo government and me.

Judge Bratton never looked me in the eyes. I would stare at him, but he never would return the gaze. The judge accused me of assaulting federal agents and confiscating their vehicles. The U.S. Attorney was Victor Ortega. He was blind to the rights of the people of the land

and full of fear of the Anglo. He was well conditioned; he jumped and whooped at the sound of the oppressor's voice. Judge Bratton imposed a bail of $5,000 each, clearly with the intent of destroying the finances of the Alianza. We had voluntarily turned ourselves in. And in cases of simple assault such as this, the judges usually allowed people bail on their personal recognizance, but not us. So this judge was already beginning to mask his true sentiments and expose the traditional attitude held by the foreign Anglo toward the people of the land in New Mexico and all of the Southwest. We noted this. It was very clear to us. I quickly learned of Judge Bratton's attitude. He had a desire in his heart to crush and destroy the people of the land.

If he would let me, I would begin to bring to light the great crimes, thefts, and destruction of archives and destruction of our own culture. Judge Bratton knew about me and my thoughts about judges, their conduct and ethics, because of my radio broadcasts. I had done these broadcasts daily for more than two years. Now, for the first time, I was face to face with one of these judges. Personally, I did not know him, but he did know me because of my television broadcasts and my newspaper articles.

The Alianza had enough money to pay for our bail, so that we did not spend a day in jail. Carlos Cedillo was our lawyer. The five accused were Jerry Noll, Cristóbal, Ezequiel Domínguez, Alfonso Chávez, and me. Immediately upon release, we went to the Alianza building to celebrate the beginning of this struggle. I said to those gathered there that the Anglo would no longer fool the world with his hypocrisy. "The struggle against judges that have suppressed the truth for the last 120 years began today. These judges are behind all the great evil done to our people. The judges have justice in their hands. They can interpret the Treaty of Guadalupe Hidalgo to their liking. If they wished, they could give us our rights by citing Article 2, Section 5, of the New Mexico Constitution, or better yet, they could cite Article 6, Section 2, of the United States Constitution. But Judge Bratton continued the practice of imposing excessive bail and continuing to flagrantly violate the Eighth Amendment of the United States Constitution."

According to this amendment, the bail Bratton imposed was excessive and exorbitant. It affected the community because ultimately it was the membership that paid the bail. Bratton violated the Constitution and, in so doing, made a mockery of the Eighth Amendment of the United States. An honest judge should not take sides in a political conflict, much less be involved judicially in supporting one side.

I continued speaking on radio and television. In that fashion I was able to counter some of the negative press and the bad seeds they had planted in people's minds. Every day, through the radio, I would answer the judges, lawyers, and press about the issues involved in the fight for the land of San Joaquín. I would ask them to come debate with me, but no one ever accepted. The public, upon hearing me answering these judges and inviting them to debate, began to understand. They were either afraid of me or I was telling the truth. Shortly after the taking of San Joaquín, I began to notice that young people started coming to the meetings at the Alianza. In the early years, only the elderly and the mature adults were interested; but after the July 4th march, and certainly after the taking of San Joaquín, the young people started gravitating toward the Alianza. To see our children march, yell, and struggle for their rights was an eternal joy to us, the parents. This awakening in our children affected us all throughout the state. In the schools, our young people had acquired inferiority complexes and learned an incorrect history. Now, our children were beginning to remove the yoke of ignorance that the Anglo had placed on them. In the schools across the state, debates ensued between children arguing these points. They became regular visitors to the Alianza offices to ask me for advice. They began to organize cultural groups. Through the radio I spoke to their parents, asking them to support and help their children.

The Anglo press began to raise a clamor: "Reies López Tijerina is dividing the people of New Mexico. He is planting hate among the Mexicans against the Anglos." One of the greatest psychological victories that these confrontations brought was that for the first time in 120 years, the Anglos in the Southwest began calling themselves Anglos in the newspapers. Prior to this time, they simply called themselves Americans and us Mexicans. But after the march and the taking of San Joaquín, all of this changed. There were other changes. In the northern part of New Mexico, some Anglo ranchers privately began admitting wrongdoing to some of the people in an attempt to placate them and encourage them not to follow Tijerina. I learned this through the words of some of those residents. They also told me of the hate that many of these Anglos began to demonstrate toward me. Anglo ranchers often would talk about me in front of their Mexican help. The Mexican help would send word to the offices of the Alianza about these comments.

I was very happy to see the participation of my children in this struggle for the land. Separation and divorce had not changed their love toward me and for the salvation of our people. During the march they acted like true, brave soldiers for justice. I never saw them tire or complain of hunger or thirst. I used to tell my children, "If we save the land, we can save our culture. If we can save our culture, we can save our families. And if we save our families, we win freedom from the Anglo's yoke." The valor demonstrated by my children gave me inspiration. In the taking of San Joaquín, Rosita and David were in front, in the first vehicle that broke through the security ring of federal agents. I did not expect anything more or less than I did of the children of the other valiant heirs. On the one hand, I did not give my children what other parents could give theirs, but my children always understood me. They knew that I was attending to a larger family, the family of our oppressed people. They would tell me, "Papá, someone has to do the work of uniting and inspiring our people." My children still bought their clothes at the Goodwill store. Every night I would pray for them. I would hope that some day my children would see a just and better world in the Southwest and that they would know the liberty and justice that the Anglo had denied us for 120 years.

When we took San Joaquín, Patricia, my wife, was expecting Isabel. She was due in eighteen days. I took her to the community of Canjilon and left her there to wait. I did not want anything to happen to her or to lose the child. Isabel Iris was born on November 10, 1966. I named her Isabel for the great woman that helped Christopher Columbus discover the Americas. Queen Isabel offered her support to this undertaking and thereby embarrassed all the men of her era. And at the same time, I named her Iris because of the logo and symbol of the Alianza, which is and was a rainbow.

Several FBI agents—Ed Martín from Los Alamos, John Bass from Santa Fe, and Wirt Jones from Albuquerque—met with Martín Vigil, state police commander for District 11 in New Mexico. The FBI agents had received instructions from Washington to investigate our claims. According to *The New Mexican,* the White House was asking for this investigation to learn firsthand the issues and their options. We all celebrated with great joy because for the first time Washington had recognized our claim. However, the local politicians in New Mexico did not share Washington's interest. They were ready to confront us and continue the 120-year conspiracy to deny us justice.

Myra Helen Jenkins

The local politicians had the historian and state archivist Dr. Myra Helen Jenkins at their disposal. In her declarations, this woman affirmed that the Alianza was an organization of racketeers that had been established only to defraud the people and to gather funds for criminal purposes. She also claimed that many of the heirs' land claims, originally made in the nineteenth century, were fraudulent.

Like the foreigners Thomas B. Catron and Bob Brown, Dr. Jenkins continued the practice of covering up a crime that her ancestors had committed. Instead of calling the Santa Fe Ring and William A. Pile criminals and racketeers, she called Reies and the Alianza "an organization of criminals." The enemies of the Alianza found a haven in Dr. Jenkins and her words. Dr. Jenkins incubated the idea of destroying Reies López Tijerina. Every Anglo in New Mexico quoted Mrs. Jenkins. On October 28, 1966, the general manager of radio station KQEO, Kenneth J. Baugh, had these words to say over the air: "KQEO has been informed that all of the Spanish land grants and Mexican grants have been explored and litigated; therefore, the promises that Reies is offering his supporters is pie in the sky. KQEO has been informed that the majority of the money contributed by the members of the Alianza will be used personally by Reies Tijerina and his family."

Although these accusations were false and defamatory, many people, certainly all the Anglos, began to believe them. This was the greatest conspiracy that the Alianza and I had to fight.

There were Anglos that supported us. And we had to be conscious of those who were not involved in this conspiracy to destroy the Alianza and its founder. At the University of New Mexico, there were many professors who sympathized with the cause of the people of the land. Dr. Clark Knowlton, professor of Southwestern History, plainly accused other Anglos of these crimes and theft of the land. The Anglo press, however, would not quote Dr. Knowlton or give him the same importance it gave to the opinions of Dr. Myra Jenkins.

The taking of San Joaquín returned to the people part of the valor they had lost over the years. In this new environment, I began raising certain issues that the people had not thought of. On the radio I pointed out that all the Anglos carried weapons in their cars and pickups, and I asked why the people of the land did not. Over the radio I explained the Second Amendment to the United States Constitution—the right of citizens to bear arms—and pointed out that only the Anglos exercised this right. I also quoted the Ninth Amendment: "Reserved rights not interpreted or ceded by the people are to remain in the hands of the people." Our people, even before the beginning of the United States, retained these "reserved rights." I felt that our struggle and uprising would take us to serious confrontations, certainly after the taking of San Joaquín. That was why I was trying to educate our public and to raise the relevant aspects of our struggle. Over the radio I began to summon people to our cause. I would say, "This is the hour for the brave among you to follow us, to come join us. Your children need you to defend them."

Finally, tempestuous 1966 came and went. The cold and heavy winter that year covered the land and the roads in the north with snow. Northern New Mexico receives winter earlier and gets spring later. Frequently there is snowfall, even in May, in that area. Radio and television, newspapers and the post office did the activities of the Alianza during these months. And, in person, we worked the southern area that hardly ever has snow. Also, during the winter months we received visitors from other places and made plans for our convention. Shortly after the taking of San Joaquín, colleges and universities began to invite me to come speak about the Treaty of Guadalupe Hidalgo and the land grant struggle. I would get calls from New York, San Francisco, Florida, and Los Angeles. The Anglo press continued to call me by my nickname, "Don Quixote," but now some began to attack me as a racketeer. Letters and telegrams continued to be sent from the Alianza members to the White House. Now we were not so much expecting a response as maintaining a record of demanding justice. We knew that the tyrannical arrogance of the White House had not changed, but we had to keep insisting. In these letters and telegrams we did not ask for anything difficult, only an investigation as to the rights of the people of San Joaquín. Why didn't they want this simple investigation? We pay our taxes like everyone else. They ask for our vote when they want to be elected. All the people had supported Senator Montoya from New Mexico. We had even asked him on the radio and in two letters to get us an interview with President Johnson. When the people had sent the president the letter on January 12, 1965, with 153 signatures of pueblo delegates, we had also sent a copy to Senator Montoya, as well as the two other letters. Montoya just gave us his word to look into the matter, and nothing else. Montoya was not ignorant of what the people or the Alianza members wanted.

We did not know what else to do in order to get through the door that had been closed forever. The title to San Joaquín had not been adjudicated. We knew all of these judges were implicated in covering up the robbery. We did not have much hope. On May 14, 1967, we gathered the members at the Tierra Amarilla courthouse. The courtroom was full, and many were standing because there were no available seats. That day the community elected new officials and voted to support the claim to the land by the people of San Joaquín. The assembly also supported a new claim to the land in Tierra Amarilla. The land grant of Tierra Amarilla has about 594,000 acres. Manuel Martínez had asked for the land grant on July 20, 1832, and obtained it. He asked on behalf of his seven sons, himself, and the families that accompanied him. The title to that grant, like all the other concessions from Spain or Mexico in reference to water, roads, and pasture, stated that the land was communal and to be held in trust for the children and future residents of the original settlers.

By June 1966, our offices were full of visitors, day and night. Some we knew were police spies and ears for local politicians. The Anglos began to round up Mexican politicians against us. These Mexicans have a mental complex put there by the Anglo. And they are well conditioned because of this mentality to reject everything I said as if it were a sin. Because of this mental complex, the Native American and the Indohispano could not expect justice from the Anglo. Hopefully, the Anglo will think about the future of his children and see the good that he could bring if he will only change his attitude, his arrogance, and his political direction. I began to notice a different thing: Anglo youths were deserting their own people and looking for a future among Indians and Indohispanos, even marrying our sons and daughters. More than fifty of these couples had registered as members of the Alianza. These young Anglos began to tell me a different version of what they felt, saw, and hoped would happen with their race in the coming years, especially in terms of the politics of the United States, both interior and exterior. These Anglo youths were interested in the disintegration of the Anglo-Saxon family. They thought that the Anglo education being supported by their parents and imparted in the schools was what was turning their society from the moral road.

Judge Vearle H. Payne

Federal Judge Vearle H. Payne came into the picture against the people struggling for their property. In all of New Mexico there were only two federal judges. One was Bratton and the other, Payne. Bratton already had us in his crosshairs. And Payne began to threaten us with jail if we did not turn over the membership list of the Alianza. The state of New Mexico, without rights nor law on which to base its request, wanted to confiscate the corporate registration of our organization and was asking the federal court to make us turn over the list of more than 30,000 names of persons who comprised our membership. This was worse than the crimes committed by the Santa Fe Ring, many of the Alianza elders told me. These tactics were worse than anything Joseph Stalin, Hitler, or Mussolini had ever used. These shameless acts showed me the contempt these two Anglo judges had for the law. This was a campaign of terror against our people. They wanted to scare our people and break their unity. They wanted our people to be disorganized, disenchanted, like sheep without a shepherd. This was exactly the way our people were when Mexico became the political sovereign over these new lands. This is the same way that our people were when

William Pile destroyed and burned the archives. That's why they did not protest. This was the same way our people were when Thomas B. Catron took their lands without their saying a word. This is how Bratton and Payne wanted to keep our people.

I was at home on May 27, about 8 o'clock at night, when my wife told me there were people in the alley and she thought they were men. I quickly looked out the window and saw two men at one end of the alley and two at the other end. I quickly called my brother Anselmo and told him to wait for me down at the cross street by the Alianza building. I managed to elude detection of the agents and had Anselmo take me to Espanola, where we had already placed our records. We had divided the membership records into two parts: the files themselves were left in a private home of a brave rancher, and Cristóbal had the alphabetical listing on index cards in his car. The district attorney for Tierra Amarilla and Santa Fe, Alfonso Sánchez, was the one who had signed the complaint demanding our membership records. Sánchez had represented some of the settlers of Tierra Amarilla in years past when in private practice. After he had taken their money and exploited them, he abandoned their cause. This was the reference the people of Tierra Amarilla gave me about Alfonso Sánchez. Judge Payne felt sure that Alfonso Sánchez would be able to carry forth this fight, but he was wrong. Our people had learned about the traitors among us. They knew that the Anglo always uses one of our own, just like the Egyptians had used the Hebrews against each other. We knew that behind all of this were the judges Bratton and Payne, not Alfonso Sánchez. He only fooled himself into thinking he was fulfilling a great mission. A few months later, on May 30, the five of us were in a car, when all of a sudden Emilio Naranjo, a federal marshall, and his five agents surrounded us. They shined flashlights into our car and in our faces, one by one. He shined the light straight in my face, but he did not recognize me, and they left. I do not know why he did not recognize me, since he knew me so well. That remains a mystery to me. I did not want to comply with Payne's court order instructing me to turn over the membership records until after the convention that was scheduled for the first few days in June. Some of the inner circle of the Alianza and I had discussed my resigning as president of the Alianza. I would not have direct responsibility over membership records, and, therefore, would not be able to comply with the court order.

Coyote, New Mexico

After the night the marshalls had surrounded us, I decided to go farther up north and sleep in the hills in Coyote. I had good friends up there, like Celestino Velásquez. Baltazar Martínez accompanied me. That night, the radio news broadcast said that Alfonso Sánchez had ordered thiry-five police cars to search for Tijerina and serve him with the court order. And through radio, television, and the newspaper, Sánchez warned the people that anybody attending the meeting with Reies at the Alianza in Coyote in June would be arrested. Of course, all the Anglos and their Hispanic flunkies were supporting Alfonso Sánchez. The name of Alfonso Sánchez began to rise in popularity. He actually thought that this would propel him to be elected governor of the state one day. In those days, the Anglos needed him and would not abandon him. The Anglos knew and feared that if Reies continued as he was, the White House would be obligated to truly investigate the land claim of the people to San Joaquín. The Anglos knew full well that the people of San Joaquín had never had their day in court. If an investigation were launched, all their hypocrisy would come out, and the Anglos would lose their possession of these lands. The Anglos, especially the judges in New Mexico, could not allow an investigation into the title of San Joaquín to take place.

All the roads leading to Coyote were closed by the state police on June 2, 3, and 4. All automobiles were searched and the passengers were threatened with arrest if they stopped in Coyote. While all this was happening, I was staying at the house of Celestino Velásquez. All the radio broadcasts said that Reies had disappeared and abandoned the people in their hour of greatest need. The *Albuquerque Journal* insulted me by saying that I was just hot air. In Coyote, some people, particularly the Anglos, began to ask, "Where is Reies López Tijerina?"

On June 2, in the morning, two federal agents came by the house where I was staying. One of them was Cristóbal Zamora and the other was an Anglo that I did not know. Acting dumb, they knocked on the door. Baltazar Martínez jumped them from behind, rifle in hand and pointing it in their faces. I was watching through the window. "What are you looking for here?" he asked. "You are trespassing on private property. And if you do not leave right now, I'm going to give you a lesson you will never forget."

The police agents turned white. Without a word, they turned and left immediately.

All these efforts were aimed at destroying the meeting that we were about to celebrate in Coyote. This in itself was a crime. The Anglo is used to legalizing his crimes and never sees it as such. They never allow themselves to consider the opinions of those they oppress. For this same reason, many of our people do not understand what is happening, and they only accept the Anglo version. The Anglos in power, with their flunkies at the front, attempted to prevent our people from meeting. In spite of these tactics being used, more than two hundred people showed up in Coyote for the convention. And every one of these individuals promised that in the next election, Alfonso Sánchez would be defeated because he had allowed himself to be used by these foreign Anglos to shut out the people and to prevent their coming together to claim their rights.

The Coyote incident remained etched in our hearts. It was here that we truly learned how the Anglo is inside. Because of this Coyote incident, we gathered greater strength of unity. The Anglo's hatred made him so blind that he could not see what he was bringing upon himself. He played and he lost. We lost in the first encounter, but the end result had not been seen yet.

When I came to Coyote, Patricia stayed by herself in Albuquerque, and Emilio Naranjo went and tried to force her to accept Judge Payne's order, but she refused. Emilio knew that the law required him to notify the person directly, not a substitute. When Emilio Naranjo tried to force Patricia to take these orders, he failed and had to tell Judge Payne that he could not find Reies. Once the days scheduled for the meeting had passed, my wife came to Coyote around midnight. We began visiting some of the people and decided to gather in Canjilon. We sent word everywhere that we would be meeting in Canjilon. By this time, the police had removed the barricades, and Joe Black, the head of the state police, had left the area. Joe Black is a Mexican with an Anglo name. He was called a "coyote." The people in New Mexico called those Mexicans with Anglo parents or names "coyotes." And they considered them more dangerous when they were uniformed police with guns at their side.

As a result of this police harassment, one very dangerous pattern emerged. The heads of the various police agencies now considered me a hunted person. Without anyone to defend me, the Anglo press created this environment and image. This dangerous new reality became clear after Coyote, when the police stopped all people on the road leading to Coyote. The people told me that the police said, "We do not have anything against you, only Tijerina." I understood the Anglo tactic, seeking to ridicule me in front of my community, attempting to prove that I was a coward, and saying that I only sought personal gain. They no longer called me "Don Quixote." Now they implied that I was simply defrauding the people to take their money. Eleven of our officials, including Cristóbal Tijerina and Félix Martínez, were arrested and jailed in Santa Fe. All of the documents we had relating to the San Joaquín land grant were confiscated. The people's weapons, ammunition, and gas masks were taken from them. All the Anglos carried weapons, but they did not take a single one of theirs. All of the leaders and officials of the Alianza were arrested, except me. The morning of June 6, I heard over the radio that eleven of the Alianza officials would be brought up on charges in Tierra Amarilla.

Tobías Leyba's ranch could not handle all the people that were arriving. The ranch looked like a huge army camp. Leyba had promised to donate four lambs for a cookout so the people could eat. Word spread that we were having a picnic at Canjilon. Before we ate, I heard on the radio that Alfonso Sánchez would be in Tierra Amarilla that day at three in the afternoon. Immediately, I thought that we should go to Tierra Amarilla and arrest this symbol of Anglo justice, Alfonso Sánchez. I gathered the head of the main families there and presented the idea. Everyone voted for the plan. Patricia suspected something, but she did not know what this was about. We all knew that the state police would be in Tierra Amarilla, because they had to arraign the eleven Alianza officials. So the biggest problem was how to arrest

Alfonso Sánchez, the main sellout, without causing injury or death. I sent Moisés Morales to look over the courthouse and tell us the number of police that were there. Moisés called a few minutes later and said that just a few were present. Rosita, my daughter of eighteen, offered to go into the courthouse with the first group. We did this so that the police would not be alarmed and cause things to get out of hand. Rosita's role was extremely important. At three in the afternoon we were ready. A one-ton truck, three cars, and a station wagon took off. I told Juan Valdez to cover the truck bed with a big tarp because we had to drive in front of the Forest Service office, and they might call the police in Tierra Amarilla if they suspected anything. I ordered those who were in the caravan, upon passing the Forest Service office, to sink down in their seats and have only the drivers show their faces. I also told them that the vehicles should be spaced apart as we went by, not one after the other, to avoid suspicion. At exactly two o'clock, the first car took off toward Tierra Amarilla. And three minutes later the second car. We all left the Leyba ranch this way. We were armed with four or five automatic weapons, guns, rifles, and a twenty-two-caliber rifle. The plan was that our vehicles would arrive at one side of the plaza. Others, on the other side, were to make sure that Moisés Morales was correct about the number of state police present. My brother Cristóbal and the other Alianza officials had just been released from court under bail. None of them was present.

The police, upon seeing that none of the Alianza members had arrived for those proceedings, left. The plaza was very quiet. When we arrived, Rosita and those who were with her went into the courthouse before anyone else. I waited for Rosita's signal. Before I had given the order to go in to the courthouse, we heard a shot. At that very moment, Rosita came out and gave us the signal to go in. We emptied the cars, truck, and station wagon. Some twenty persons, including my thirteen-year-old son Daniel, who did not want to stay at the camp, and David, the oldest in the family, came along. We had come for Alfonso Sánchez, but Alfonso did not have the courage to be at Tierra Amarilla in person. The radio had said he would be there, but he wasn't.

When we entered the courthouse, we wanted to keep everybody there so that no one would leave and go talk about the goings-on. Many of our people yelled at Eulogio Salazar not to leave, that he was not going to get hurt. Eulogio attempted to jump out a window, and shots were fired trying to make sure everybody stayed put. A bullet hit him. I saw his blood and recognized the consequences that would result from that. It upset me. My spirit burned because Eulogio Salazar was a loyal friend. The Anglo ranchers and police knew that also. Baltazar, others, and I ran after him. As soon as he had hit the ground, he started running towards his car, which was about thirty meters down the road. I wanted to tell him what we were trying to do, that he was not the one that we were after. We caught up with him, explained to him what was going on and that an ambulance would arrive shortly, if he would just wait. He would be treated better by the ambulance personnel than at home. I also asked him, "Why did you run? Didn't you hear us yelling at you?" And he did not respond. I took him to another car and told Baltazar and David to call the ambulance.

As soon as I took care of Eulogio, I ran back into the courthouse. I saw a young man telling an official, "Pray to God because you are going to die," and the policeman was totally scared with panic, looking at the young man and saying, "Yes, yes, I am praying."

Juan and Ventura and I went looking for Alfonso Sánchez in the various rooms on the second floor. Many were empty, and we came to one room that would not open. We tried forcing it and could not. A bullet was fired from inside, and it came through the door and just barely missed us. We got highly irritated. We had come on a legitimate mission to arrest a felon, and one of them was firing shots at us to obstruct our mission. We fired the automatic weapon through the door latch, which flew into the air in a fraction of a second. Daniel Rivera, deputy for Sheriff Benny Naranjo, was hiding inside that room. When he heard the automatic weapon fire, he was terrorized and put his pistol back in its holster. We opened the door, and one of our men hit Daniel Rivera in the face, and he fell down bleeding.

We asked him where Alfonso Sánchez was. "He did not come to the trial," he responded. And so we left him alone. I realized at that moment that it was he, Alfonso, who was not around and not Reies who was hiding.

By this time the state of New Mexico knew what was happening in Tierra Amarilla. "Let's go," I told Juan and Ventura when we had finished searching the second floor. And I told the people in general, "Let's go. Alfonso Sánchez is not here."

As we were leaving the courthouse, I saw two state police cars approaching. I immediately thought that if we encountered each other, there would be gunfire. Immediately, we fired in the air as we exited. They stopped their cars about a hundred meters away. Both police cars stopped and took cover as we sped away. We were still near the courthouse when the ambulance came for those who had been wounded. We looked for Eulogio Salazar, but we could not find him. He had already disappeared. An unknown person came and told me that Tito Salazar, Eulogio's brother, had already taken him to the hospital in Espanola.

Here I should get a little ahead of myself and explain the events. When Salazar left the courthouse, he went to the home of Oralia M. Olivas and Rose Mary Mercure. Oralia, Rose Mary and her husband were eating in a restaurant when they heard the gunshots. They came out and saw Eulogio running. The three took him into their house and attended to him. Every one of those persons asked Eulogio, "Who shot you?" He told each of them "the Tijerinas." Later, Robert Gilliland and Thomas Richardson, of the New Mexico State Police, used this testimony against me. Eulogio Salazar told his story to Robert Gilliland on June 21. In this report, Eulogio repeated what he had told Oralia, his sister-in-law Rose, and Plácido Mercure, that the Tijerinas had shot him. Robert Gilliland, after interrogating Eulogio and having him sign the declaration, changed Eulogio's testimony from "the Tijerinas" to "Tijerina had shot him."

About five in the afternoon, we got in our vehicles and we returned to Canjilon. During the time we took possession of the courthouse, an Anglo reporter, Larry Calloway was there from United Press International. He was at a public phone booth across the street talking to UPI about the arraignment when he saw us arrive. He heard the first gunshot. Larry was smart enough to begin narrating the events as they were happening by phone over the UPI wire. Immediately, the news from UPI in New York was carried live across the nation, into Mexico, all over Latin America, around the globe. That same day, *The New York*

Times sent a special reporter to the communities of Tierra Amarilla, Canjilon, and Coyote.

Baltazar Martínez was so preoccupied with what was going on that he did not hear me when I said for us to return to Canjilon. As we were coming back, we saw a police car hidden behind some pine trees. At this time the Forest Service agents must have been asleep. By the time we got to Canjilon, our women were already alarmed. All the radio stations and television stations had suspended their regular programs and had special bulletins about the events at Tierra Amarilla. I heard General Jolly's order calling the National Guard into service. This was on every radio and television station. I gathered the heads of the various communities and explained to them what had happened in Tierra Amarilla. I talked about the mobilization of the National Guard. Meanwhile, I sent the women to prepare food for three or four days for six or seven persons, got a portable radio, binoculars, raincoats, because the rain was falling and had been falling for the last five days. I told them of the victory and the benefit of what had happened that day, June 5, and that many years would pass before we would actually see the real fruit from this event. I said, "God bless the Almighty Judge, the three angels of justice. Justice sometimes is seen by others."

We took the automatic weapons. I told Patricia not to be afraid of anything and to take care of Isabel, who was six months and twenty-five days old. Patricia never really knew what we had done at Tierra Amarilla, what she heard on the radio.

Juan Valdez and Moisés Morales knew the mountains like their hands. Every tree, every valley, every peak, they knew by name. We headed toward the mountains as the sun went down. It was about seven p.m. From Tobías' ranch we could see part of the plaza in Tierra Amarilla, and we could see the state police gathering and beginning to form their caravan to come search for us. The Anglo voice was very changed now. It was no longer making fun of me, the community, or the Alianza. The funny thing about destiny, at the same hour that we had taken Tierra Amarilla, Israel had taken the city of Jerusalem.

After walking into the hills some twenty-five minutes, we began to hear the first helicopters. Within minutes, a second and a third passed overhead. They were searching behind the Tobías ranch, thinking that was the only route we would take. We really had no other way out. We moved quickly like deer. The seven years of my life as a fugitive served me well to control my nerves and control my nervousness as well as those who were with me. In addition to the helicopters, three other small planes went by overhead, and a large four-engine airplane was photographing the area.

We listened to the radio broadcast that evening. KNX, out of Los Angeles, was announcing a revolution in New Mexico. KRLD in Dallas, Texas, was saying, "An insurrection by the Mexicans in the state of New Mexico has taken place." Eight hundred and fifty soldiers and all the state police gathered there in Tierra Amarilla looking for us. All night long the radio did not talk about anything else except that the manhunt was about to begin. One particular news item bothered me a great deal. The head of the state police, Joe Black, had arrested my wife and taken the baby from her. He had sent the baby to an orphanage, explaining that this would force Reies López Tijerina to come down from the mountain. When I heard this over the radio, I thought that Joe Black did not have the balls to chase Reies like a man. Why was he taking a mother and child, innocent kids, to catch Reies Tijerina? Or did he think he was alone? Did not the soldiers and state police make him brave? On the other hand, did he really think that I was going to come down from the mountain with that trap? In reality, Black did not know me.

The first news item from United Press International began to come over the radio. UPI called me "King Tiger," and from then on, all the news media began calling me by this new nickname. King Tiger was a rather loose translation of Reies Tijerina.

Like deer, we climbed into those mountains trying to escape death. We knew that we had broken the Anglos' barrier of silence of what they had done since they had gotten their backs wet crossing the Mississippi while coming into our lands. All night we climbed into the Pedernal Mountain that lies in front of Coyote. In the darkness we lost Jerry Noll, an Anglo that had helped us a lot in the struggle for the land. The next day we heard over the radio that he had been arrested. We crossed the main road that goes from Espanola to Tierra Amarilla really early with great difficulty. Airplanes had been searching the area; they thought we would cross there heading toward San Joaquín. When we were atop Burro Mesa, we saw many of the army vehicles down below. We saw tanks and armored vehicles among them. Briefly we talked about the necessity of leaving the country, but to where? Mexico did not want me due to the defamatory letter the White House sent against me. An alternative was Cuba, but what would we do in Cuba if we did not share the ideological convictions of the Cubans?

We walked all night and the next day into the afternoon; we finally reached the Chama River. We crossed that river with some difficulty and got to Los Encinos, which is also called Youngsville. This was a name given to the place by an Anglo who did not like the name in Spanish. Moisés and my son David went to get horses from the ranch of Don Celestino. Many of the loyalists came to see me that evening, and for a couple of days we rested and had discussions. Many other leaders from other organizations came to see and talk to me. All of them were blindfolded, and nobody was allowed to look at our whereabouts. Once inside the house, the blindfolds were removed.

I told Peter Nobokov, who wrote the first book (ridiculous) on the taking of the Tierra Amarilla courthouse, that I thought perhaps I would remain a fugitive. But as I meditated more, I thought it was best to continue my confrontations with the courts. I had been a fugitive for seven years. I had escaped major police ambushes more than seventeen times. Back then, I did not have good friends. My instinct to overcome danger was like the animals of the jungle. Now, this virtue was useful. But that was not the wisest thing to do. The day had not arrived that we would have to do something like this. Besides, I was free on bond, and Bratton at any moment could withdraw that bond. And Judge Payne also was after me, although not as much. Payne already had what he wanted from the Alianza. No one had ever taken the membership list from any organization. Judge Payne, with this unconstitutional maneuver, was showing everyone his fear of the Alianza. The police had taken the membership list from Cristóbal on June 2 in Coyote. No sooner had they taken this list than a campaign of police terror began against Alianza members, similar to what Hitler's Gestapo did to the Jews. The FBI and the state police began to visit the homes of each member of the Alianza. They had an address for each one of the members. I was still in the mountains when they were already violating the rights of our people to gather together and associate, free of harassment from the police.

The Anglos themselves had brought the taking of the Tierra Amarilla courthouse upon their own heads. For the past nine years we had been writing to Washington, asking for justice and demanding an investigation. On December 12, 1959, we wrote to Dwight D. Eisenhower. In September 1963, we wrote to John F. Kennedy—on January 12, 1965, to L.B. Johnson. In addition to these extensive letters, we sent large numbers of telegrams and letters to all the different departments of the White House. We were citizens. They ate from our hands and labor, our taxes. They ran their affairs in Washington with our money. Yet, they treated us worse than dogs without an owner. We did not ask that they return the land to the heirs. We simply demanded that they investigate the title of San Joaquín. What was so difficult about this simple petition? Why didn't they want to investigate this particular land grant? Did they prefer blood and war over uncovering what had been covered up?

For this reason, I felt justified in the taking of Tierra Amarilla. All the people felt I was. Celestino Velásquez, an elder going on ninety years, told me that he knew the two Anglos of the Victoria Land and Title Company from England who attempted to take the 600,000 acres of the San Joaquín land grant. Mr. Velásquez knew the criminal conduct of these Anglos and was ready to cooperate in everything that I would ask him. He let us sleep in his house while he went to stay with his son. Many delegations came to this ranch to see me and to talk about what to do next.

Alfonso Sánchez reportedly was livid because he was being blamed for what had happened in Tierra Amarilla. They were still looking for me, but he did not want to confront King Tiger. Day and night the news media kept talking about King Tiger and playing a ballad composed by Roberto Martínez entitled "The Ballad of Río Arriba," because Tierra Amarilla is the county seat for Río Arriba.

While at the house of Don Celestino Velásquez, my closest confidants and I decided that it was best for me to surrender in Albuquerque. There wasn't any better option. We had already gotten worldwide attention. The focus now was on our oppressors. I was in danger, however. That next Monday, I would have to appear before Judge Payne, and now Judge Bratton threatened to raise my bail. But I had something in my favor. The taking of the courthouse in Tierra Amarilla was more serious than the taking of San Joaquín park land. The federal judges had left me in the hands of the state courts. I asked Uvaldo Velásquez, the son of Don Celestino, to take me to Albuquerque so that I could surrender to the federal officials. I also asked Juan Valdez and Moisés Morales to join me in surrendering. So we said goodbye to everybody else and left Coyote about eleven at night to arrive in Albuquerque the first hours the following Sunday morning. In San Isidro, about thirty-five miles from Albuquerque, Uvaldo stopped to gas up. He was about to leave when I told him, "Wait. Let me drink some water. I'm very thirsty." I got off, drank water, and a young man saw me. I knew he would call to turn us in.

Coronado's Bernalillo

Coronado founded Bernalillo in 1540. From there it is only seventeen miles to Albuquerque, a city founded in 1706. It was about two in the morning when we arrived close to Albuquerque. It had been a week since we had taken Tierra Amarilla, and the state police were on full alert. Joe Black had been waiting by his phone twenty-four hours a day during all this time. Patrol cars with Mexican police passed me. Not a single Anglo was looking for me at that hour. In fact, reporters got to the site before the other police. There were more cameras and reporters than there were police officers. When I was arrested in Bernalillo, the general public thought that I had been arrested under adverse conditions, but that was not the case. The truth was that I was coming to Albuquerque to surrender and answer to Judges Bratton and Payne on Monday, June 12.

Patricia later told me about the treatment she had received at the hands of the state police. While all the others had not been handcuffed, Patricia was cuffed with her hands behind her back. They took away our seven-month-old baby and accused Patricia of being involved in the takeover of Tierra Amarilla. All of this was totally false. And the newspapers repeated the words of Joe Black: "Patricia will be the bait we'll use to bring King Tiger down from the mountain." Black was using the same savage tactics that the Anglo marines used in Vietnam. The rest of those arrested were kept in a corral near the ranch of Tobías Leyba. Patricia was taken to prison in Santa Fe on June 5. About 8 p.m., my daughter was taken illegally from her mother because Patricia was totally innocent in the taking of Tierra Amarilla. Patricia did not see Isabel for more than forty-eight hours, and Patricia was pregnant again, about five months. That's why I took care of her a great deal and did not want her to be mortified over anything. I had, in the past, lost children from premature births.

In Canjilon, Alfonso Sánchez finally showed up with hundreds of police armed with rifles. Now he was demonstrating valor, Patricia told me. It was later confirmed by my daughter Rosita, Tobías, and others who had seen the police and the National Guard and James Evans looking for me everywhere. Many of the Chicanos, veterans of the Vietnam War, told me that Canjilon looked like a Vietnam military camp, with more than a thousand soldiers, tanks, helicopters, small aircraft, and large, armored cars.

On April 20, 1968, the *Saturday Evening Post* stated that I had given myself the name of King Tiger, but further down in the column it said, June 5, "Don Quixote" Reies had converted himself into El Cid. Larry Calloway, the UPI reporter at the Tierra Amarilla courthouse, said, "War in the United States? Revolution? It is not possible in this great nation."

When all this happened, Cristóbal, my brother, told me he had spent three days in Canjilon when the army was camped there and began house-to-house searches. For three days, Cristóbal did not eat or drink water. Several times the soldiers and self-appointed Anglo militia came near the house, but since it looked abandoned, they did not take interest in it. My warriors took Cristóbal from there in the middle of the night, passed him through several ranches, into the mountains that surround the community of Peces. Then, Cristóbal spent more than forty days with the Penitent brotherhood, who attended to all his needs. After all this time, Cristóbal then decided to surrender. He was never charged, however, with the taking of Tierra Amarilla.

Baltazar Martínez and Baltazar Apodaca remained at the Tierra Amarilla courthouse once we had left. They had not heard our call to retreat and leave. When they did return toward Canjilon, they took as hostages a federal agent named Jaramillo and Larry Calloway. The police attempted to arrest them. Martínez was able to escape into the mountains. They chased him on horseback, with helicopters, dogs, and jeeps, but never caught him. The governor offered a $500 reward for information leading to the arrest of Baltazar Martínez. After some forty days, Baltazar sent word to his mother, "Go and collect the $500 and give them to me so I can get married." So his mother turned him in and bailed him out. He got married with the money that the governor had offered for his capture.

After June 5, all kinds of organizations and groups became aware of our struggle. The Mexican people responded to the events of June 5. People came to visit from all corners of the nation to congratulate our warriors and me. We had confronted the giant of the world. Telegrams, long-distance phone calls, and letters from Mexico, Spain, and the rest of the world arrived daily. Finally, my community had lost its fear of the Anglo. While this revolution was taking place, the FBI and the state police and other agents kept around-the-clock vigilance on the Alianza headquarters. During these days of tribulation, the person in charge of our office was Eduardo S. Chávez. Gordon Jackson, the FBI agent, visited Eduardo early in the morning several times to take him to the Alianza office. He knew that Eduardo did not have a car. Eduardo, however, never lost faith nor weakened. Many others during these days did weaken.

We received hundreds of letters from all over the world, some simply addressed: Reies Tijerina, New Mexico, and United States. The postal service would deliver them to our office daily. Regardless of how badly the Anglos thought of me, my community was now on the map: San Joaquín, Tierra Amarilla, Coyote, and Canjilon. In spite of all of this, the Anglos still refused to investigate the title to San Joaquín. They still preferred confrontations instead of a peaceful investigation.

Alfonso Sánchez had many political ambitions. When he learned that Governor David Cargo was talking to Eduardo Chávez, secretary of the Alianza, to find a peaceful solution to the issue in Coyote by meeting with me, Sánchez immediately ordered our arrest so as to beat Cargo to the punch. Cargo wanted the same thing I wanted from the U.S. Department of Justice: an investigation into the title of the San

Joaquín. If the investigation proved that we had not been robbed of our land, right then and there, I would dissolve the Alianza without asking for any investigation of the other 1,715 land grant titles in the Southwest. What more favorable offer did the Anglo want?

A false rumor began in northern New Mexico that caused panic among the Anglos. The rumor was that all Anglos would be decapitated in northern New Mexico. This wasn't hard to believe because in northern New Mexico, between eighty to ninety-five percent of the population is Mexican. In Río Arriba County there are just a few Anglos. In Tierra Amarilla there is not a single Anglo. This is where the land grants of San Joaquín, Coyote, Canjilon, and Tierra Amarilla are located. This is what gave merit to the rumor that the settlers of the old land grant families were going to kill all the Anglos. Naturally, the Anglo used the press to propagate these untrue rumors. Agents like Alfonso Sánchez and State Senator Edmundo Delgado further aggravated the problem. Delgado said the Alianza and its members "are a conspiracy against law and order." And he said that I personally had "made false promises to the people and fooled them," and that the full responsibility lay on Governor Cargo for having shown a willingness to even meet with the Alianza.

My Wife in Jail

Patricia waited in jail for me to arrive and obtain her liberty. Patricia was only nineteen years old. She had never been in jail. Her daughter was in the hands of strangers, and the National Guard and the state police were hunting her husband. For two days she did not eat or drink for fear that they would give her drugs or poison. Patricia told me that Alfonso Sánchez, Joe Black, and four others came to visit her regularly, asking her where Reies was. "If you tell us, you can save his life. If you don't, we will kill him in the mountains or wherever we find him, like an animal in the jungle." According to her, Alfonso was full of hate. He, among all, wanted to catch the main prize. No one was bothered more by them than my wife. During the two nights that she spent in the Santa Fe jail, she did not have blankets. She could not sleep, being worried about what was going on. She felt sick, but because of the way she was being treated, was afraid to say anything. The pressure the guards put on Patricia was incredible. Since she was arrested at the Leyba ranch, she was marched with a rifle at her back. Two or three agents dragged Patricia, with her hands cuffed behind her back, in and out of various automobiles. They injured her wrists. She told me that several of these agents took liberties on her body with their hands. This conduct of the state police indicated the blind hatred and envy they had toward us. The terror, pressure, and bad treatment Patricia received provoked her body to have a miscarriage two days after being freed. The doctor confirmed that this was a direct result of what had happened to her while detained.

The State Prison

Alfonso Sánchez and Joe Black came to see me in the Santa Fe jail so that the reporters and cameras would put them on the front page. The people were with the Alianza. Now the people felt real proud of what had happened on June 5. The next day, I was taken, along with the other warriors, to the central prison for the state of New Mexico. They had about seven police cars surrounding our caravan to take us to this jail. Upon our arrival, my heart felt full of joy when I heard hundreds of prisoners yelling, "Viva Reies López Tijerina and his warriors." This was a reception that my warriors and I did not expect. It took us by surprise. And then, when we were taken to our individual cells, I heard "The Ballad of Río Arriba." This song described exactly what had happened in Tierra Amarilla. The song began, "In the year 1967, the day was the 5th of June . . ." Upon hearing these words, my heart broke and, although I tried not to, I did shed tears. When I got out of prison, I met Roberto Martínez, the composer of this ballad. But while in prison, I was only allowed visits from my family and my lawyers. Many of the reporters from New York, *The Washington Post,* and *Los Angeles Times,* were denied an opportunity to interview me. Patricia came to see me and gave me her side of the story of what had happened to her. The thirty days we were in prison were the happiest in my life. Many of the warriors will always be in my heart and in the hearts of the people. Some of them were Juan Valdez, Baltazar Martínez, Moisés Morales, Tobías Leyba, José Madrid, Baltazar Apodaca, Cirilio García, Ezequiel Domínguez, and Rosita and David, my children, who were also in prison with me. Also, Ramón Tijerina, Jerónimo Barueda, Adelicio Moya, Marino Moya, Félix Martínez, Cristóbal Tijerina, Jerry Noll, and others I can't remember right now. The lawyers sought to have bail established for us. But Alfonso Sánchez fought to have us held without bail. The state supreme court was careful not to name an Anglo judge to the case and assigned Judge José Angel from Las Vegas.

On the 35th day, we were released from prison without bail. I immediately went to my radio and television programs and began broadcasting what had happened. I told them about the events in Tierra Amarilla, Coyote, and Canjilon. I refreshed their memories about the great Santa Fe Ring conspiracy, now being maintained by Judges Bratton and Payne. I again made a call to the community to join us in our efforts. I repeated my offer to debate Mary Helen Jenkins on an open microphone or anyone else who wanted to challenge our title to the land of San Joaquín. No Anglo ever accepted my offer to debate. I made the same offer on television, but no one ever responded.

Robert Gilliland headed the investigation into the taking of Tierra Amarilla. Sheriff Benny Naranjo gave his opinion about what had happened. Benny, in an interview given to Bill Leverton of Channel 4, said that he heard the gunshots and the words "Reies said not to hurt anyone." He repeated this statement several times. He said this to the police in Canjilon and to the National Guard troops. For some strange reason, once his father, Emilio Naranjo, visited, he changed his testimony. The same thing happened to Eulogio Salazar. Once Emilio Naranjo visited him, he radically changed his testimony. Robert Gilliland was a real good friend of Emilio Naranjo.

When we were released from prison, people from throughout the Southwest began to invite me to speak. The Pueblo Mestizo, Indohispano, had finally awakened. Everybody wanted to meet me. *Excelsior,* Mexico's greatest newspaper, sent a reporter to interview me and write our story, including the taking of Tierra Amarilla. *Excelsior* wrote a series of front-page articles.

Militant groups emerged from everywhere. One of their leaders, Rodolfo "Corky" Gonzales from Denver, Colorado, came to visit me in New Mexico. I was in prison when he came to see me the first time, and he wasn't allowed to see me. More than ten carloads of people had come with Corky. These urban groups had sprung up throughout the nation. I felt the fight that I had started in 1956 had changed our youth overnight. They had a new spirit and were looking for justice and struggling for the land. Young Anglos also began deserting their race and joining our cause. Only the racist conservatives resisted our efforts. The old racists, however, will soon pass into history. Our young Mestizo youth will take their place under the sun.

The Supreme Court

The Supreme Court of the United States was one of the instruments that the Anglo government used with great efficacy to remove our people from their lands. Although many legislative acts were passed and political maneuvers were used to steal our land, the biggest and most powerful was the Supreme Court of the United States. They closed the door to justice for our people. They left us outside the halls of justice with their famous decision over the land grant of San Miguel del Vado rendered on May 24, 1897.

Let me explain a bit of the legal tactics and maneuvers that the Anglos worked within the Supreme Court of the United States to steal the land from our people and cover their footprints. The Treaty of Guadalupe Hidalgo was signed on February 2, 1848. Since that date, the United States took political sovereignty over the land that Spain and Mexico had governed for more than three hundred years. The treaty imposed judicial and political obligations on the United States regarding the land, and the United States had to adjudicate these titles in ordinary tribunals.

The government of the United States, however, decided to deny us access to ordinary tribunals. We were without justice for forty-three years because the United States Congress did not establish the Court of Claims until 1891. During this forty-three-year lapse, all of the violations of the Treaty of Guadalupe Hidalgo occurred. Anglo governors destroyed the Spanish archives holding the titles and evidence that the land belonged to our people. The first Anglo governor of New Mexico was a soldier who came to this territory with General Kearney. According to historians, he burned the Spanish archives in his chimney the first winter. He stoked the fire with our archives while he warmed his feet by the fireplace. He burned document after document that forty-three years later Anglo judges would ask for as proof. Then came William A. Pyle in 1870. He destroyed and/or sold another great part of those archives. The historians Hubert Bancroft and Ralph Twitchell have confirmed this crime. The next governor, Bradford Prince, disposed of the remaining archives that belonged to the northern district of New Mexico from 1889 to 1893. He sold them to a private businessman. These documents have recently become the basis for litigation in a federal court in Kansas City, Missouri. This was only one of many savage destructions of property that was commited in order to steal the land from our people. Another was the arbitrary establishment on the part of Congress of the Surveyor General on July 22, 1854. They established contact with Thomas B. Catron. Catron was, according to Anglos, the expert on land matters. According to historians, "Catron was considered by the Anglos, the king of New Mexico during fifty years." He arrived in New Mexico in 1860 and died in 1920. He came from Missouri in a wagon loaded with flour. Among the first things he did was to live with a Mexican family and learn Spanish, the language of the people.

On February 14, 1873, the first Surveyor General confirmed Claim #71 as belonging to the people of San Joaquín del Cañón de Chama. He recommended that Congress approve it. This and thirty-four other land grants were approved. But the politicians in the White House did not approve of these recommendations. If the governor of New Mexico had burned, destroyed, and otherwise sold the general archive, how could the Surveyor General confirm these titles of the people? Congress sent another surveyor, George W. Julian, who was under express orders from the commission to re-examine and investigate these thirty-five land grants that his antecedent had approved. Upon re-examination of them, and under instructions from William Andrew Jackson Sparks on July 23, 1885, he rejected twenty-three and approved twelve of the original thirty-five land grants. In spite of all of this, the claim by the people to San Joaquín was still validated. San Joaquín had passed the test that the Anglos had invented to disenfranchise them. And Judges Bratton and Payne had the gall to say that "the grant of San Joaquín does not exist."

The office of Surveyor General did not function with executive power. So Congress created the Court of Claims on March 3, 1891. Again, all the people of the land had to take their titles before this court, comprised of judges that owned slaves. This court disavowed any knowledge of what the surveyor generals had recommended. This court demanded that original documents be presented to them. The very documents that Anglo governors had burned, destroyed, or sold were required as a pre-condition to hear a title case on any land grant. One of the best examples of this case involves Santa Fe, the capital of New Mexico.

This city lost its communal land because its title did not appear before the Court of Claims. The Supreme Court of the United States ruled against the city on March 1, 1897. Fifty years later Lansing Bloom of the School on American Research found, in the General Archive of the Indies, the document that contains the date and the order founding the city of Santa Fe (March 30, 1609). Luis de Velasco, the viceroy for Mexico, to Don Pedro de Peralta, signed the document. If the governors had protected this document, the city of Santa Fe would not have been denied its title. The court used the argument that Santa Fe was settled by soldiers that had deserted Coronado in 1543, and not by Pedro de Peralta. Through this brief study, we can see how the bad faith of the Anglos of the United States has predominated since the beginning. Notice, however, that Congress, just like the Supreme Court, accepts, recognizes, and confirms the grants of May 8, 1822, to the city of San Augustín, Florida, and of April 1911, for the city of Manila. San Francisco, California, has had good luck. In all these latter cases, the Anglos already had control of municipal power in these cities, while in New Mexico the Hispanic settlers were the majority. The discrimination by the Supreme Court against the original settlers is something that leaves no doubt. All the cases brought by Mexicans to the Supreme Court were lost. All the cases brought by Anglos were won. Example: Thomas B. Catron sued for 1.5 million acres of land and won. The last case was Sandoval versus the United States.

Ten years after the signing of the Treaty of Guadalupe Hidalgo, many of the documents in the Guadalajara, Mexico, archive were mysteriously burned. The United States, based on stipulations in the treaty, was to have requested these documents since 1848, but waited until February 3, 1873. On ratifying the treaty, the Senate of the United States passed a resolution ordering President Grant to ask Mexico for certain titles of lands. The initiative reached Mexico twenty-five years later. About that same time, President Grant sent William A. Pile as governor to New Mexico. He burned, destroyed, and sold the documents. What a great farce! When Mexico finally answered the United States that there were no documents in the Guadalajara archives, the U.S. should have cared for the documents left in New Mexico and Arizona. One governor after another, with Thomas B. Catron as advisor, destroyed all the written evidence that favored Hispanics.

The gigantic conspiracy is so large that I can only briefly introduce it in this book. It would be impossible to include all the events, but I hope that this recollection is enough so that our children, students, and historians will investigate and make everything clear. This great conspiracy, without parallel in history, is one of the reasons why I cannot abandon the struggle for the lands. I have opened people's eyes. I have documented the right of my people to the land and the crimes of the foreigners. That is why they hate me so much. I have not violated any law. What we did in Tierra Amarilla, we did within our constitutional rights. The Anglo judges that hate me so much have twisted the law in order to find us guilty under "any pretext." Judge Bratton used everything at his disposal. He violated our rights by trying us elsewhere than where supposedly the crime was committed. The crime that we were accused of took place in San Joaquín in the County of Río Grande. There, ninety-five percent of the population is Hispanic, and all of them have been deprived of their land by the Forest Service agents. Judge Bratton did not want to be in the midst of this community. The judge also was afraid to come north. That's why he violated our rights and instead took our case to Las Cruces, New Mexico.

The Bratton Court in Las Cruces, New Mexico

Knowing full well how difficult this would be for us, Judge Bratton moved the trial to Las Cruces. In essence, Judge Bratton kidnapped us and took us to Las Cruces. He knew that it was three hundred and fifty miles from San Joaquín, where the incident took place. My five hundred-plus witnesses would not be able to attend the hearing in Las Cruces. Judge Bratton knew how poor my community was. Moreover, Bratton knew that the majority of the area residents of San Joaquín were Hispanic. Those persons, heirs to the lands, hated the Forest Service. Since 1904 when President Theodore Roosevelt sent the Forest Service into that area to begin taking the land and grazing rights away from the people, the heirs to this land, the people have resented the service's presence. The Alianza published a leaflet entitled *The Land Grant Question.* This twenty-page booklet is our study, legal and judicial, of the origin of our communities and our right to the land throughout the Southwest. This booklet caused the Anglo, who dominates politics in New Mexico, great irritation. The judges themselves hated the new orientation that the Mexican people, this forgotten community, were now taking.

In September, we had the fifth annual Alianza convention in Albuquerque. We invited leaders from the Native American and Black communities. The Anglos had oppressed us all.

All the Anglos are united in corporations, such as lawyers, judges, politicians, teachers, actors, and workers. All of these unions and corporations are cogs of a great engine that are connected to the White House, Congress, and the Supreme Court of the United States, in order to pursue their interests. They dominate and maintain the natives in complete submission. All of these corporations (small governments and private entities) support judges like Bratton and Payne when it comes to the rights of the people. All of them are in bed together.

In 1967, President Johnson came to El Paso to participate in a ceremony returning land known as El Chamizal to Mexico. For more than one hundred years, Mexico had pursued its right to this land against the United States, but the United States ignored and refused to abide by legal decisions until now. Many Chicano groups across the United States invited me to attend and protest with them in El Paso. In El Paso, Chicanos approved of the declarations I had made to the press. Vice-President Hubert Humphrey also made declarations to the press in favor of the people of the land. He criticized the Department of Agriculture, in particular its Forest Service branch. These declarations helped our cause a great deal and gave hope to our people. But Johnson's government was not interested in the land question. His own ranch, El Pedernal, in Texas, is on land owned by Cecilia Saenz Montes. If Mrs. Montes could only prove title to that land, it would be very shameful for him. The methods used by Anglos in Texas to steal the land from the original owners were cruder and bloodier than in other states.

After this trip to El Paso, we got ready for the trial that Judge Bratton had prepared for us. Judge Bratton had ordered me silenced, denied me the right to speak about the Treaty of Guadalupe Hidalgo, the land claims, and our culture. I was not to be intimidated, so I ignored the order. As expected, the trial began as a farce. During jury selection, Judge Bratton would not let us question the panel over such things as what the name "King Tiger" meant to them and whether they were influenced by such nicknames. The nicknames were given to me by United Press International after the taking of Tierra Amarilla. On the other hand, the prosecutor, Alfonso Sánchez, was allowed to present sixty-four indictments, thirty-four of which contained my name, as well as "King Tiger." In this manner the potential jurors were mentally prejudiced to assure my conviction. The Anglo press and magazines made the words "King Tiger" and "bandit" appear synonymous. They linked them to me throughout the nation and the Southwest. That was the image that the Anglos wanted the people of Las Cruces to have of me.

The 700-mile round trip from Tierra Amarilla to Las Cruces was financially impossible for my people and witnesses. Judge Bratton did not allow us to explain the reasons for the taking of San Joaquín. The jury was comprised exclusively of Anglos. Judge Bratton, with the help of two Coyotes, fixed the jury and case as he wanted. He closed the door to justice. We were reduced to asking questions only about the assault on two Forest Service guards, Phil Smith and Walt Taylor. That was the only matter I was allowed to speak about. I was limited in my defense because I had no money or political power, and I was a stranger in this part of New Mexico. The press, in the meantime, had labeled me "the most hated man in New Mexico." Ultimately, I lost in Las Cruces. Judge Bratton and Jack Love won. We returned from Las Cruces to our homes. We began to prepare for the greater trial about to occur, involving the taking of the Tierra Amarilla courthouse. It was amazing how I was found guilty on a simple charge of assault without having touched those guards with my finger. Bratton announced the sentences on Cristóbal, Jerry Noll, Ezekiel Domínguez, Alfonso Chávez, and me on December 15, 1967.

Weeks before the taking of San Joaquín, an Anglo Forest Service agent had savagely beaten José Morphine. The Anglo was never brought to justice. José Morphine was an employee of the Forest Service. He had been with the service for years. This is how he was paid for his complicity in the theft of our lands and his obedience to the Anglo.

It was very clear to me that the trial in Las Cruces was a prelude to the trial over the taking of Tierra Amarilla on June 5. Bratton and Payne wanted to make sure the federal trial poisoned the Anglo mind. They provided ammunition for negative publicity to the machine that was working against me. They wanted to make sure that "King Tiger" would not be set free by the state judge at the next trial.

The Impact of a Murder on the Tijerina Family

Joe Black, head of the state police, said, "The Alianza has operated within the law until today, but now there's a burden on its back. There's nothing bad or illegal about the Alianza, but with Eulogio Salazar's death, they will have to prove they did not kill him before they are clean in the eyes of the public." But Joe Black has never made the investigative report public, so that we will not be able to exonerate ourselves of this accusation nor get the "monkey" off our backs until he does so. They accused us and only they could absolve us. The Anglo's plan worked out just the way he wanted. Salazar's death, as Black said, was a "monkey" on the back of my family. The impact of the murder was felt in every corner of the state, and more so at the schools my children attended. Anglo teachers, without taking into account the way the crime was being covered up, blamed me, the founder of the Alianza. My children suffered this ignominy every day. My children could not stand the hate Anglo teachers were generating against the Tijerina name. I did what I could for my children. But I was in prison during their most critical school days. I could not defend my children from the absurd racist attacks of these Anglo teachers.

The politicians made Salazar's death possible. Now, they were covering up the crime, and the Anglo press was spreading the poison.

Not only were the Anglos attacking us, but also some native Indohispanos were accepting the false propaganda.

The investigation into the death was kept quiet. All the politicians, as well as the clergy, kept their mouths shut. Time went by. If Bob Brown, editor of the *Albuquerque Journal,* had been murdered, the Anglo politicians and clergymen would have waged war worse than the one waged against China to accept opium in 1839. But to the Anglo, who is implicated in the great theft of our land, silence was convenient.

Judge Angel freed us on February 8, 1968. I tried in vain to get the governor and the police to make some announcement about Salazar's death. I called and knocked on as many doors as possible to pressure them, but I was unsuccessful. I still did not know the Santa Fe Ring well enough. I still did not know the relationships between the Anglo bosses and their Hispanic flunkies.

Eulogio's murder and Senator Montoya's declaration of December 29, 1967, were the ammunition and propaganda the Anglo needed to call me "the most hated man in New Mexico." They tortured my family. Anglos believed they could force me out of the state. But the Anglos, together with their flunkies, were very wrong. They would continue to see me in the land they stole from my people. What's worse is they would be the first ones to leave, unless they wanted to be confronted with their own crimes.

My children lost their education and couldn't find jobs. Eulogio Salazar's murder has been covered up by the police, the press, and bad politicians. But what they do not know is that the Fair Judge of this Earth has promised me that I will get to see the punishment for those guilty of spilling Eulogio's blood. No power or political influence will save them from the blood they spilt. Each one, in due time, will be found and will receive his deserved punishment.

On January 12, 1968, the state pretended to hold one of the most important trials in the history of the Southwest. Santa Fe was filled with police to impress the press and the world. Alfonso and his bosses wanted to sell the lie that we had killed Eulogio. They wanted to make us appear to the world as Salazar's murderers. By then, the real murderers had been protected and the crime covered up. Nobody could enter the courtroom without being frisked from head to toe, even getting penholders and women's hairdos examined. New Mexico had never seen anything like this. The Anglo press agitated and frightened the Anglos. They used "King Tiger" and "bandit" in their false propaganda to alarm the people. They did not use the name "Tijerina" as much. The more Bob Brown's press tried to kill my name, the more the people appreciated me.

Judge Angel, after hearing witnesses from Tierra Amarilla, suspected someone was blocking the investigation of Salazar's death. He changed the charges against us from "kidnapping" to "false arrest." The charges went from first-to-second-degree felonies, and that changed the amount of bail.

On February 8th, I came out of prison for the second time. The leaders and groups from other states were waiting for us. Bert Corona had already organized a series of events and convened several groups for me to go talk to in California.

Dr. King and the Poor People's Campaign

On March 5, Dr. Martín Luther King sent me a telegram inviting me to Atlanta, Georgia. Black, Native American, Chicano and Anglo leaders would meet on March 14. I was honored at a dinner hosted by Dr. King. He seated me at his right and congratulated me. After dinner, Dr. King proposed that each group meet separately to select its representative. The Chicanos unanimously elected me to be their representative to Dr. King's historic Poor People's Campaign. Dr. King had proposed we protest the following summer.

On September 22, 1967, I went to Chicago to meet with Dr. King. I talked to him about the need to create an alliance between our peoples in order to obtain justice in the United States.

I was very busy with the great fight for the hundred million acres that belonged to our people. I was receiving invitations from all over the nation. César Chávez also sent me a telegram. He wanted me to be with him at the end of his twenty-five-day fast in Delano, California.

The New Mexico press, at the service of Bob Brown night and day, was dedicated to a nonstop campaign to fulfill the "prophetic" words of Senator José Montoya that "Tijerina is dead." He had also said, "I guarantee that ninety-nine percent of Hispanics hate Tijerina."

The Saturday Evening Post on April 20, 1958, had labeled me "Don Quixote." Now, after Tierra Amarilla (June 5, 1967), the national and international press referred to me as "the Cid." But to Bob Brown and his Santa Fe Ring, I was a simple thief or "King Tiger." The more I was accepted by the world as a voice of the oppressed people of the United States, the more that Montoya's bosses became irked. Bob Brown dedicated himself to preparing the public's mind so when the Tierra Amarilla trial was held, the jury would see me as the suspect for Salazar's death. Bob Brown has never asked that the report on that death be made public. The public was tired of waiting for this report. I wanted to get Joe Black's tag, "the monkey," off my back. But how could I? Black had suppressed and covered up the results of the investigation.

Sympathizers of our cause and three state police officers gave us information that implicated some of Montoya's good friends in the murder. They said an Anglo was behind the murder. The people and I knew it. But the "supreme pontiff" of the press wanted the public to be suspicious of me. We held large meetings to ask the governor to report on Salazar's death. But someone stronger than the governor would always stick his hand in, and the incident remained covered up. The public always received the same response: "We cannot publish the report yet, because that would hurt the investigation, and the murderers can go free." Joe Black gave that reply to the public, for years and years. To this day, they have never given the public a word of information on this murder. How does Joe Black want us to get the dead man off our back, if he was the one that put him there? In reality, the ones carrying that death on their backs are Joe Black, Martín Vigil, his successor, and Bob Brown. However, the one with the most power and influence to demand the public be given information about the circumstances of Salazar's death was Senator Joseph Montoya.

I must confess here that I have never stopped asking the heavens for justice. I felt that one day justice would uncover what the police and the politicians were covering up. I knew, but I could not prove, that the murderers were insignificant figures. The true responsible parties were very important politicians. The political machine was very strong. It is an old and well-established machine. All my friends were poor and without influence. But I had faith and confidence in the mission the three angels had given me. I had faith that the great political machine of New Mexico and the White House would disintegrate some day. If the politicians were covering up Eulogio's blood, they could not do it forever. And if justice is delayed in revealing what they were covering up, it was because Eulogio's blood had not yet reached all those implicated.

The March of the Poor

While the public was busy with the mystery of Salazar's death, Dr. Martín Luther King announced his Poor People's Campaign. United Press International broke the news that I was leading the "Chicano" delegation. The news irritated Brown of the *Albuquerque Journal*. The next day Bob Brown denounced me in an editorial as a person undeserving of representing my people in the March of the Poor. He accused me indirectly of Salazar's death. Brown's press saw to it that I had no peace.

Then came Dr. King's assassination. The nation was shamed by the spilled blood of one who asked for equality and justice.

Reverend Ralph Abernathy called me from Atlanta, Georgia, and asked me to be with him in Memphis, Tennessee, on May 2. The Poor People's Campaign would begin at the same motel where Dr. King was assassinated. When Dr. King had asked me to participate in the march, I presented the conditions under which Indohispanos would participate. "We do not want scraps nor charity," I said to Dr. King. "We want justice. We want the government of the United States to swear by the Treaty of Guadalupe Hidalgo. We want the return of the land stolen from our populations. We want our culture to be respected, and we want the foreign, compulsory education removed." Dr. King accepted our proposals. The other condition I presented to Dr. King was for the indigenous people, Native Americans, of all nations and tribes, to lead the march and that their rights be presented first; it would be like an arrowhead on the list of demands to be presented to the White House. Following them, the rights of Black people would be presented, and at the end of the list would be ours, Indohispanos (Chicanos).

I made this presentation to Dr. King in front of the Chicano leaders. I have copies of these conditions in the order mentioned above in my files.

The international press reported these conditions and agreements. So the politicians in New Mexico and Bob Brown knew it. They got together and reached agreement. The day before my departure for Washington, D.C., Alfonso Sánchez jailed me for the takeover of Tierra Amarilla. He did this so the world would see me as a bandit and not as the head or leader of all Mexicans living in the United States.

As always, in trying to wrong me, they benefited me. Dr. King was the most prominent figure Blacks had in their nonviolent struggle for justice. Anglos in power in the United States did not want me to be seen next to King. Even the heads of "religion" in New Mexico joined this campaign. The voices attacking Tijerina came from everywhere. Brown headed them. His voice and that of the press were used more than ever in trying to keep me from going to Washington.

I called Reverend Abernathy and proposed he come to Albuquerque before I went to Memphis on May 2, the day we were to begin the March of the Poor. Reverend Abernathy came, and we marched through downtown Albuquerque, ending at the old Plaza, the true center of Albuquerque. The other reverends and heads of the different churches were in trouble. They did not want to turn their backs on the Poor People's Campaign because it was Dr. King's and he had just been assassinated. But they also did not want to support the Albuquerque march headed by me. Complaining in a thousand ways, they found themselves under my orders, the man about whom Senator Montoya had said, "As a figure, he is dead."

They were able to put me in jail when all the leaders of the Black, Native American, and poor whites were to meet in Washington. But my enemies did not anticipate what Reverend Abernathy did on opening day of the campaign. Instead of presenting the cause of the poor first, he made a demand for my freedom. He accused the U.S. and New Mexico governments of conspiring against the March of the Poor. This tormented even more those who called me "King Tiger" and "bandit."

Montoya was the "big" figure of the Mexican race in the capital of Great Babylon (Washington). And it bothered him that I would show up in Washington to talk about the poor. To stop me, all the political machinery in New Mexico started moving. The University of Texas at El Paso invited me in April. I went accompanied by Cristóbal. As soon as my speech at the university ended, we left for New Mexico. As soon as we passed the Native American nation of Isleta in New Mexico, we were arrested. They took us to prison. That's how they detained me, and that is how "the law" was used by Alfonso Sánchez, the Anglo's flunky.

The Anglo press continued its campaign against me, the "bandit." I was in solitary confinement for four days. They charged me with sixty-four counts for the takeover of Tierra Amarilla. The police harassed our people daily during 1967 and 1968. In those days, paid police spies trying to learn our every step plagued the Alianza. They wanted to find flaws. They did not let us rest. The police were waging a campaign of terror against the Alianza. Many people lost their jobs. Many others had to leave the Alianza.

Bob Brown's reporters spread the rumor that we had paid William Fellion to plant a bomb at the Alianza's headquarters, which detonated early, taking off part of his arm. It was not difficult to comprehend this Anglo reign of terror. The Anglos wanted to cause me to have a nervous breakdown. I knew they wanted to frighten me. Every hour of the day and night they bothered us with threats, curses, and all sorts of insults by telephone. Threats and terror surrounded my family. But this campaign of terror did not make me change my mind.

During the four days the judges kept me in jail, Reverend Abernathy and his followers surrounded the Department of Justice in Washington, asking for my freedom. The judges, without a reason, raised my bail to an amount ten times greater than the previous one. The people's protest was heard around the world. The judges imposed unfair imprisonment on me. Every time the international press mentioned my imprisonment, they also mentioned that the White House had stolen our land. Against the wishes of our oppressors, our cause grew.

At the end of four days, I was released from the state prison. And, as I had promised Reverend Abernathy, I left for Memphis the next day. I was with Dr. King's widow and the Reverend Abernathy for two days. The March of the Poor started without the man who had planned it. Once the march officially began on May 2, I returned to New Mexico. We left in three Greyhound buses from New Mexico headed for Washington, D.C. In Denver, three more buses joined us, then three more from Los Angeles. Texas joined us in Kansas City with three more buses. When we arrived in Washington, we were twenty buses of Chicanos. The black people had formed a small city in Washington they called "Resurrection."

In Washington

We were there a week before I chose Hawthorne School to house our people. Rodolfo "Corky" Gonzales from Denver, Reverend Nieto from Austin, Texas, two young Puerto Ricans from New York, and a young woman, Escalante, from Los Angeles, assisted me in the school. We were more than five hundred strong, brave people from the entire Southwest. All of Indohispano origin met the following day. Native Americans from several states decided to join us and work together. The Native Americans and the Indohispanos had the same claim and complaint against the government of the United States: the violation of treaties to the detriment of our land and culture.

Black people had their objectives: more jobs, more and better education, better public assistance. But before marches and demonstrations started, I asked Reverend Abernathy to have all the leaders meet to refresh our memory and reorganize our stay in Washington. This first meeting was very heated. Words were used that did not harmonize with the words and agreements we had with Dr. King before he was assassinated. Reverend Abernathy wanted harmony among all groups and races at any price. But some of his assistants were not in agreement with Abernathy. My biggest fight with them was over sticking to the agreements made with Dr. King in Atlanta. That is to say, Native Americans and their complaints were to be presented first and foremost. It was only fair. If we wanted the Anglo government in the White House to open the doors of justice to us, we had to appeal to the world. And to get the attention of the latter, we had to give Native Americans the principal place before the eyes of the world. It was easier to move the Anglo's conscience with the sacred and just rights of Native Americans. If we achieved justice for Native Americans, it would be easier to obtain it for oppressed Blacks. And, at the end of that list, for Indo-hispanos. That was the agreement we had reached with Dr. King. But Abernathy, as was to be expected, did not enjoy the same respect Dr. King had from his followers.

When I had attended Dr. King's funeral, I met again with the leaders of the March of the Poor. Stockley Carmichael, Marlon Brando, Sammy Davis Jr., Abernathy, and many other leaders were there. I presented, in detail, the rights of the Native Americans to justice. I explained that if Native Americans did not obtain justice, nobody could. If we do not ask for the Native Americans first, then we are not asking for us.

This was my biggest conflict with Abernathy's followers. But the Anglo press never wanted to mention this. The Anglo did not want to make me appear as a defender of the Native Americans. This was the origin of our break-up with the Black leaders in Washington, D.C. But the white press, as much as Abernathy's assistants, prevented this fact from becoming public. I never had any conflict with Abernathy. It was some of his subordinates who took a new course, forcing us to follow ours.

Finally, on May 27, I was forced to speak more clearly. The press, especially the New Mexico press, took advantage of the opportunity. Bob Brown altered the truth and told lies and falsehoods. He published that I was fighting with the Blacks because they were not giving me the first place. This was more than false. It was still part of the plan and conspiracy of the Anglo and their flunkies to fulfill Montoya's words, "As a figure, Tijerina is dead." I never asked for Mexicans to have the first place. All Abernathy's followers knew that I had fought with Bernard Lafayette to cover the travel and expenses of leaders of the Native American nations, such as Mad Bear from the Toskarora reservation in New York, Clifton Hill from Oklahoma, Hank Adams from Washington State, and many others.

The Evening Star published on May 27 that Abernathy's lieutenants and I had clashed. And on May 28, *The Washington Post* published that Abernathy and I had made peace. Hank Adams (Enrique), the supreme leader of all the Native American tribes and nations during the Poor People's Campaign, came to my door on May 29 at 2 a.m. He told Juan Roybal and Wilfredo Sedillo that it was urgent for him to see me. Before waking me, Juan and Wilfredo wanted to know what this was about. Hank insisted it was a life or death situation. They knocked on the door and woke me up. I listened to Hank's story and told him that, in light of the hour, I would wait until morning and call all the leaders. But, he did not want to wait.

"Call Ralph D. Abernathy right now," he told me. "I called him, but his lieutenants did not want to wake him. They told me I had to wait until 8 a.m."

Enrique was hurt. He and the other Indian chiefs had been present on several occasions when I had advocated on their behalf, not only before Dr. King, but also before Abernathy, Andrew Young, Hosea Williams, Jesse Jackson, and others.

At that moment I called Abernathy. They woke him up immediately, and we spoke about the affront against the Indians. The Washington State Police had arrested a group of Indians, violating a treaty between the Indians and the government. Among the arrested was Dick Gregory, a black actor. Since I had been given the right to present his case to Abernathy, I told the latter that the Indian people wanted to demonstrate in front of the Supreme Court of the United States. The day before, Abernathy and I, with our respective assistants, had told the news media that our differences had disappeared. I wanted to know if Abernathy was really for Native American rights. I presented the idea of surrounding the Supreme Court, maximum symbol of the judicial structure of the United States. I explained to Hank Adams that it was necessary for him to be at the front with his people, and that we would be with them at the rear.

I did not say this due to any fear whatsoever. I did it to avoid jealousy and envy. And what moved me to take this precaution were the rumors that the press was spreading about different leaders. At the beginning, Enrique did not think it was a very good idea to confront the embodiment of the maximum power of the United States. I had to spend around ten minutes explaining why the judicial branch is greater than the legislative and the executive power in the United States. The judicial structure is the one that interprets the law of the nation. It is the one that carries the biggest blame in the theft of our land. It is the one that orders, at gunpoint, our language be taken from us and a foreign one taught. It is the one that forces us to pay taxes without representation. It is the one that interprets to its own convenience the treaties made between the Native American nations and the United States, between Mexico and the United States. The Supreme Court of the United States is behind our poverty. The judges are the most deceiving masks behind which the Anglos hide. The Supreme Court is the most powerful weapon the Anglo has against the Indian, the Black, and the Indohispano.

Judicial power has committed so much wrong against the Indian, Black, and Chicano, that the Liberty Bell refused to ring on July 8, 1835, when John Marshall, the first Supreme Court Chief, died. On the contrary, it broke as a sign and act from God (the Fair Judge of All Judges). But that has never moved the conscience of the Anglo toward his brother, who was on this continent way before him. I explained this to Enrique. I did not even tell him anything about my personal war with the state and federal judges of New Mexico.

I finally convinced Enrique that this was the best venue. I did not sleep anymore that morning. I called Reverend Nieto, Mrs. Escalante, Sullivan, Corky, and others. And I prepared to convince Reverend Abernathy on this. I expected strong resistance. And that is how it was. He tried hard, without success, to convince us that we would all be arrested. "Everything but that," Abernathy said. "That has never been done." His subordinates all abandoned him; only a few bodyguards stayed.

Enrique did not need help with words. He had the necessary valor. He was young, but he was courageous.

I sent messengers to all the Chicanos (approximately five hundred brave ones) to prepare and be ready. There were more than one hundred brave Indians from the different tribes and nations. The Blacks accompanying Reverend Abernathy were no more than fifteen. Some Anglos, pretending to be poor, also accompanied us. My children David, Rosita, Daniel, and Raquel were with us also. As I said before, Bob Brown and his army of journalists had already sold the nation, with Montoya's help, the idea that Reies López Tijerina was a "bandit," that "Reies is an impostor," and that "Reies seeks publicity." But not everyone swallowed Brown's hook. *The Saturday Evening Post* presented me before the nation and the world as the Cid of the Indohispano people (April 20, 1968).

I only mention this in my memoirs so that the public, victim of the "bad" press, learns that Bob Brown's opinion is not the only one.

When Black leaders and my people had words of discord in "Resurrection City," the capital newspapers published the truth, although not all, because they spoke of the rights of the Native American I was defending. The UPI put that out over their wire. But what Brown of the *Albuquerque Journal* published on May 28, 1968, not only omitted part of the truth, but also fabricated a lie. It was so raw and cowardly that it will not be erased by time. This is the *Albuquerque Journal*'s lie: "Tijerina affirmed that according to his opinion, during the marches the different racial and ethnic groups should appear in descending order of importance: First, the Mexican Americans, then the Blacks, and in third place, the Puerto Ricans." Note well, my brothers, that Brown did not even mention the Native Americans. No other national paper that received the UPI wire published this diabolical sentence. The *Journal,* being under Brown's control, added a false sentence. It deserves to be mentioned. All our blood brothers, the Native Americans, should understand the psychopathic spirit of this man. The Anglo is trying to plant hate among Indians and Indohispanos. This man has undertaken a dirty labor against the Alianza and me. We have the hereditary right to represent our people. I will later mention other things concerning this man. For now, I continue with the takeover of the Supreme Court.

That May 29th morning, I carried on a war against the "judges and their empire" in my heart. Abernathy and Enrique, chief of the Indians, did not know this. I knew the eyes of the world were on the Supreme Court of the United States. I could not let this opportunity pass. My people had to lose its fear of that ghost.

Taking over the Supreme Court would symbolically be the greatest education for my intimidated brothers. At the same time, it would be the victory of victories. We could not lose that day. Even if they sent us to jail, the Anglo would never be able to repair the defeat of this great symbol of justice. The Anglo was not prepared to understand the disaster we were going to create. I had years of studying this monster. Judges are the pillars that support white-collar criminals. They are the ones that strengthen and legalize the corrupt politicians who manage the people's money. What was going to happen on May 29 was like a dream for me.

I could not believe that hundreds of brave ones and I would come face to face with the maximum symbol of judicial power of this nation. I was accompanied by five of the participants in the Tierra Amarilla courthouse takeover. They, together with my son Danielito, climbed on Athena's statue. This was done as an act of symbolic conquest over Anglo justice. A reporter took several pictures of this symbolic conquest and gave me a couple. When I received this gift, I felt a good spirit was moving this young man. *The Washington Post* also published a photo of this symbolic conquest. The courageous ones of Tierra Amarilla were immortalized on May 29, 1968.

The Albuquerque Tribune made more noise about the takeover of the Supreme Court than any other paper. It headlined the event with these words: "The Poor Take Over the Supreme Court," and in smaller letters, "they broke windows, hit doors." A large picture appeared in this paper with the caption "Angry Indians invade the Supreme Court yelling 'We want justice!'"

For an instant, it seemed there would be a big confrontation between the people and the police. But the brave ones from New Mexico and the Southwest created a human barrier by linking their arms. The police remained on the opposite side of the street. They seemed to receive new orders and calmed down.

A tense moment occurred when radio stations exaggerated in a news bulletin that four Supreme Court windows had been broken. Some brave ones, irritated when the large doors of the main entrance were closed, made a provisional entrance. They left a button with the words "We will overcome." I did not see this incident. But the radio and the press talked about it. I had expected violence from the police that day, but there was none.

Hank and the Indian people asked for a meeting with the judges, but they refused. John Davis, main clerk of the Supreme Court, agreed to meet with four delegates: one Indian, one Black, one Indohispano, and one Anglo. Hank refused the offer. John Davis finally accepted the 20 delegates. We had triumphed! We did what had never been done with the Supreme Court of the United States. The youth exhibited great delight in their faces; they jumped and ran. Men and women, old and young—everyone reflected the new spirit of victory. The moment was joyful, a spirit of celebration, as those who find lost treasure overcame us. The people had recovered their lost bravery. Nations that trembled before the United States were perplexed at seeing what these people had done with the judges in the palace of the judicial emperors.

The White House and the Supreme Court would never forget this defeat and humiliation. They knew who originated the plan to take over the Supreme Court. *The Evening Star* published a photo with a caption, "Reies Tijerina, Mexican American leader, in the Campaign of the Poor." The United Press International made me the author of the plan against the Supreme Court. *The Albuquerque Tribune* published the same in the May 29th issue. I knew what awaited me in the future.

When we left the Supreme Court building, we walked toward the White House. A black man and a white woman were behind us. The police arrested them. When I saw this, I asked myself, Why does this poor black man have to pay for what the Indohispanos did at the Supreme Court? The black man was Ray Robinson, and the woman was his wife, Shirley. Five policemen were needed to carry him away.

The police's plan was revealed when my son Danielito and the brave ones from Tierra Amarilla crossed the street. A cop on a motorcycle ran over them. It was deliberate. The cops used their batons. It was chaos. I saw it was not a matter of law and order. It was personal revenge. With the same sadistic spirit that moved them in Hiroshima and Nagasaki, they fell upon these youngsters. My daughter Raquel, fifteen years old, was hit. The savage blows gripped my soul. Had my brave ones not stopped me, I would have stained my hands with the blood of these cowards. We got the youngsters out of jail that same night. I felt joy seeing my two sons free.

After the monumental victory over the Supreme Court, the Anglos started trying to divide us from the Indians. I went to a great Indian celebration in Henrrieta, Oklahoma. When I returned to Washington, I learned that the press had published another shameless lie. The Anglo press told the world that the Native Americans, Corky, and I had fought over leadership because of jealousy: "Reies returned to New Mexico because he lost his leadership." Many people actually asked me about the fight with Corky. I received a call from people in New Mexico asking me about the fight. But after seeing me come back from Oklahoma accompanied by numerous Indian leaders, they did not know what to think. We unraveled the Anglo conspiracy to divide us. It was clear to me the Anglos were hurt over their defeat at the Supreme Court.

On June 5, I convened the whole community, Corky included, to celebrate the first anniversary of the takeover of Tierra Amarilla. Everybody demonstrated a joy and spirit of celebration on that great and significant day of our liberty. While we celebrated, the news spread that an Arab refugee from Jerusalem had shot Robert Kennedy. It was hard for the nation to accept it. Two months earlier they had assassinated Dr. King; five years before it had been President John F. Kennedy. I thought, "Maybe these tragedies will touch the conscience of the Anglo, who robbed us of everything: our land, our culture, and the joy of our spirit."

The next day, June 6, we presented our claims before the State Department. Dean Rusk agreed to see us. "More or less, four can come in," said Rusk. "No," we answered, "twenty delegates and the press." Rusk answered, "Twenty can come in, but without the press." We refused.

Here, I must clear up a sad truth. Not only did the Anglo rob us of our land, culture, values, and virtues, but they also robbed us of the right to know. This robbery is not committed by the White House, but by the publicity mechanisms controlled by Anglos and their "allies."

The Anglo does not recognize our right to demand justice for our property and for our culture. But it recognizes the right of the Jewish to reclaim their land two thousand years after they abandoned it. An Arab, one thrown out of Palestine, spilled Robert Kennedy's blood. That blood was part of the price the United States paid for wanting the land Jews claimed as theirs. And this is what the Anglo must recognize: the land that I demand for my Indian and Indohispano people belongs to us in all truth. Just like the Anglo concedes reason and justice to the claims of Jews, he should concede reason and justice to us.

If the Anglo wants justice for the Jewish, he should want it for us. The Anglo has been involved since World War II in the Jewish land reclamation. Well, so be it. But why does he want to take away our right to demand what is ours? The Anglo did not hesitate in taking measures to deprive us of our inheritance.

The Arabs, children of Ishmael and Abraham, did not burn the property titles of the "Jewish land" the way the New Mexican Anglo did. I think that the Arab claim, as small as it may be, over the disputed land, is more legitimate than the claim of the Anglo over ours. This is what the Anglo and his allies cannot accept nor want to hear: the big difference in attitude he exhibits toward the Jewish land claim and his intransigence toward the land we claim in the Southwest. This is the bone stuck in the Anglo's throat.

I considered the march and the Poor People's Campaign one of the best opportunities to give our own version of our history, not the Anglo version, to the world. The Anglo knew what I wanted. And that is why he twisted the truth and deceived the public on everything related to the events in the capital of the United States.

After the victory we had achieved against the Supreme Court on May 29, we went to visit the Mexican Embassy and the Organization of American States to present our case.

On June 3, with more than three hundred brave southwesterners, we went to the Mexican embassy. We did not find the hostile Anglo attitude we had seen since our arrival in the capital. The Mexican ambassador accepted our petition. He greeted us with a hug and offered us delicious sodas. He opened his heart and the doors of the Mexican Embassy to us. He offered to help with the Treaty of Guadalupe Hidalgo. For more than an hour, with an open heart, we presented the truth of the matter, the bitter story we have lived over the last one hundred twenty years, and that the Anglo has frozen so the world will not find out. We gave him statistical proof. The whole world knew of our visit to the Mexican Embassy. The Tierra Amarilla victory on June 5 had resonated in Mexico. This victory was feared most by the Anglo. The publicity given this date hurt Anglo pride. Since that day, many Mexican friends have told me that the United States has changed its attitude toward Mexico, but with the interest of having Mexico forget about the Treaty of Guadalupe Hidalgo and the fifteen million Mexicans oppressed in the United States.

For the first time, Spain and all Indohispanic America knew our version of the history of the Southwest. The United States presented us to the world on June 5 as "rebels without a cause," to the point that a large Mexican daily headlined their article, "To Jail for Rabel Rousing." Now, we were neither in Tierra Amarilla nor in New Mexico, where Bob Brown and his allies controlled all news mechanisms. Here, there were correspondents from all nations. I spoke directly with journalists from Mexico and Spain. The Mexican magazine *Tiempo* put me on its cover. *ABC* of Spain headed a morning edition with "The tide of racial protest threatens North American society." Our case was presented to the world. In spite of disagreements between Francisco Franco and the White House, *ABC* wrote very positive stories about the Southwest settlers stating, "North America is discovering the mystery of its history these days." The Spanish journalists did not stop reporting on the symbolic takeover of the Supreme Court of the United States. The Mexican ambassador sent a special envoy to interview Mexicans in the Poor People's Campaign. He was a very courteous young man. The interview was published in the *Official Daily* of the Mexican government. These were the screams from Washington we were sending out to the world. Anglos, like Bob Brown, did not appreciate that.

I must say that during the time my brothers and I were in Washington, three Anglos and a Native American were in charge of the Alianza office and all matters. They wrote and gave news of all campaign activities to local news agencies. Bob Brown did not trust his Anglo brothers when they wrote or said anything in my favor. The two largest Albuquerque newspapers with correspondents in the capital left out all the favorable things said in the Washington newspapers about my people and me. The *Evening Star* issued two good, long articles related to our confrontation with Dean Rusk at the State Department on June 13 and 16. Washington reporters favored us, but the New Mexican press published, "Dean Rusk Disproves Tijerina." In reality, I never talked to Rusk, because he would not allow the press in.

The Anglo accuses me of violence. Those who criticize me have their hands full of blood. They have spilled blood of innocent people in the United States and all over the world. What for them is "liberty, justice, and the free world" means they have crossed the seas of earth, planting hatred, racism, and war among nations. So, it has been in Korea, Germany, China, Vietmam, Cuba, Colombia, Panama, Mexico, the African countries, those of Indohispanic America, Europe, Asia, the Far East, and now, the Middle East. The Anglo and his criminal Central Intelligence Agency, a "secret government," use the Bible and the church to accomplish their diabolical objectives. They use press reporters and their publicity apparatus to violate all international treaties. They have not left a single Native American unhurt. They have not respected the property or culture of a single one. They have conditioned Black people in such a way that now that they aspire to their freedom, they find themselves divided by the confusion the Anglo has created among them. And now, their offspring, the children of this shameful history, dare label me violent.

When the campaign for the poor was coming to an end, an Anglo approached me and offered me legal help. I did not have any money to pay lawyers and so I accepted this Anglo's help. Patricia was expecting another child. She had accompanied me to Washington during the last weeks. Patricia told me from the beginning that she did not trust Bill Higgs, but I convinced her that there were some good Anglos in the world. We returned to New Mexico after sixty days in the U.S. capital, satisfied that we had achieved our objectives.

I had to appear in court on some pending motions upon arrival. While I was in Washington, Beverly Axelrod had represented me in the New Mexican tribunals. She had not appealed Judge Bratton's sentence of December 15, 1967. That was the main reason I accepted Bill Higgs' offer in Washington. It was already late and Beverly still had not prepared the motion. She was embarrassed and even cried once. Bill pulled us out of that one. The truth was that the New Mexican judges had me in a corner. They wanted to paralyze me. And I had no money to buy justice at the price demanded by the Anglo.

Judge Bratton and Jack Love brought new charges against me. I arrived just in time to appear before another jury in another "trial."

Second Sentence

The trial took place in the Santa Fe Federal Court. In this second trial, the Anglos prosecuted Jerry Noll and me together. I felt good because the people were behind me and supported me. As I expected, we lost the federal trial. The Anglo jury arrived at a verdict immediately. They gave us six months in prison and a $500 fine. We had defended our right to speak freely. The Anglos did not like Jerry Noll. According to Jerry, the United States did not have a legitimate right of sovereignty over the Southwest. Jerry's ancestors had denounced the United States since 1833.

Now I had been convicted twice and had two sentences over my head. I was free on bail, pending appeals. The federal judges were tying me up, as spiders do with flies. They had intimidated my race and thought that I would give up. Bill Higgs moved fast. He started preparing my two appeals. I did not expect to win them, but I needed to buy some time against their organized political power. And I had to take away the fear the Anglo had instilled in my people. There was a lot of work to be done. My only weapons were spiritual, moral, and cultural. These weapons are slower than the Anglo ones.

The new history of freedom was being written. The children of the people of the Southwest were uniting. The spirit of the Indohispano people was reviving, and my brothers were learning about themselves with the Laws of the Indies. The Alianza was a new hope. The march from Albuquerque to Santa Fe we had on July 4, 1966, was my people's signal and message to the government of the United States. The taking of San Joaquín was the rallying cry of the people, who clamored for justice. The taking of Tierra Amarilla was possible thanks to the power of freedom. The redemption of our spirit came that precious June 5, 1967. The march and campaign of the poor in Washington, D.C., was the last call to the Anglo's conscience and that of their allies before the coming of justice. But the "judges" could not see the new history. They believed I was mentally ill.

The New Mexico Supreme Court assigned Judge Paul Larrazolo to try my brothers and me. He gave us two dates by which to file the final motions before the trial. He set the trial date for November 12. This was the trial for the takeover of Tierra Amarilla. The Anglo press had done its part to poison the mind of the public. They blamed me for Salazar's murder. Now, judge Larrazolo had to do his part. During the last eighteen months, the press, radio, and TV were cultivating the public, convincing everyone that "King Tiger" was a "bandit," a "criminal," a twice-convicted felon by federal judges.

But my people were praying for me. They lit candles by the thousands to hundreds of saints so that God, the Fair Judge of All Judges, would free me from Anglo hands. I had faith. I was supported by just and peaceful people, and by their pleas.

Before the trial, reporter Pete Herrera of United Press International was assigned by his Anglo bosses to write a brief, but fair story, about me: "Tijerina is Moses for the Mexican-Americans." Bob Brown did not allow this story to come out in his newspaper. The people of New Mexico were deprived of this publication. But it was published outside of New Mexico. The *El Paso Herald Post* printed it. Brown did not allow a good thing to be said about me. Brown knew that my big trial was near, and he did not want to see me exculpated of Salazar's blood.

The people of the Alianza met and decided to print our own copies of the article. We distributed them by mail to all the friends and family of the Alianza, with an explanation of Brown's conduct.

My people commented on the changes over the last year and six months. The Anglo was different. The changes in employment, in the schools, among politicians, and in the clergy were evident. Now the Anglo showed respect and attention to my people. Although the changes were superficial, my people saw it and told me about it. I saw it, too. But what many did not know was that the Anglo was doing this so my people would not follow me, so my people would not listen to me. They also did not know that the Anglo's hate toward me was now even greater and more destructive. I knew this because I observed it and felt it.

My people are conditioned to discrimination, to misery without justice. The Anglo made some changes in the treatment of my people after June 5. The people qualified them as a major blessing. This was too much for my people. They had never received such gentle treatment over the past twelve years. Of course, to souls thirsty for justice, this seemed like justice. They almost did not want to believe it. In their new joy, my brothers did not see that the Anglo disdained me even more.

On August 9, the press announced that Boston Witt, the state prosecutor, had said he would not publish the investigation about the Alianza and me until after the trial on November 12. This investigation was expected to reveal that Tijerina was a "Communist and was stealing money from the poor." As if the Anglo government and its allies left much money in the pockets of the poor for me to get my hands on. It was almost as if these "vampires" were interested in the well-being of the poor.

My tasks multiplied and work at the Alianza increased daily. I was pulled in many directions and others had to help me with all the duties and responsibilities brought on by our people's renewed interest in our culture and heritage. The people were no longer timid and fearful as they had been in 1956, when I first met them. There was a new spirit and courage. I could see that this new spirit would bear fruit in about ten years. I felt responsible for the birth of spirit and mental development among our oppressed and enslaved people.

On July 26, I filed suit against the State Board of Education for abuse and discrimination of our children. The educational system was in violation of Articles 2, Section 5, and Article 12, Section 8, of the state constitution and Article 6, Section 2, of the United States Constitution. Our language has been abused and stolen, just like our property has been. Back in February 26, 1968, my daughter Raquel and fifteen other students had protested the education they were receiving in the public schools. The police came and beat our children. In the land of the free there is no room for our language.

Toward the end of July, I thought of going into electoral politics. I had never bothered with politics, but thought that this was an avenue to expose the corrupt judges and politicians, unmask them. I realized that one person against the political machine would not prevail, but it was another avenue. Besides, many people had urged me to run for governor. I knew I could not clean up the corrupt political machine. It was hopeless. But I ran, to surprise the media, judges, and politicians. I announced my candidacy when I returned from the Poor People's Campaign on the day I stood before Judge Larrazolo on July 23. People from all quarters called to congratulate me and express their support. I drafted a twelve-point platform that included the land issues, educational reform, and my stand against white-collar crime. Those most responsible for white-collar crime are the churches (organized religion), then government and the corporations it permits to operate. Together, these entities are destroying the institution of the family. The disintegration of the family is key to the continuing destruction of western civilization. As candidate for governor, I could speak to these issues. My campaign slogan was "Justice."

But I was denied ballot status, so I went to court. I was denied there, also. I never thought they would close this door on me. This was the second door closed to me in my long struggle. The first door had been the court case, Sandoval v. United States in 1897.

The lawyers that represented me in court for the taking of Tierra Amarilla also represented me before Judge Bratton. Because they lost this rather insignificant case, I fired them. They had already cost us close to $20,000 in attorney fees. It was too much money for too little effort. I made strong statements against my lawyers in Las Cruces and said that I probably would defend myself in the future. I had already gained legal knowledge from studying the Treaty of Guadalupe Hidalgo, the various constitutions, property rights, international law, and federal statutes. I knew the judges were the real enemy of the people. I never expected to lose my cases to these judges.

Eventually, I had to confront the judges. My confrontations with the police in San Joaquín and the military in Tierra Amarilla were really confrontations with the gunslingers of the judges. Judges are behind the powerful; they are the real power. They had me in their sights, and I was already under a two-year prison sentence and free on a $50,000 bond. These judges did not lift a finger to prosecute William Fellion, when he attempted to murder my family and me at the Alianza building. The judges did not punish Fellion; he punished himself by blowing up his left arm while attempting to bomb us. Similarly, once before in October 1966, two Anglo men attacked Anselmo and me a few blocks from the office. We managed to fight them off. These same Anglos then complained to the police that we had assaulted them.

Consequently, all of these dangerous events forced many Alianza members to do double duty as security and spies. Police agents infiltrated the Alianza. We knew our telephones were tapped. We spied on these police agents and informers, while they kept vigilance on us. The FBI kept close watch on the Alianza members. They had the membership list. Judge Payne had forced us to turn it over to the police. Each of the thirty thousand members was visited by the police and with lies and falsehoods they tried to get the members to break with the Alianza. In the Albuquerque area alone, we had over 9,000 members.

Judge Larrazolo moved the Tierra Amarilla trial from Rio Arriba to Albuquerque. Upon the advice of Beverly Axelrod and Bill Higgs, I accepted John Thorpe from San José, California, to help, *pro bono,* with the defense for the ten of us accused in the taking of Tierra Amarilla. Thorpe had defended some of the Black Panthers in their trials. All together we had fourteen lawyers on the defense team, four of them representing me. The defense team worked for eighteen months preparing our case.

On the eve of the trial, a defense attorney surprised us with a motion to sever his client's trial in order to avoid my bad influence. I never expected this move. I also did not expect Judge Larrazolo to grant this motion and to sever me from all nine defendants. I was to be tried separately. The night before the trial, I made a decision to represent myself. On opening day, I got up and said, "May it please the Court, from this moment forward, I terminate my four lawyers and wish to represent myself. . . ." Judge Larrazolo was shocked and visibly upset. Now, he had to give me time to prepare my own defense. He only gave me thirty minutes to get ready. My lawyers and family tried to dissuade me from this step. I listened to my son David ask me if this decision was not based on my pride. I told him, "Son, my entire struggle has been for the people. My spirit is on trial. They have released a raging bull. I have to face the bull that is charging me." The judge assigned lawyers to assist me at the suggestion of the state prosecutors. They did not want me to make procedural errors that could overturn a conviction due to my ignorance of the law.

The trial took place from November 12 through December 13, 1968. I taped the entire trial and that copy is in my personal archive.

My first legal step was to examine rigorously the jury panel. I disqualified most of the panel members because of bias held against me for the death of Salazar. Bob Brown's defamatory campaign now worked in my favor. I was proving the great harm the press was doing to our cause and me. The majority of the Anglo jury panel members were convinced that I had murdered Eulogio Salazar. Judge Larrazolo had no choice but to dismiss each potential juror for bias. When I finished my examination of the jury panel, I had a jury comprised of seven Indohispanos, a black woman, and four Anglos. Jack Love had successfully prosecuted me in Las Cruces. He was now Alfonso Sánchez's assistant prosecutor in this trial. The people had just defeated Jack Love in the November 5th general election. He had run for attorney general. And, Alfonso Sánchez had also been defeated in his bid for reelection as district attorney. Both of them were demoralized by their electoral defeats and were seeking revenge against me. The Alianza membership and I had worked hard against them in that election.

I faced sixty-four charges, and Judge Larrazolo made the state choose only three. They chose their best accusations, which were assault, assault and false imprisonment of Daniel Rivera, and a third charge similar to the other two. The state's best witness was Daniel Rivera. While he was on the witness stand, I made Rivera detail the history of the Tierra Amarilla land grant. I made him admit that he did not know federal civil rights law. His knowledge of the law was very shallow and poor. I made him explain Emilio Naranjo's predominant role in the county. Daniel got nervous on the witness stand. He perspired profusely. The courtroom and hallways were filled to capacity with our supporters and the press from all over the country. I questioned Daniel over different themes and finally got to his role in the quashing of our meeting in Coyote, New Mexico. I made him explain to the jury the various police agencies present that day—FBI, state and county police, and the Forest Service agent (James Evans)—that violated the civil rights of people and prevented them from lawful assembly. The state prosecutors could not help Daniel Rivera on the witness stand. He was all alone. Love made a motion for recess when he saw how I was effectively destroying their star witness. I objected, stating that I was about to finish and proceeded to question him over what happened in Tierra Amarilla. I asked him point blank if he thought I was responsible for all that happened that day. He said, "Mr. Tijerina, I do not blame you for anything that happened in Tierra Amarilla." Hearing those words, I told the witness that I had no further questions of him. The momentum of the trial shifted in my favor at that moment.

That afternoon, Bill Higgs brought me a copy of the *Albuquerque Tribune,* which carried an article on my courtroom performance and compared me to Clarence Darrow. I asked him who that was. I never knew his fame until Higgs told me.

The state presented more than sixty witnesses against me, and I called fifty on my behalf. Among the witnesses were Governor David Cargo, General Jolly, Joe Black, head of the state police, and many Rio Arriba County employees. I questioned all these witnesses on civil rights and the right of citizens to arrest a person that commits a crime. The jury and the public in attendance were surprised to learn, as I was, that they did not know civil rights law. I asked the witnesses, "You carry guns with which to kill people without knowing the law? Does Joe Black allow you to carry a gun without informing you about the rights of people?" They all had to answer me in the affirmative, including Nick Sais, who had been wounded in Tierra Amarilla. I asked him, "Do not you think that being armed, without knowing the rights of people, that you are a danger to the society?" He admitted he was. I went further and asked him, "Who do you think is at greater fault, you or your superiors, in arming you without teaching you the rights of people and the law?" He twisted and turned in the witness chair, but finally answered that his superiors were at fault. In a surprise move, I asked that Alfonso Sánchez take the witness stand. I wanted to prove to the jury and court with his expert testimony that these law enforcement officials were ignorant of the law and, therefore, incompetent to enforce the law. That is why things turned out as they did in Tierra Amarilla. Jack Love jumped to oppose my request, while Sánchez turned pale. Judge Larrazolo took the matter under advisement. Ultimately, he protected Sánchez and did not let me cross-examine him.

My Defense

The state rested its case. I began my presentation with an opening statement in which I explained the supreme law of the land found in Article 6, Section 2, of the U.S. Constitution and the guarantees afforded by the Treaty of Guadalupe Hidalgo under that section and how the

Alianza was created because the United States was not fulfilling its obligations to us under the law. I explained that it was not Mexico's responsibility or ours to comply with the law; rather, it was the U.S. government's responsibility. I pointed out that the U.S. was not only irresponsible but also looked the other way when archival records that could prove we were the descendents of people that had settled the Southwest more than 300 years prior were destroyed, burned, lost, sold, and otherwise made to disappear. Our forefathers left their legacy in the names of the geographic monuments found all around us. I explained that under Articles 8 and 9 and the Protocol to the Treaty of Guadalupe Hidalgo, our cultural rights, especially our language, were violently attacked under unconstitutional laws. In this regard, we were no different than Native Americans and Blacks complaining of civil rights violations. I told the jury how the Alianza began employing peaceful means to draw attention to our demands for justice by writing letters to all the presidents, from Dwight Eisenhower to Lyndon B. Johnson, without a single response. I told them about the Anglo historians Hubert Bancroft and Ralph Twitchell, who also concurred in their research that our land was stolen by violence, fraud, government complicity, and deception. These scholars validated our claims to the land in New Mexico, Texas, Arizona, California, Utah, and Nevada. Yet, the government pretends we do not exist. It makes fun of our demands and laughs at our efforts. I told them how the San Joaquín land grant was three-times adjudicated and found to belong to the people. Yet, Judges Bratton and Payne, the White House, and Bob Brown of the *Albuquerque Journal,* say it does not exist. I told them this was a political case and not a judicial one. I explained that we had been residing on these same lands since 1526, before any foreign Anglo. Now, we were treated like the foreigner in our own land. The Anglo has never respected our property rights.

I called Dr. Frances Swadesh, an anthropologist with the University of Colorado, as my first witness. Her doctoral dissertation was on the Spanish land grants and settlements in northern New Mexico. Her research focused on the legal maneuvers utilized by Anglos to steal the land from our people. She was an effective witness. I wanted the Anglos to hear our story from another Anglo. Next, I called Dr. Clark

Knowlton, formerly with the University of the Highlands, Las Vegas, New Mexico. Both of my expert witnesses helped prove my opening statement. They testified that from the White House to local governments in New Mexico, all had conspired to steal the people's land by not abiding by the terms of the Treaty of Guadalupe Hidalgo. They had allowed injustices to be committed against the people, especially in Tierra Amarilla. Jack Love did not like my witnesses' testimony. The more these two experts testified, the more his case got away from him. The jury began to understand what was at the root of this case. Public opinion shifted to our side because of the testimony of these experts.

I called some of those who were with me at Tierra Amarilla to the witness stand, including myself. First, I testified about my childhood and my life, how I was not allowed to speak Spanish. I told them I was an orphan at age six and that I had seen my father robbed of his earnings by unscrupulous ranchers on three occasions. I narrated the education that my mother had given me and how I wanted to study for the priesthood or become a minister. I told them of the Valley of Peace and how I first came to Tierra Amarilla in New Mexico. When I came, I learned of the theft of the land by the Anglos, and I began to petition for an investigation into the land grants of San Joaquín and Tierra Amarilla. I repeated the letter-writing campaigns we initiated to the White House and other public officials with no result. I then told them how up to this point we had been peaceful citizens using nonviolent means to present our demands, but District Attorney Alfonso Sánchez had violated our rights to assemble and freely associate by preventing our meeting in Coyote, New Mexico, on June 3, 1967. I told them that the police violence against us began in Coyote and ended in Tierra Amarilla. I explained to the jury the right to arrest someone who has committed a crime, citizen's arrest power. I told them we went to Tierra Amarilla to arrest Alfonso Sánchez for violating our civil right to assemble and associate. But he was not there, and the local police were ignorant of our rights under the law and mishandled the situation. They had caused the violence at the courthouse in Tierra Amarilla.

The state offered a few rebuttal witnesses, but the jury was already more favorably disposed to my defense. The judge gave each side an hour for closing arguments. Jack Love and Alfonso Sánchez divided their time between them. Both of them simply exhorted the jury to find me guilty. I anxiously waited for my turn. During my time, I refreshed the jury's memory on the legal history of the land grants and our rights under the Treaty of Guadalupe Hidalgo. I reminded them that our meeting in Coyote was to be peaceful and that the police came with their guns and prevented our meeting in violation of our First Amendment rights under the U.S. Constitution. I told them how ordinary Anglo citizens all carry weapons in their cars and trucks, but not our people. If we carry weapons, we are arrested. I told them how my wife Patricia had been treated in jail and her subsequent miscarriage of our baby.

The main point I made in the closing argument was the people's right to arrest others who have committed a crime. I stressed the citizen's arrest power as being the ultimate civil right because the police are all armed and dangerous. The people have been disarmed. When we went to Tierra Amarilla to exercise our constitutional rights of citizen's arrest, we were met by police officers ignorant of the law.

When I finished, Alfonso Sánchez, instead of reviewing the evidence they had presented against me, proceeded to defend himself against my accusations. He apologized to the jury for not knowing that Patricia was pregnant and that she had aborted the baby. The jury now knew there were two murders resulting from Tierra Amarilla: Eulogio's and our baby's. Sánchez's face reflected his shame, while I was happy. Sánchez was putting himself on trial and having to defend himself. Jack Love had gotten help in trying in Las Cruces from Judge Bratton, and my lawyers had simply given up. Here, Judge Larrazolo was not helping them, and I was doing a good job in defending myself. The judge then asked us for our requested instructions to the jury. I submitted four questions on citizen's arrest. Love protested my submissions, but the judge allowed them. I wrote, "To effect a citizen's arrest, the person has the right to use the necessary force to do so."

The Victory

After four and a half hours of jury deliberation, the verdict was announced: Not Guilty. Each "Not Guilty" was read for the three charges against me. We were elated! Those words were the most beautiful I had heard in my entire life. Love and Sánchez were devastated, sad, and confused. Judge Larrazolo left the courtroom quickly. Some jurors wept with joy at our victory.

The media waited for me as I exited the courthouse. They asked me, "How do you feel after this great triumph?" As my wife, daughter Raquel, and I crossed the street, a carload of Anglos yelled out, "We're still going to get you."

Congratulatory messages arrived from around the nation and the world. I became even more sought after by people. Now, I was even asked by people for legal advice on their problems. The local press had to put our victory on their front pages. The victory resulted in an increase in membership in the Alianza.

On December 20, I wrote the governor asking for an appointment to discuss the Salazar investigation, and we sent a telegram to the Spanish government, which cost us $100 to send. We never got a reply.

A Growing Police Conspiracy

Now that I had beaten my enemies at their own game, I was in greater danger. From that day forward, they decided to play even dirtier and unleash more criminal activity in my direction. Within days of the victory, my former wife's home, where my older children lived, at 618 W. Lead S.W., was bombed. My children were terrorized. The television cameras arrived and reported on this attempted murder. But *The Albuquerque Journal* buried this news item. My house was shot at three times within two weeks following the trial. Windows at the office were stoned and broken. They thought that their terrorizing my family would weaken me. My family had been made stronger over the years, and, during my seven years as a fugitive, they had lost their fear.

When I was speaking on January 23, 1969, at the University of California at San Diego, an Anglo friend, Ross Benedict, rushed to the speaker's stage to tell me that my home had been bombed. He had just heard it over the radio. My three-month old son, Joaquín Carlos, and two-year-old Isabel were but five meters from the explosion point. Patricia and Rosita were on the second floor. Wilfredo Sedillo and Juan Roybal were on security duty at the time. All of them escaped serious injury. Again, the electronic media reported on this attempt, but the *Journal* suppressed the information.

Robert Gilliland, once again, was put in charge of the investigation of this bombing, the third one aimed at my family and me. He never investigated. He did not even question my family on what they might have heard or seen. An FBI agent did question my wife and her parents. The rumors were that we were bombing our own facility.

We had no police protection. William Fellion, the old bomb expert, was loose. He never was tried for his attempt on our lives. He lost his left arm in the previous attempt, but his friends bought him a metal prosthesis.

We celebrated the second anniversary of the Alianza on February second. We had a great turnout. The people did not fit in the building. We announced that we had obtained the use of a larger building near Taos for future meetings and to set up our school. An Anglo had made that offer. Our lawsuit against the educational system was going forward in federal court with Judge Payne. We sought to educate our children in Spanish and concerning our own history and culture. We never got to use the building. Within days of our announcement, it was burned to the ground.

The Albuquerque Journal

No sooner had my innocent verdict been announced than John McMilion and Bob Brown were editorializing for a retrial. They did not want to accept the jury verdict. They wanted to place me in double jeopardy. In less than four days after my victory, the *Journal* was clamoring for my skin.

They were not concerned that William Fellion was never charged for his attempt on my life and was roaming free. On March 15, 1969, another bomb exploded next to the Alianza building. The blast destroyed fifteen automobiles, broke countless windows in the area and the doors to our offices. The bomb was placed underneath Mr. Anaya's automobile. We usually used his car to go and come on errands. The car was blown to smithereens. Pieces were found some four blocks away. The blast made a two-meter hole in the street.

While the television cameras covered the damage done by this latest and largest bomb explosion ever, I got a call from Tomasito Gallegos. His house had just been bombed. He was an Alianza member, the one that had made the special steel for our building to protect us from this type of blast. The *Journal* reported that these bomb blasts were "the doings of the Alianzistas to draw attention to themselves." We submitted a resolution to the U.S. Congress in March, but Senator Joseph Montoya and Representative Manuel Luján did not want to introduce it. The representative from Texas, Henry B. González, introduced House Bill 1729, asking for an investigation into land claims in the Southwest.

We also entered into negotiations with the Presbyterian Church over the land they occupied in the Piedra Lumbre grant; they called it "Ghost Ranch." The family of Pedro Martín received this land grant of 49,748 acres in 1766. I wrote William P. Thompson, head of the Presbyterians, on November 14, 1968, providing him with the legal history of this land grant. I asked him to return the land and set an example for justice. The secretary general of New Mexico, William A. Morrison, telegraphed a response asking that we meet on April 23 to discuss the land question.

Meanwhile, the federal court subpoenaed the Alianza secretary-treasurer Eduardo Chávez to bring all financial records of our organization to court on February 27, 1969.

In January, we found out that more than seventy-five thousand school children, many of them in the Albuquerque schools, had been eating horsemeat. The meat was bought from Walter Jaramillo. He was vilified in the press for more than forty-five days. We knew he was not the main culprit. Julián Soto y Soto had told us who was. Mr. Soto y Soto, however, was from Mexico, without documents or passport. He told us that he worked for Walter L. Fields at $40 a week, although he had been promised $80. He had worked for him for eight months, and Fields had only paid him the $40 and kept the other $40 in reserve. Soto y Soto was paid to kill the horses and dress the meat that Fields sold to Jaramillo, White's Cut-Rate Market, and others. I called Rees Lloyd of the *Journal* and John Leahigh of UPI and told them what we knew. The story was published, but without credit for our role in discovering the real villain. Bob Brown would not allow mention of my name in the story. If the people knew how we had helped in this case, they might see me in a better light, but the *Journal's* main interest was in seeing me tried again for Tierra Amarilla. The date for my other trial, however, was approaching.

The News

On April 4, the mayor of San Joaquín offered land to anyone wishing to live on their land grant. Mayor José Lorenzo Salazar received letters of interest from all over the country. This action scared the Anglos a great deal, especially those who were holding land illegally within the San Joaquín land grant. On this same day, the U.S. Department of Justice responded to our letter of March 17. I had asked that it investigate the *Albuquerque Journal* and *Albuquerque Tribune* in light of the recent U.S. Supreme Court case, U.S. v. Citizen Publishing Company.

Meanwhile, Dennis Sanders from Hollywood was proposing a film on the taking of Tierra Amarilla and my life story. *The Boston Globe* ran a lengthy feature story on April 6 on the Alianza and our struggle for the land.

I got a letter from my court-appointed attorney, John C. Wheeler, on April 9, informing me that Jack Love was getting a trial set for May 19. I also got a letter from Harold Kent, my attorney representing me on the film project in Hollywood. He wanted ten percent of the deal as attorney fees.

I went to New York and addressed the National Lawyers' Guild at the Hilton Hotel. I spoke about the Treaty of Guadalupe Hidalgo to more than two thousand lawyers gathered there. Upon my return, I found out that I would be tried on June 16 in Judge Burks' court. To make matters worse, I got a letter on April 14 from Morton Stavis in New York, advising me that the 10th Court of Appeals had affirmed Judge Bratton's sentencing decision. He was going to appeal to the U.S. Supreme Court, so I could remain free on bond.

We met with William A. Morrison regarding the Piedra Lumbre land grant. He promised to do all he could so that justice would be done for the people of Piedra Lumbre. And, over in San Joaquín, Mayor Salazar was putting many young people to work on the land belonging to that grant. The Forest Service was very upset with this development. These Anglos occupied more than six hundred thousand acres of our land.

I left for California at the beginning of May to speak at various colleges and universities. I spent eight days on the speaking tour. When I was at San Bernardino, I saw the NBC program *The Most Hated Man in New Mexico.* The thirty-minute documentary reached into millions of homes. U.S. society was beginning to learn of our cause and struggle. CBS had previously broadcast two other documentaries on our struggle. And, McGraw-Hill Book Company offered to publish my life story. Samuel D. Stewart, executive editor, came to see me.

On May 17, we celebrated the 443rd anniversary of the Spanish language with a march through downtown Albuquerque to the old plaza. We had to celebrate our heritage because the Anglo had prohibited our language for the past 121 years. We had a great celebration. June 5 was rapidly approaching, and we wanted to reoccupy the lands belonging to the San Joaquín land grant.

One morning, Wilfredo and others came running to my house to show me the morning edition of the *Journal,* which was reporting that the National Assembly of the Presbyterian Church meeting in San Antonio, Texas, had approved a resolution to return the land they occupied in the Piedra Lumbre grant to its rightful owners, along with a $50,000 grant with which to obtain legal services to press other land claims. Bob Brown, also a Presbyterian, opposed the resolution and sought to divide us. I called a meeting of potential heirs to the Piedra Lumbre land in El Rito de los Encinos, also known in English as Youngstown. More than five hundred persons attended. We decided to ask the church to postpone the return of the land. We did not want those who opposed us and those who had not joined in the fight for the land to be involved in the administration of this first devolution of land. We sent Morrison a telegram to that effect.

Coyote

The Presbyterian Church leaders invited us to meet at Ghost Ranch. We went. The heirs to the Piedra Lumbre grant spoke eloquently and told the Presbyterians they did not want the land returned if the Alianza was not involved.

All the oppressed people in the U.S. knew that President Richard Nixon was a racist and the enemy of the justice we sought. He appointed Warren Earl Burger as chief justice of the Supreme Court. The Native American, the Black, the Indohispano, we all knew the Supreme Court was the exclusive instrument of the rich. I was asked by many people to do something to protest this appointment. Nobody was doing much to protest other than privately, and a few made press declarations. The militant leaders were afraid of taking action against the supreme judicial power. After meditation, I decided to travel to Washington and execute a citizen's arrest of Warren Burger. I called *The New York Times* and told them what I was going to do. CBS correspondent Joseph Benti carried the news on television for three consecutive days.

I went to Washington, D.C., on my mission. June 2 was a beautiful morning in the nation's capital. My wife and I went to the mayor's office in the nation's capital. I registered my intent to execute a citizen's arrest. I sought out the police chief and asked him to witness my arrest, but he declined. I read him the law on citizen's arrest and told him it was illegal to refuse to assist me. The press was around me like bees after fresh flowers. I went to the Senate office building to meet with the committee that was conducting the hearings on the appointment. This was not an easy task for me. I knew that I would go to prison any day now, but I wanted to do all that I could for our struggle while I still had my freedom. An hour and a half went by, and the nominee did not emerge from the Senate Chamber. Finally, Senator Everett Dirksen from Illinois emerged and spoke to the reporters. Warren Burger did not come out. He hid from me and went out the back door. The media asked me what I was going to do. I said, "This judge has set a bad example to the world, going out the back door. Only fugitives go out the back door." The media asked Dirksen about my coming to arrest the judge. He said, "It is perfect stupidity." I interjected, "Then why did he go out the back door?" Ever since the Supreme Court has been in existence, the nominee, once confirmed, emerges out the front door. Burger has been the exception. Perhaps this was a symbol that the imperial power of the judiciary was beginning to wane. I saw all of this as a spiritual victory for my people and our cause.

I then went to the Supreme Court building to leave my arrest warrant and declare Burger a fugitive from justice. I met with John Davis, the clerk of the court. I registered my warrant and got a receipt. This was the end of one of the most difficult missions I have undertaken in my life.

Upon my return to Albuquerque, my people, especially the Alianza militants, met me at the airport. Our office had received hundreds of telegrams and letters of support for my action against Burger. Rodolfo "Corky" Gonzales sent me a congratulatory telegram expressing his admiration and respect for what I had done.

We immediately left for Coyote, where our people were meeting. There were leaders representing many other groups. The mayor of San Joaquín welcomed me. Reporters from everywhere were there, including Samuel Stewart from McGraw-Hill. I did not want to write my story in English. I wanted to write my memoirs in Spanish.

We spent a week in the area and the last three days by the dam in Abiquiu. This is one of the oldest settlements in northern New Mexico. Settlers went from Abiquiu to establish San Joaquín, Tierra Amarilla, and other communities. Representatives from many communities came to the meeting: Chilili, Las Vegas, Tierra Amarilla, San Mateo, Seboyeta, Atrisco, Santa Fe, Espanola, Taos, Pecos, Albuquerque, Ojo Caliente, Cuba, San Miguel del Vado, and people from the plazas in San Joaquín, which are: Las Cebollas, Canjilon, La Gallina, Mesa del Poleo, Coyote, and Cañones. We measured the limits of the San Joaquín land grant and made our future plans. The Alianza leadership was there also: Wilfredo Sedillo, Juan Roybal, Abraham Sánchez, José Lorenzo Salazar, Ubaldo Velázquez, Samuel Córdoba, José Martínez, Rodolfo Manuel, Belarmino Maez, Santiago Anaya, and others whose names escape me at this writing. My children were there also, David and Daniel, Raquel and Lita. Rosita was in the hospital.

The Forest Service agents were out in full force. They were not supposed to be armed, but they all were. James Evans was there. We never lost sight of him. He had promised that I would get it next time. There were also fifteen uniformed police officers, including Robert Gilliland.

After breakfast one morning, my wife Patricia told me she wanted to do her part in our struggle. She said, "Besides, if the gringos put me in jail, I am better off because I do not want to be free while you are in prison." I acted as if I did not hear her. She insisted, and I told her to consult with the senior advisors, but that it was too late, we were leaving for home. She looked for them. Some were reading the newspaper articles where we had made the news. During our stay in Coyote, we had gone to arrest Governor David Cargo for his part in the coverup of the death of Eulogio Salazar and the scientists at Los Alamos National Laboratory for fabricating atomic and hydrogen bombs, weapons of mass human destruction.

Patricia made her presentation to those gathered in Coyote. She wanted to burn the Forest Service sign at the entrance to Coyote. They supported her idea. And, when we were on the way out of the area, she set fire to the sign. The police arrested her on the spot. Wilfredo was tape recording everything being said. Patricia told the police that she had set fire to the sign as protest. I went to the car where Isabel, our thirty-month-old child, was sitting. I had to care for her now that Patricia was under arrest. The Forest Service agents, armed with automatic weapons, surrounded us. Our people were not armed. I was the only one with an M-1 and 30 rounds, but it was in the car. I heard someone yell out, "Reies López Tijerina, you are under arrest." Robert Gilliand and James Evans approached me. I told them they had not witnessed anything. I told them the police who were present already had arrested Patricia. I believed they were here to disturb the peace. And I told them, "If you do not leave right now, we will arrest you." Gilliland had a twelve-gauge shotgun, double barrel. Evans had a rifle pointed at me. My son David jumped between Evans and me. A young Anglo woman, Carol Watson, pinched Evans' hands to release my son. Only the Anglo police assaulted us; the Indohispano police just watched.

When Evans pointed his rifle at me, I felt rage. I told him he was acting out of personal motive to try my courage. I turned away from him and quickly walked to my car for my weapon. As I reached for it, Jack Johnson pointed a 30-30 rifle in my face. I saw him pull the trigger and heard the rifle misfire. I thought I was going to die. I got my rifle and walked toward Evans, yelling for people to get out of the way. All the Forest Service agents aimed their weapons at me. I did not care. I was blind to the danger and only wanted to confront Evans and show him all his gunmen did not intimidate me. Evans and I faced each other. Everyone had moved aside. The Chicanos were lined up on one side and the Anglos on the other. When Evans saw me, I loaded a cartridge into the chamber and aimed at him. More than one hundred fifty people were witnesses to the faceoff between us. I represented the oppressed Indohispano people and he, the most powerful government in the world, "Great Babylon." Another Anglo agent took aim at me and fired. His weapon also misfired. All the people screamed, including my children. But Evans ran from me like a scared coyote. When I saw that, I returned and placed my weapon in my car.

Several of us were arrested: my brother Ramón Tijerina, my son David, Carol Watson, Karim Hamarat, Rudy Manuel, José Aragón, Patricia, and me. We were taken to jail in Albuquerque. Patricia was charged with destruction of federal property, and I was charged with assault on Evans. I had confronted Evans and made him run. We were all released without bail on our own recognizance. I had but two days left of freedom.

Prison

On June 11 we traveled to Santa Fe to press charges against Evans and his gunmen. There were five witnesses to Jack Johnson's attempted murder of me, including two news reporters. Our people had gone to Evans' home with a warning to leave the state. We had an arrest warrant for him. He did not sleep in his house. Like Burger, he became a fugitive.

Within hours of pressing charges against them, I had my bail revoked. The U.S. Marshalls picked me up at two that afternoon. I had $4,241.75 on me for my family. The police confiscated that money. I called my wife, with the help of a Chicano policeman, and told her to come for the money. Chief Duffy refused her the money. My wife had to ask for welfare assistance to survive.

While in prison, only my family could visit me. I was cut off from the Alianza leadership and friends. The Anglos were now going to show me what I did not know about them. I was now completely in the hands of Anglos, and they could do with me what they wished, when they wished.

From then on, I knew very little about the Alianza. Emilio Naranjo took me from the Albuquerque jail and transported me to La Tuna, a federal prison in Texas. There, I was placed in solitary confinement. I was without radio or newspapers. After two weeks, I was returned to Albuquerque. William Kunstler, the famous attorney, came to help with my appeal. At my trial, Robert Gilliland stated he wanted to kill me. Rees Lloyd of the *Journal* said he had heard Evans also say he was going to kill me. Judge Payne was embarrassed to hear his gunmen testify that they wanted to kill me and then not have the courage at the last moment to do so. Judge Payne had to use more diabolical means to stop me.

Emilio Naranjo again transported me back to La Tuna. Between June and July, I was taken back and forth about four or five times. In prison, the Mexican inmates received me like a hero. La Tuna had about eight-five percent Mexican inmates. That is why I was segregated from the inmate population.

When the media reported on the money I had when arrested, Frank Tenorio, a state police officer, approached my wife. Tenorio assured her he was not like the other police agents. He promised to help her obtain the money she was entitled to. We had a secret Alianza member employed as a U.S. Marshall, Edwin Berry. He kept me informed of what was being plotted against us. Tenorio was lying to Patricia in order to gain her confidence.

We were set for trial in September for the Coyote incident and in late October for the second trial over Tierra Amarilla. Patricia and I were to be tried together, but Judge Payne severed our cases. He wanted Patricia isolated to take advantage of her. He knew she could not read. The court-appointed attorney for Patricia was an ex-CIA agent, David Kelsey. I advised her to fire him. Her next attorney was Peter J. Adang, and he moved her case into the future. I was tried in September and Patricia in February 1970. Judge Payne told my wife to vacate the family home and that I would be released sooner, if she cooperated. They wanted her to testify that I had induced her to set fire to the park signs in Gallina and Coyote. Patricia refused. She knew it was her idea. How could these men, supposedly judges, do this to a woman? I thought they would respect my wife. I was wrong. They would do with her what they wanted. I was transferred to the prison in Santa Fe. I was kept going back and forth like this for months.

I found prison life restful and tranquil. My throat rested. I rested and reviewed in my mind all the history of our struggle. I had time. Outside, I never had time. My cell and my solitude were not harmful to me, but what they were doing to my family hurt me.

Judge Payne tried me in September. It was a ridiculous trial. I was not allowed to question the jury panel. I had an all-Anglo jury, except for one postal employee who was a Mexican. I was not allowed to present evidence that the forest signs were within the property owned by the San Joaquín land grant claimants and not the federal government. Judge Payne said there was no such place as San Joaquín in New Mexico. U.S. Attorney Victor Ortega assisted Judge Payne in denying me justice. He struck the other three Indohispano jurors on the panel. I faced more than thirty witnesses, all police officers. How could I be guilty of assault with more than thirty policemen around? The fact that Jack Johnson had tried to kill me, but his rifle misfired twice, was of no consequence to them. Robert Gilliland testified he wanted to kill me because he hated me. And he repeated his testimony to the jury at our request. He said it again. The jury was not moved. They had their minds made up from the beginning. I was going to be found guilty, no matter what. I did not have a jury of my peers. New Mexico is mostly Indohispano and the jury was Anglo. They violated their own constitution. Patricia testified that she burned the sign at her own volition. I was also charged with aiding her in the destruction of federal property. I was tried first and found guilty. She was tried later and found innocent. I got a nine-year sentence from Judge Payne for the sign my wife burned.

Judge Burks set my second trial on Tierra Amarilla right away. In the meantime, Edward Schwartz, editor of *The New Mexico Review and Legislative Journal,* wrote a letter to Bob Brown of the *Albuquerque Journal* asking for the reward money offered by the newspaper for information leading to the arrest of Salazar's murderers. The *Review* had published that very information in their September issue. The article entitled "Who killed Eulogio Salazar?" named the killers and the accomplices in the article. He had given the information to the district attorney in Santa Fe and the U.S. Department of Justice.

On December 16, 1967, Judge Bratton sentenced me to two years for Tierra Amarilla I. Now, on October 21, 1969, I would be tried for Tierra Amarilla II. Jack Love wrote to Judge Garnett Burks asking that I not be allowed to examine the jury panel or bring up any land grant issues as a defense. The judge not only granted the prosecutors that request but also prohibited me from bringing up my right to a citizen's arrest.

While I was in prison, I recommended that my brother Ramón head the Alianza. He was the provisional president for a while. Ramón tried to keep the organization together. His strong arms were Eduardo "Lalo" Chávez and Wilfredo Sedillo. We were badly infiltrated by police spies. Their sole purpose was to divide and fracture the organization. The accusations now were that I was a Communist and had murdered Eulogio Salazar. The only good thing was that they did not deny the Anglos' theft of our land or the fact that they had burned all the records we needed to prove our claim.

Lalo and Wilfredo had been with me from the beginning. Lalo never missed a day at the office, except once when he went to the hospital for surgery. Wilfredo was the best detective we had. He could spot a spy instantly. Wilfredo had gone to school as a child with Judge Bratton. He knew those who now harmed our people. David Reies, my son, was in charge of intelligence.

My Letter From Prison: August 15–17, 1969

I write these reflections from my prison cell in Santa Fe. I feel I am a victim of the racism and hate of the bad politicians who govern us. My appeal bond was revoked at the request of James Evans, a Forest Service agent. He tried to kill me and failed in Coyote, New Mexico. Evans is from Georgia and has a reputation of hating Blacks. He was transferred from there to avoid harm from those that would avenge his wrongdoing and sent to intimidate the heirs of the settlers in the Southwest. First, I thought I would remain silent about the attempt on my life, like many others have done. But then I thought, What if I am assassinated and my people never know what happened? President Kennedy, his brother Robert, and Dr. Martin Luther

King were assassinated, and they had no time to tell the people what was happening. That is why their assassin escaped. If I keep silent, my silence will contribute to their plans. It is best that my people know before it is too late.

The dreams and happiness of the rich depend on the land they stole from the people of New Mexico, and they do not want me to raise that issue. In fact, they do not want anyone to speak for the poor.

Rees Lloyd, reporter for the *Albuquerque Journal*, testified under oath that James Evans had told his friends that he wanted to kill me. Bratton presided over this federal trial and heard Rees Lloyd's testimony. Judge Bratton knew of this conspiracy and instead of doing me justice, he condemned me.

My home and my office have been bombed four times. William Fellion placed one of these bombs. He was arrested and set free without punishment because he is a friend of those who would destroy us. The other is an Anglo scientist who was also freed because of insufficient evidence. My home has been riddled with automatic weapon fire three times.

My brother and I were physically attacked once a few blocks from our office. The police report was made but the crime was suppressed. Judge Bratton knows about all of these assaults because they have been reported by the media. And still the racist element would have everyone believe that I am the threat to the community.

The right to arrest someone is not a right to use violence. On the contrary, it is law and order, unless the person resists or flees. No honest person should avoid arrest, if for no other reason than to prove his innocence in court. The Jews accuse the Pope in Rome of keeping silent while Hitler persecuted the Jews in Germany and other countries. I also accuse those who have kept silent in New Mexico while the bad Anglo steals our property, violates our culture, and assassinates those who would defend themselves. I know of no church in the Southwest that has risen in defense of our rights under the Treaty of Guadalupe Hidalgo.

The press and other publicity organs have fooled the people. They have twisted all of my words. They keep the people ignorant of what is happening.

In Coyote, New Mexico, a miracle saved me from two *coyotes*. One is Robert Gilliland and the other is Jack Johnson. Both have Mexican mothers, but refuse to identify with the Indohispano people. That is why they are called *coyotes* and are the best instrument for the Anglo's dirty deeds. Jack Johnson is a state police officer and was in plain clothes the day he attempted to kill me in Coyote. I was told that the government would use *coyotes* to kill me and then claim that I was resisting arrest.

When I wrote this letter, I had been in prison for sixty-five days. My crime is defending the rights of my people under the Treaty of Guadalupe Hidalgo. I am in prison because of our land and our rights. Our claim is as legitimate or more so than that of Israel. Yet, many in New Mexico will support Israel's petition, but will not acknowledge our rights. And what's more, they are helping those who cover up Salazar's death. With one hand they hid the killers of Salazar, and with the other hand, they point at me.

Daily I see new prisoners, and they bring news of what is happening outside. Every day I spend here is not in vain. My people will benefit from this. I am what I am because of my people.

Bratton put me in prison on June 11, 1969, and Wilfredo sent a telegram the next day to President Nixon. He asked for them to stop my persecution and to charge with their crimes the Forest Service agents that made attempts on my life and assaulted more than one hundred men, women, and children in Coyote on June 8. He reminded Nixon that we had told him previously of the bomb explosion at our building and not received a response.

The letter I wrote in prison was more than thirty pages long and I had great difficulty getting it out. One of the guards confiscated it, but another helped me get it back. My letter was published in *El Grito del Norte* newspaper.

It was now five months since the money I had left for my family had been confiscated and not returned. The money was being used as bait to get my wife to comply with their wishes. They knew that women who lose their husbands to jail would do anything to get their husbands back.

During the time I was in prison, a couple of Anglo kids stole a forest park sign like the one Patricia burned. They were tried by one of my judges and fined $25. My people sent Nixon another telegram with this information and offered to pay $25 for the sign that was burned. They received no response.

I was in prison when I saw a copy of Peter Nobokov's book *Tijerina and the Courthouse Raid*.

The Second Trial

My brothers Cristóbal and Anselmo had gotten the Anglos' message. They had had enough and distanced themselves from the Alianza. Judge Bratton had tasted victory and was glad my brothers had left the cause. He reduced Cristóbal's sentence from six months to two. Cristóbal and I spent part of our prison time together. I also served time with Alfonso Chávez and Ezequiel Domínguez. I never criticized my brother for leaving the organization. I knew he had a family to care for.

While I waited for the second trial, I wrote another lengthy letter on October 13, 1969, in which I outlined what I had gone through and the revelations by the *New Mexico Review* on Salazar's murderers. My enemies thought that the Alianza would die with me in prison. On October 18, the organization celebrated its seventh annual convention. My brother Ramón took my place as titular head in my absence.

I was now in Montesa Park prison and had more liberty to visit with other inmates, not like at La Tuna. I would talk to the prisoners about our land recovery movement. When the Anglo came into the Southwest, our people had rights to 34, 653, 340, 616 acres of land. The U.S. government helped to take away 32, 718, 354, 226 acres and left us with only 1, 934, 986, 39. I do not count the six hundred thousand acres of San Joaquín because that claim was never adjudicated by the U.S. Court of Claims.

My wife and children came to visit me from time to time. Her visits always left me sad because I could see how they were using her. She would tell me things that bothered me a great deal. I could not tell Patricia what evil lurked around her; she would not understand. I was taken to my fifth trial on October 22. I was totally helpless. Only a miracle could help me. The morning of the trial, Judge Burks summoned me to his chambers, along with my appointed attorney Jack Wheeler, as well as the prosecutors Jack Love and James Maloney. The judge told us there had been jury misconduct involving the jury chair, a woman. She had also been on the jury in my other trial before Judge Payne. I asked the judge to dissolve the jury and drop the charges against me. He refused but reset the trial for November. During this time, Edward Schwartz had published his letter to the *Journal* asking for the reward money. Everyone now knew the assassins of Eulogio Salazar. I asked Judge Burks and Jack Love to recuse themselves from the case for being personally involved with state police officers and for having a conflict of interest with these officers being witnesses in the case.

The Alianza membership had a special meeting in November and passed a resolution calling for the creation of a new nation in the Southwest. Those who pushed for this resolution wanted to show they were more militant than I. The judges, however, were not afraid of mere words. I was not imprisoned because of my words, but for my deeds. By then my wife was ill. My wife was being pressured by Frank Tenorio to say that I had killed Eulogio Salazar and to accuse the senior advisors of the Alianza of being Communist sympathizers. The judges knew my wife was falling apart in little pieces. When the Alianza called for a separate nation, I resigned from the organization to save my family. The stronger the people spoke, the more the police would punish my family. When I was tried in September, the people learned that Patricia had a low IQ, a 69, which was below average. I was prepared to fight the judges and those who would deny us our rights. I was not prepared to see wolves devour my wife. She was an innocent mother of two children.

I was taken in shackles to my fifth trial on November 15. The courtroom personnel were the same: Judge Burks, Jack Love, and James Maloney. My family was there. I did not expect to win. All the

Anglo forces were now combined against me. At this trial a new witness was produced, Lee Woods, a cripple. At the Salazar murder scene they had found footprints belonging to a cripple. Woods was a rancher from Tierra Amarilla, but I tried to question him. I was not allowed and was found guilty. I was now sentenced to twenty-six years in prison from all the trials combined.

I made a motion to Judge Burks to reduce my sentence. He rejected my motion. My family was broken. Patricia's last court-appointed attorney was encouraging her to divorce me.

The First National Hero of Aztlán

My son David was my right hand. The police tried to disguise their conspiracy against him. He was charged but not tried for the taking of Tierra Amarilla. David would come to visit me frequently. He was the one to come and tell me that at a conference in Denver, Colorado, the delegates had passed a resolution designating me the first national hero of Aztlán. Baltazar Martínez of Canjilon had presented the resolution. I felt especially proud that Baltazar had made the resolution.

While I was in prison, a movement began in New Mexico calling for a constitutional convention. The Anglos wanted to limit our rights that the Treaty of Guadalupe Hidalgo had given us. They wanted to remove Article XII, Section 8, that provided for both languages to be used in school for instruction. I told David to advise our people to vote against these measures and they did. The revisions were defeated.

The World of Prisoners

I had known life as a fugitive and had gotten used to being hunted like an animal. I had not known the horrible world of prison life. While my appeals were in progress, I had hope of liberty. While I had this hope, prison life was tolerable. I began to lose my appeals and my hopes were dashed. The weight of facing twenty-six years in prison began to press on my mental faculties. I lost my faith and lost my feelings. Only the prisoner knows how much he suffers in prison, especially his mind and his spirit. I began to lose contact with my reality. I was in limbo. But I learned that the human body will adjust to everything, given time. The prisoners lose all rights, and the guards take advantage of that power they have over them. On the outside, those that control the land and have power oppress the poor and the ignorant. But the oppressed can at least rebel. In prison, you can only tolerate your situation. The guards can with impunity increase your terror every minute, every hour, every day. Time is on the side of the guards. Time for the prisoners is on hold. The guards develop an appetite for brutality and agony.

Witnessing my wife's agony and suffering further broke my spirit. She was being broken and used by Frank Tenorio on orders from Judge Payne.

Reies with father and friends. Margarito, Reies, Antonio Tijerina (father) and friend.

María and Reies' wedding portrait.

Family portrait circa 1950. María with Rosa on her lap, David and Reies.

Tijerina's children with horsedrawn buggy used to take children to school, in Enseneda, NM, circa 1959. Top row: María Tijerina (mother), Margarito (Celestino's daughter), David (deceased) and Celestino Manzanares. Second row: Rosa and Daniel (deceased). Bottom row: Ira de Ala, Raquel and Willie (Celestino's son).

María and Reies' younger children circa 1961. From left: Noe, Ira de Ala and Raquel.

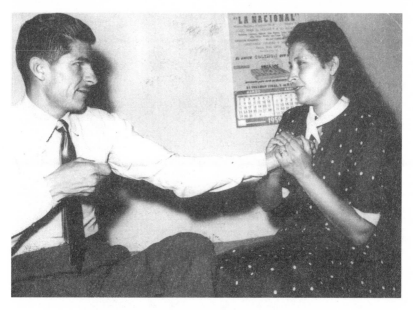

Reies and María in Mexico, March 1959.

Members at the Alianza Convention, Albuquerque, NM, Civic Auditorium, September, 1966.

Reies at New Mexico State Board of Education Meeting, Santa Fe, 1966.

Alianza meeting, Albuquerque, NM, circa 1968. From left: Tomas Ben Yacya, Hopi Chief; Ralph Featherstone, SNCC; Ron Karenga; and Reies.

Poor People's Campaign kickoff, in Albuquerque, NM, 1988. Second row from left: Rosa, F. M. Casaus, and Odelicio Moya. Bottom row from left: Ben Yacya, Reies, Rev. Jaramillo and Anselmo Tijerina.

On location, filming "Chicano!" in Mexico. On left Jaime Fernández, Jaime Casillas (kneeling), Reies (to left of camera) and Rosa.

Reies at Alianza building, in Albuquerque, NM. He is followed by a policeman and Rosa.

Chapter 3

1970

On January 4, a poll among the principal dailies of New Mexico indicated that the first-place story was that of the struggle for the land, while the war in Vietnam took second place. This bit of news from the Associated Press favored our cause, but irritated the Anglo judges. My family continued to suffer because of the popularity of our cause. I don't want to hide the fact that I wish for a new government. The present government is the most corrupt that I have seen, and it is this government that has me in jail. This government has destroyed values and human virtues more than anyone else has. It's the worst in the world. Only the Anglo, with his sick mentality, has been able to produce such great harm under the name of "democracy." Putting me in jail did not result in the destruction of our movement, as the Anglo government thought it would. Instead, more and more people have picked up the cause and are joining our movement. Those closer to me have gotten more militant, people like Eduardo Chávez, Juan Roybal, Wilfredo Sedillo, Antonio Griego, Ambrosio González, Juan Lorenzo Salazar, and a few others.

During the past 110 years, the Anglo has intimidated and terrorized the Native American and Indohispano. But this ended when I arrived in New Mexico and began telling people that the Anglos' days were numbered. The Anglo knows that there is no human power in the world available to him to stop what this spirit has begun.

Exiled to the Land of the Insane

To aggravate my agony, Judge Bratton tried my wife at the same time that he sent me to a federal prison hospital in Springfield, Mis-

153

souri. There I found myself among the mentally ill, mentally retarded, and psychopaths. I am not a psychopath. Judge Bratton knew this, so why did he send me there? Who ordered this judge to put me there with the insane? Richard M. Nixon, then in the White House and a known enemy of militants, was the one who put me there with them. While I was in that horrible prison dealing with the mentally infirm, Judge Payne and his wolves took advantage of my wife, despite the fact that several psychiatrists testified that Patricia was not in a condition to be tried because she could not read or write. She did not understand even the most rudimentary elements of law, much less what was said in court. They tried her anyway. The jury was an all-Anglo jury. They were more embarrassed than Judge Payne and refused to condemn my wife. Judge Payne wanted the jury to find Patricia guilty of the destruction of the forest sign in Coyote. Regardless, the jury refused to condemn my wife. The Anglo judges were embarrassed that I had been found guilty of assisting my wife in burning the sign and my wife was found not guilty. She was the principal person charged with the crime. Peter Adang, my wife's lawyer, represented her in these matters very poorly. Patricia came to Springfield, Missouri, and told me all that was going on. Ultimately, all of these trials were adjudicated. Payne sentenced me to nine years for a crime that I had not committed.

Meanwhile, I began to listen to the strange stories told to me by the psychiatric patients and psychopaths in the prison. Day and night I heard these prisoners cry out. This was a strange world to be in. Not only was I in jail, but I had to live among truly insane inmates. To survive in this environment, I not only had to listen to the insane, but to the psychiatrists, and accept their medications. If I didn't, I'd be put in solitary confinement. The stories I heard from the inmates were incredible. Some told me they could see their brains on the wall. Others told me that Mrs. Richard Nixon, the president's wife, had come to visit them in prison. These were prisoners who had committed serious crimes—bank robberies, murders—and many of them had more than ten years in that prison. Others, I discovered, became mentally ill and unstable because they had been in prison for such a long period of time. This is a reality and the judges know that better than anyone else.

My wife was intimidated and forced to move out of the house where I had left her. To give myself therapy, I began writing daily to my wife to help in her hour of need. She was being harmed and I was in prison. An inmate who worked near the prison records made my private prison file available to me. That's where I discovered all the evil being done against me. The prison file referred to me as a psychopath, as schizophrenic. They said that I thought I was a god. The prison had about five thousand inmates separated into three sectors: the dangerously insane, the least ill, and then, the psychopaths. I was with the most dangerous. I stayed there for quite a while until I was moved to the second category. This inmate population had exercise privileges of two hours daily. From the first day that I arrived, I resigned myself to being a model prisoner; I would not give them any excuse to lengthen my incarceration, trump up new charges, or suffer any greater harm. I knew that I had to get out for my wife and family. So I had to endure and suffer whatever came my way and get out quickly.

Many of the prisoners knew about me before I got there. *The New York Times* had published articles; the book *Tijerina and the Courthouse Raid* had been published. There were several copies circulating in the prison. One of the guards had a copy and asked me to look at it. The prison population was comprised of Indians, Chicanos, Blacks, whites, Jews, Italians, and many other nationalities and races. I saw many important, powerful figures as inmates, having feigned temporary insanity, to escape true justice and punishment. On the other hand, there were many without money and influence that became insane while in prison. I worked in the kitchen as an inmate and made friends with many of the staff, including an Anglo psychologist who befriended me. He would tell me what other psychiatrists were saying behind my back and what was coming in my future. There was no doubt in my mind that I was a political prisoner.

The Biggest Psychopath of Them All

Patricia would come visit me once a month, but I wouldn't tell her my agony. I would listen to her problems. She told me of her relocation to another place called Las Colonias, some ten miles from Pecos,

New Mexico, and thirty-five from Santa Fe. She never got the money that was confiscated by the police. While in prison I began reading up on psychiatry as best I could, without being detected by the prison psychiatrists. I could not understand how it was possible that the Anglo judges could do so many injustices at the same time against my family and me. They were covering up Eulogio Salazar's crime. They looked the other way when my house and my office were bombed. They turned loose William Fellion, a known killer. They abused my wife, and now they withheld money from my family that was rightfully ours. I couldn't understand why they did this. It must be that the Anglo sees in me his criminal history, and that's why he cannot tolerate my claim for the rights of the Indohispanos and the Indians. The White House put me in this prison for the mentally ill so that the whole world would dismiss me as being crazy. My Mestizo community would say that I was crazy. The Anglos hated me and I also began to hate them back. They were mad at me and I was even madder. I could not demonstrate any of this because I was behind bars. The Anglos hated me because I had placed doubt about their right and legitimacy to govern. I had done it because they were destroying all the rights and human values on earth. The rich and powerful use psychiatry to avoid paying for their crimes, while the poor, defenseless individuals pay for their own faults and the faults and crimes of the powerful as well.

Psychiatry is useful to the one that applies it. Psychiatry is in the hands of the enemy of the people, so they destroy the powerless. I studied psychiatry fundamentally so that the government psychiatrists would not declare me a psychopath. What is psychiatry? Is it a science? When and where did it begin, how is it used, who uses it? What's the correct interpretation of a psychopath? I had to find the answers to these questions. I had to, because psychopaths and psychiatrists surrounded me. My total environment was penetrated with the agony of these inmates. Some would laugh at themselves all day; others cried incessantly.

Every prisoner was a sad mental case. And many of them sought refuge in my advice and counsel. I also found how damaging the loss of consortium from loved ones is. The psychiatrists began studying you by studying your childhood, and they began studying why a person would fight the biggest power in the world without a weapon and without resources. Only a crazy person would have to do this; therefore, Reies had to be crazy. The Anglo psychiatrists believed that I was abnormal because normal people don't take on a powerful enemy like the United States government.

I began to reason that if a person could be a psychopath, so can entire races of individuals. And I began studying the history of the Anglo and came to the conclusion that, as a race, he is psychopathic. I believe the origins of the Anglo psychopathy began when the English were excluded from the Treaty of Tordecillas, signed June 7, 1494, between Spain and Portugal. The treaty was a deal brokered by the Pope. It was at this time that the Anglo not only rejected the legitimate body of the era, but also the religion that went against them. The Anglo, without respect for authority and religion, and to get back into the colonization game, legalized piracy. They had to operate outside the law to become the law. Over the last 480 years, the Anglo complex of psychopathy has worsened. His conscience torments him, and his thinking grows demented for having violated his own religion, his own law, and humanity.

The Anglo was at peace with himself until I arrived and began accusing him of committing crimes against our people. I knew Anglo history fundamentally. While I was in prison, I was able to dedicate and further my studies. I became very illuminated. I saw Anglo history in the United States in a different light. I learned, for example, that 1) the Anglo destroyed the buffalo to force the Indian into hunger instead of fighting him face to face; 2) they killed all the Indian chiefs by treachery and proclaimed false peace treaties; 3) the Anglos immortalized the words of General Sheridan, "A dead Indian is a good Indian"; 4) the Anglo developed the black legend against Spain; 5) the Anglo has broken every treaty he ever signed, beginning with the Indians; 6) the Anglo proclaimed the Constitution with liberties that were for a select few and destroyed the most sacred of honors in society, that of family; 7) the Anglo maintains an English-only policy in the "land of the free and home of the brave"; 8) the Anglo takes his oath of office swearing on a Bible, yet maintains a strict separation of church and state; 9) the Anglo legalized piracy, and protected illegally what he could not lawfully; 10) George Washington, supposedly the Father of the Nation, never could father a child; 11) the Liberty Bell has never been able to ring out without cracking (three times it happened).

These attributes are characteristics of a psychopath individually and as a race. This was my analysis of the character and mentality of the Anglo. This is what I found and discovered among this giant race of people. And all of the people of this earth should take great precaution against this psychopath and should treat him like a mental patient. This patient suffers from a fever of super grandeur. He does not just exaggerate his history, but also his culture, with much-exaggerated images as Tarzan, Superman, Lone Ranger, Buck Rogers, Wonder Woman, Six Million-Dollar Man, etc.

This great psychopath had me in prison and wanted to declare me a psychopath. This biggest psychopath of them all legalized opium and drugs, just like it legalized piracy. From 1839 to 1842, the Anglo race made war against a respectable and honorable people in China to obligate them to accept opium. This war was immoral. Since then, the Anglo has brought on the drug plague. His own children are its victims. Now they have brought not only drugs, but also a sexual revolution. His own children proclaim sexual liberty, free love, and sexual equality. This giant psychopath is capable of destroying our families and human values. And now, he is threatening the world with atomic, hydrogen, and nuclear bombs. Normal people of the world should figure out how we can pacify this giant and contain him because he is in a sick mental state. If the Anglo is to die, he wants everyone to die with him.

Discoveries and Revelations in Prison

Losing life is the closest one can come to justice. Here the inmates pay for their crimes and find justice. Unfortunately, it's the poor and defenseless who are in prison. The rich and powerful, and their friends, never know a prison. If they were to be imprisoned, they would meet justice face to face, and the world would become a different place. The rich, powerful allies own and direct the government. Prison life would be more beneficial to the wise than the ignorant, to the rich than the poor, to the powerful than the defenseless. Those who kill each other in prison are not the rich, wise, and powerful, but the ignorant, the weak, and the poor. The world has not made just laws. The rich make the laws for the rich. And if anyone has to pay for the violation of those laws, it's the poor and defenseless. The "Christian world" pretends to celebrate when a "sinner" converts to its religion. Why, then, don't we celebrate when a prisoner has completed the sentence and is set free? Isn't that paying your just dues to society and becoming a new convert? And it is not just the inmate that pays for his sentence, but also his wife, children, and parents. Everybody pays except those white-collar criminals who have destroyed our good way of life, violated all the laws while stealing money that the public has paid in taxes and for products.

In prison, men lose all their courage and cry like children. I saw many things. I learned to study and investigate my own mind, strengthen my recall powers, and appreciate my time. During the nights and long days that I was in solitary confinement, I would review my childhood, my adolescence, and my teenage years in my mind. I could distinguish one period from another. Like an archivist, I came to know my mental record very well. I learned to treat and arrange each memory like a chapter in a book. This reflection, study, and mental discipline helped me a great deal, because not only did I discover things about my life, but also the impact these events had on me. I discovered that my mind was more than just a computer of memories. I discovered that my mind was alive, had a world of its own and was organic. I would study these memories and discover the importance they had for my family. I soon learned that my family was the axis of my world. Meditating and studying the value of my family, I did, of course, experience great agony and hurt. I was not able to see them.

I was in prison when the United States spacecraft landed on the moon, July 20, 1969. I compared that to the building of the pyramids in Egypt, on the backs of the oppressed. This lunar exploration stirred in me a new thought and interest in the universe. This was a new dimension and reach for people. I began to develop a new spirit, and my conscience had to find a new relationship between my existence and developments in the world. Many of the prisoners wanted to talk to me about these kinds of things, but I was careful not to trust inmates that served the administration and guards. I would pick my friends with great care, and even those I would not tell what was in my heart. I would only confide in them what would not hurt me in the least. The ten years that I had struggled against organized religion helped me in prison, just like my four years as a fugitive. In prison, I had to step softly like a cat. I had to live in peace with my oppressors, the guards, and have contact with others, but avoid the dangerously insane. I had to be alert day and night, but not arouse the suspicion of my jailers. Many times, inmates provoked me. I'm sure superior authorities goaded them. This happened to me in all of the prisons that I was in: Santa Fe, Albuquerque, Montessa Park, La Tuna in Texas, and now here in Springfield, Missouri.

One time, I was taken back to Albuquerque. While there, the FBI arrested one of the white militia members called the Minutemen, an extreme right organization. Robert De Pugh and Walter Payton were arrested some five kilometers from Truth or Consequences, New Mexico, about 150 miles south of Albuquerque. The FBI confiscated some five tons of weapons and ammunition. The next day, for the first time in my prison life, I had a cellmate: Walter Payton. I was unaware of his identity and talked with him for more than four hours. Walter was about twenty-five years old. Payton told me a most interesting story about being processed in Albuquerque. According to Payton, one of the arresting officers asked him, "Do you know whom we have in jail here? Reies López Tijerina, 'King Tiger.' Payton said to me that he had told them, "Well, you better not put me in there with him because I'll kill him." I asked him if he would make that declaration before a court of law in the future. He said he would. When the jail officials realized that we were getting along and that he had not killed me, they transferred him out of my cell. I never saw him again.

While in La Tuna, I had another interesting experience. I became a cellmate to Joseph Valachi. He was the Italian mafia member that testified against them. Valachi's cell was carpeted and large. I thought it was very strange that I would be in such a luxurious cell. Prison staff that befriended me told me not to eat my food. I was being placed in Valachi's cell to eat poisoned food, so they then could say someone tried to kill Valachi and poisoned me. Our people would blame the Italian mafia, and the Anglos would be free of any guilt in this. I believed this to be true because all my cells have barely been the size of a bathroom. I had to eat my meals right next to the toilet hole on the ground. My cells usually had no windows or sunshine. I didn't eat any of the food and drank only water in Valachi's cell. The Anglos never suspected I was fasting. My food was going down the toilet hole. Other inmates would give me candy and food tidbits while I went through this situation. Mexicans were eighty-five percent of the inmates in La Tuna.

Since January 19, 1970, when I was taken to Springfield, I couldn't get medication for my chronic throat problems. Even though I complained to the authorities and asked my family for help, the prison officials denied me throat medicine. They only gave me tranquilizers, their medicine for "a mental condition." One time I almost died from a reaction to this medication that I didn't need.

When I was in prison, Bill Hicks, a lawyer that I trusted, received $40,000 dollars from a group of churches on behalf of the Alianza. I thought Bill would be different from other Anglos, but I was wrong. He ended up being the same.

During this time, I thought of writing a letter to President Richard M. Nixon. But then, I told myself, "If neither Johnson nor Kennedy nor Eisenhower answered me when I was free, what would make me think that I would get a letter from Nixon, now that I was in the prison for the criminally insane?" My family and members of the Alianza sent a telegram to President Nixon, asking him for my liberty or for medical attention in prison. He never answered them. I finally thought that it was best to write to Nixon, so I would have proof that I had asked for justice and had been denied. So I wrote him a long letter. My letter was returned within a few days. The note attached to my letter said that the Springfield prison provided all the medical attention I needed. While in prison, I lost thirty pounds, and I finally decided to write a writ of habeas corpus and file it with the court in Kansas City, Missouri. In this writ I detailed my seven months in solitary confinement, the attempts on my life by guards and other police. I also cited the lack of medical attention and my being housed with mentally ill prisoners as evidence of cruel and unusual punishment. I provided a list of ten or twelve witnesses, including Walter Payton and Robert De

Pugh. The news of filing my writ of habeas corpus was publicized throughout the United States.

I finally received medical attention for my throat and was operated on June 1, 1970. By then, I didn't want an operation, but I had no choice in the matter. They took more than forty x-rays of my throat; in and of itself, that damaged me more. The x-rays revealed a tumor in my throat. After the operation, my wife, David, and Juan Roybal came to see me regularly. It was not long before rumors began circulating that I was dying of cancer and was insane. To this day, people still ask me if this is true.

Towards the end of June, Patricia told me a story that hit me like a bomb. Three men had raped her. Patricia went to the state police, someone named Sánchez, but he didn't listen to her. When Patricia insisted on police protection, they threatened to put her in jail. Patricia told me there were witnesses to what had happened. Neighbors came to her side and offered protection. The neighbors loaned her a gun. Within days, an officer, Richard Martínez, came and took the gun away from Patricia. This is what Bratton and Payne wanted: to destroy my family and destroy me. The White House also wanted to destroy me. Within the Albuquerque police there is an intelligence unit with orders to finish me. That's why the Chicano police, like Martínez, would not protect my wife.

These Anglo injustices against my family accumulated. I felt powerless to do anything to help my wife. There were many nights when I couldn't sleep because all I thought of was the high price that I was paying for fighting for my people. In my eyes, my wife was the perfect symbol of the condition my people suffered in an Anglo world. I came to the conclusion that my wife was my people. Just as they abused my wife, the police and judges abused my people. The government abused my people and others. It tried to destroy my family and home just as it tried to destroy our culture and our community families. My wife could not compete with the Anglo in reading or writing. My people could not compete with the Anglo and his foreign culture and language. Although there are many different people in the United States, no one has forced his language on anyone else, except the Anglo. For example, there are more Germans than Anglos in the United States, but they don't impose their language or culture by forcing violence on the rest of us. There are millions of Italians, but they don't impose their language on anyone else. Only the Anglo. The Anglo loudly proclaims, "All the peoples of Europe and the East give up their languages to come to the United States. This is America. Why don't you all do the same?" My answer is as follows: "The immigrants from other countries came voluntarily, leaving their lands, their flag, and their roots. The foreigner has no reason to hold onto his cultural baggage. In the case of my people, it's not the same thing. We did not immigrate to the United States like the Italians, the Germans, the French, the Asians or the Anglos. We lived in the Southwest three hundred years before the Anglos ever arrived. By the time the Anglos arrived, our parents, together with Indians, had populated the continent, had named all the rivers, mountains, valleys, and cities. The Anglo did not promise to respect the language and culture of other people as in the Treaty of Guadalupe Hidalgo."

My wife is my flesh and blood; her blood lives in my spirit. What all these cowards did against her I felt in my own flesh and blood. I began to think about justice and to study justice.

While in prison I made friends with Bill Barkley Truitt. Bill was the nephew of General Douglas MacArthur and grandson of former U.S. Vice-President Barkley, under Truman. Bill was not a regular Anglo. He believed as I did. He thought that Anglos were headed in the wrong direction and that they would soon fall as a people. In Bill I saw the mentality of the Anglo youth rebelling against their parents. During 1970, the entire nation began to see the white youth rebellion. In Chicago, New York, Los Angeles, Detroit, and many other places, you could see the voice of protest from white youth. President Nixon did not know what to do. He used all he could at his disposal in terms of weapons and propaganda not only to triumph in Vietnam, but against his own rebellious children, and he failed. All the major cities of the United States were going up in flames and riots.

In Mexico, a great surprise occurred. The attorney general of Mexico, Luis Echeverría Alvarez, became president. Back in 1964, Mexico was afraid of the United States. That's why they had deported me. But now in 1970, Mexico was not afraid of the White House. My heart was filled with joy at the news that now he was president. In my lifetime I had seen the psychopathic giant reach his peak in August 1945. And during the days of my life, from 1926 to 1976, I had seen this giant go through many important events. But while in prison, I had the premonition that the end of the Anglo domination of the world was near at hand. All the other prisoners were also in agreement. They used to tell me all the time that the United States would not last much longer. Many nights when I was alone in my cell, I would recall the memories of what all the Anglos did against the courageous Mangas Coloradas, Cochise, Victorio, and Jerónimo, between 1836 to 1886. During those hours of silence, I would ask with all my heart of the Just Judge of Judges to grant me life to see justice done.

The Value of Time

Way before the Anglos had ever put me in prison, I had studied the value of time and the significance of time in the life of animals, plants, and persons, even communities. This interest was born when I began to study and read about communities, nations, and languages. I began to study the history and the age of each people. Time is very important in the life of a human being, as it is in the life of a nation, community, or language. Time matures all things. Just like a child of tender age cannot be compared to an older person, neither can the intellectual be compared to a people of relatively young age. A child needs time to develop virtues and values. And in the same way, people need time to develop their values and virtues and convert them into power of the people. There are races of people that are in stages of development: infant, young, mature, and old. People also go through stages as children, youths, adults, and elders. Time separates each different stage, as it does with individuals. Now that I was in prison I understood more than ever the significance of time in the life of people and communities. The science of time began to help me better understand the development of our people, a new race born out of the clash of east and west in the American continent. According to the law of time, the European races are maturer. Upon coming to the New World, the old and the new clashed. From that union, a new infant race was born. This new race was legalized on October 19, 1514, in Title 1 of Book 6 of the Law of the Indies. In 1970, this new race reached the age of 456 years old.

Compare this relatively infant race of 456 years with the more mature and older races of the Spanish, the French, and the English. It's like comparing a child of five years with an adult of twenty-five or thirty. A race develops its national consciousness like a child develops its familial consciousness.

Fraternity and Harmony

As a prisoner, I was totally isolated from liberty and all those activities related with liberty. The Anglo had tied my hands. But at the same time, my mind and my spirit were given liberty. With time on my hands, my mind and spirit had no boundaries. I began to study many things I never had time for before. In the outside world I had to worry about food, clothing, shelter. Now, the prison took care of all of these things. I just worried about understanding the Anglo and studying the science of time, trying to understand the origin of war, jealousy, hate, envy. Time was the most expensive item in my life; therefore, I had to utilize it as if it were ground gold. Finding the solution for peace among humanity became a goal of great importance to me. I told Rita Pino in November 1969, and my brother Cristóbal, when we spent jail time together, that I had a new project. I wanted to promote fraternity and harmony among human beings. I told them that I didn't know how or when I would do all of this, much less how I had arrived at the decision, but I was convinced that this prison life was a great college to study that. My interest was heightened in this area right after the lunar mission of July 20, 1969. Aristotle, teacher of Alexander the Great, told him, "The marvels of the world are many, but none is as great as the marvel of man." I thought man had everything, but was careless. Humanity has everything except harmony and fraternity with one another. Human beings have the secret to harmony and fraternity in their heart.

The Family

The heart of human dignity is the family. The family is the source of values, virtues, and the love that nurtures harmony and fraternity. Our mothers are the first teachers and then, the nation. Our homes are where the human plants are born. The parents are the gardeners that water these human plants with love water. There is no better school for a child than the home and the family.

I came to realize that the family is the root of society. The institution of the family has outlived governments. And, regardless of government ideology, the family remains the same institution. In certain times, government protects the family. In other times, government casts the family aside. In the United States and white European countries, the family has been abandoned. The family has outlived all kinds of governments, in spite of their ideology, including "democracy." In fact, the family has lost ground because "democracy" has robbed the family of its sovereignty. The son cannot take the place of the father until he leaves and forms his own family. Even then, the son remains indebted to his father. The home and the family cannot be governed by democratic practices. The father is the head and king of the family; the mother is the heart and queen of the family. Together, they make a perfect government.

The U.S. Constitution is silent with regard to the family. The families of a nation are what make a people great. They are the pillars of society. The family was substituted by the corporation in this country. The corporation was given all the power taken away from the family. There is more protection for business than for the family. Anglo education is also destroying the family. Many of our children are falling under the influence of the "American way of life." We must fight to regain the family and its honor.

Prison Psychiatrists

Psychiatrists surrounded me while at the Springfield, Missouri, prison. Day and night, day after day, one would come and another would leave. They all thought highly of themselves. They bored me with their questions. I had to answer their questions. And they were not true to themselves. Some of them were homosexuals that took perverted liberties with their patients. I had to tell them my life history against my better sense. Over and over, I had to repeat my life story, from childhood to my confrontations with the White House. They wanted me to relate a life story that was not real. For example, I told them of my childhood poverty and how that was not unpleasant because I lived in the midst of love, joy, and happiness. I told them of how I got food from garbage cans but thought that was normal at the time. They would ask me if I harbored ill will toward the rich. My childhood did not now influence my view of the world. They wanted falsehoods. They wanted to know my childhood fears and how many fights I had. I told them that I was afraid of the dark until I was about fifteen years of age. I told them I never had a fight as a child, but I did love wrestling. I was asked if I was afraid of lightning. I told them that lightning and storms made me feel happy and extraordinarily joyful. I told them my mother taught me not to fear snakes by handling them in her hands.

Once I had a psychiatrist from Dallas, Texas. He taped everything we discussed about my family. I suspected he was a White House operative, and friends in the prison hospital control room confirmed my suspicions. This is how it was in prison. I had to watch myself against the psychiatrists, guards, and inmates. Often, I had dangerous, insane inmates in my cell. On those occasions, I would not sleep. The cowardly Anglo guards did not want to hurt me with their own hands. They wanted another inmate to do the job for them.

My Family Alone in New Mexico

While I was in prison, my family was alone and defenseless. The politicians had their reasons for wanting to destroy my family and me. On July 14, 1970, however, Judge Bratton's wife died. I remember the date because that is the same day I married the first time. I also remember that Bratton never gave my wife an appointment. He also did not listen to my plea regarding my wife's legal defense. I wanted to tell him she was not mentally capable of understanding the issues involved. I interpreted Bratton becoming a widower as a sign that the Just Judge of Judges was on my side.

The rapid rise in membership and interest in the Alianza caused them concern. Jealousies and envy surfaced among Indohispano politicians and us. The White House very astutely exploited these emotions. Some politicians hated me and others envied me. The union of Anglos and enemy Indohispano politicians was powerful. They had political reach from New Mexico to the White House. They covered up the

police theft of my money, Fellion's bombing of my home, the assassination of Eulogio Salazar; and they have tried me twice for events in
Tierra Amarilla I did not commit. They protect Frank Tenorio and other
puppets that have violated my wife, while they keep me in a mental
institution. These politicians attacked me as not being from New Mexico. They said, "We must get him out of New Mexico." Why didn't they
say that when the Anglo came into New Mexico as a foreigner?

Tijerina Park

I spent my time thinking of what I would do when I got out. I had
elaborated a plan. I would do more and bigger things against the White
House and the Anglos. Upon release, I thought I would return to New
Mexico and produce a real history of our people. I had to get out of
prison and leave the country to be able to tell the truth to the world,
especially to Mexico and Latin America.

The Anglo has ground my people into the dirt. The Anglo's mortal
error has been to grind my family, my wife, and me into the dirt. If the
Anglo thought that prison and the abuse of my family would break my
spirit, he is mortally in error. He has made my spirit grow bigger like
that of a giant, and I have sworn to fight them until the White House
no longer exists.

The federal judge in Missouri made me go through a lot of discovery and legal maneuvers over my writ. He finally denied it.

During the time I was in prison, many things changed. The Anglo
press revolutionized the word "Chicano." We use it, but they use it to
divide us from Latin America. The Anglo will use anything to create
more borders and barriers and differences between us, particularly ethnic divisions between Indohispanos. In New Mexico, young people are
stealing and burning Forest Service signs. No sooner are they replaced
than the people take them again. They even changed the words on one
sign from "Roosevelt Park" to "Tijerina Park." I knew all these things
were symbols of what I was looking forward to rejoining.

I was in prison for 775 days, when suddenly I was taken from
Springfield, Missouri, to the Albuquerque airport and released. Hundreds of supporters and family were there to greet me. My wife and
children cried joyfully at my return. My people loved me.

Conditional Liberty

The White House set me free on July 26, 1971. I was not completely free. I had difficult and hard conditions of parole. I could not hold any leadership position in the Alianza for three years. I was to be on parole for fifteen years and had to report monthly to Richard Martínez. I thought this was only for the sentence that Burks had imposed. I thought I would begin my time for the sentence related to Tierra Amarilla. Judge Gallegos, however, allowed me to remain free on $10,000 bond. Cirilo García posted the amount. He had been with me in Tierra Amarilla on June 5, 1967. The White House let me go, thinking the New Mexico judicial system would lock me up to serve its sentence. That is not what happened.

In Washington, D.C., the politicians of Hispanic ancestry—Montoya, Luján, González, Badillo—got together and planned a unity conference. I was not invited. César Chávez and José Angel Gutiérrez were invited. Montoya now called himself a "Chicano." He thought this conference would place him as the undisputed national leader of our people. Many people urged me to attend. José Angel Gutiérrez called and asked me to attend. He offered to pay my expenses to Washington, D.C.

When I arrived, the people present demonstrated their affection and love for me. I felt like a hero. On the first day of the conference, Montoya was there, but the people did not let him speak. They demanded to know why I had not been invited. A group of women began to demand that I be allowed to address the assembly and threatened to shut down the conference if I did not speak. A quick resolution demanding I speak was drafted, introduced, and passed unanimously. A delegation of twenty people came to my room and told me of the resolution. I accepted to attend. Montoya was on the stage. I bet he never imagined that his organizational work at uniting all the different groups at the nation's capital would be so that I would speak to them. Montoya was crushed, and I thought this was but a dream.

I gave the assembly a detailed account of what the police had done to my family, how they had conspired in the rape of my wife, and how they almost murdered my eighteen-month-old child, Carlitos. I also told the delegates the history of the Alianza and our struggle to regain our property rights. *The New York Times* and *The Washington Post* carried my story. They were not interested in the unity conference; they wanted my story. The fact that this information was now in the public domain made me feel better because my soul was relieved.

My wife was very concerned that I would seek revenge for what had been done to her, so she did not give me the names of her assailants. She feared that if I acted on that information, I might be returned to prison. Even my closest advisors and friends cautioned me to wait a while before looking into the matter. I had to threaten her with divorce if she didn't tell me who raped her and almost killed my son. I finally got the names from her and began to place them in the larger conspiracy out to destroy me.

Upon return to Albuquerque, I was congratulated for my taking over the conference. Even the *Journal* and *Tribune* said I had taken control of the conference. They had to admit, even if indirectly, that the people were with me. I felt that another link of the conspiracy chain had been broken.

I also received a copy of *Land Title Study,* the report on the land grants in New Mexico. Supposedly, the 261-page study cost $80,000 and four years to produce. The land title study covered land grants in New Mexico, Colorado, and Arizona. It did not include Texas or California. Later, I received 135 copies of the report and used them effectively. This was a major victory for our cause. The report clearly was a public admission that what I had been saying was true. We owned the land and it had been stolen. Our ancestors had claim to thirty-five million acres of land in the Southwest, and the U.S. Court of Claims validated only two million acres. The Anglos and the White House stole thirty-three million acres, almost ninety-five percent of the holdings. How does the White House expect me to remain silent? Many Anglos are divided on this question, with many of them in our favor, such as Dr. Donald Cutter, professor of history at the University of New Mexico. This was my second victory upon release from prison. My third was about to happen: *The Tribune* published a story alleging that the police had stolen the money I left for my family when I was taken to prison.

Toward the end of 1971, the police killed Rito Canales and Antonio Córdova. They were members of the Black Beret organization. They were both friends of mine, and I had repeatedly warned them of police informants and spies within their organization, but they took my information lightly. The police took Rito and Antonio to an abandoned area where dynamite was stored and murdered them. The police version was that they had been apprehended in the course of stealing dynamite and shot. The people got very angry with these police murders.

I began to lay plans for a conference on harmony and fraternity. I organized Blacks, Native Americans, Anglos, Chicanos and others, and called the first annual conference for April 8, 1972. My wife and I had a child born that day, and we named her Harmony. We as a people needed to be in harmony with other peoples. Some people thought I had changed directions in my struggle, that I was abandoning the struggle for the land. I was apprehensive about some of the people that were around me. I knew that I could be returned to prison under the slightest pretext. I knew that I was appealing another fifteen-year sentence. I had to be careful. Yet, some people wanted me to confront the police and were pushing me. We identified those we thought were spies and police agents. I left the affairs of the Alianza in the hands of trusted members and merely gave them advice. I spent my time on lecture tours and searching for Salazar's assassins. Between 1971 and 1973, I spoke throughout the United States.

June 17, 1972

Shortly after I was released from prison, Judge Garnett Burks died. He was young and strong. He once said, "Reies could have been set free had he had a good lawyer." In other words, Burks was admitting that I was innocent but had ineffective legal counsel. I had been condemned, just like the poor always are.

Another federal judge, Ed Mitchum, heard the horsemeat case. He found the Anglo rancher innocent but awarded the Mexican Soto y Soto only $75 in back wages.

While I was in Washington, D.C., my daughter Rosita was kidnapped. Men, posing as Black Berets, called her about attending an urgent meeting of the organization. She was without transportation, and they offered to come and take her to the Black Berets' meeting. En route, she became suspicious of the men and jumped out of the car near the Chesterfield Bar in south Albuquerque. She hurt herself escaping but managed to get away and call her mother. I was told about this incident when I returned.

David Norvell, who once had said that Carlitos was not my legitimate son, came to ask for my help. The 1972 elections were approaching, and he wanted to run for the U.S. Senate. I asked him to help me get my brother Margarito out of prison. Norvell was the state attorney general and could help Margarito. He went to see him. Margarito was released from prison in September, after seven long years.

Jacqueline Bernard published a book for fifth through seventh grades, *Voices From the Southwest*. The book contains three short biographies: Antonio Martínez, the priest from Taos; Elfego Baca, the famous sheriff; and mine. I was thrilled that the children of the Southwest were learning about our struggle and the great theft of our lands. In spite of all that the Anglo was doing against our movement and me, the story of our struggle was now in the classrooms.

September 4, 1972

The Raza Unida Party, founded by José Angel Gutiérrez, held its first national convention in El Paso on September 3–4, 1972. José Angel asked me to honor them with my presence. I went happily. I spoke to the delegates about the importance of the land recovery movement. I also said, "We have to cleanse ourselves of the Anglo's immorality. This is the time to do it. This is the hour of the brave." At the conclusion of my remarks, I invited Corky and José Angel to the stage and presented them with a copy of the land title study published in New Mexico. I urged them to place unity above personalities, groups, and organizations. Unity comes before leaders and ideology. I invited the delegates to attend the National Congress on Land and Culture to be held in Albuquerque on October 21–22.

I had developed the idea for such a conference on land and culture over time and had proposed it at a conference held in San Jose, California. My plan was to prepare our people for a movement of independence, if the Anglo government continued making a mockery of our sacred rights. Everyone in attendance at the San Jose conference supported the resolution for this conference.

At the conference I discovered that many, not all, of our youth have been mentally conditioned by Anglo education. And in trying to repudiate the Anglo, they have embraced foreign ideologies. Without ridding themselves of an Anglo mentality, they have embraced foreign ideologies. This embroils them in a state of confusion, and, without realizing it, they are serving the interests of the Anglo.

Almost all the Chicano books have been written from an Anglo perspective. The authors completely ignore the true Indohispano history. Those who pass themselves off as authorities harm the spirit and mind-set of the Mestizo more than the Anglo. To my view, these authors simply wish to put their names on their little books, sit behind a desk, and proclaim themselves judges of the movement. Some of them have written about me. For years I have wanted to write my version of history to tell the truth and expose them. But I thought that time would rid us of them. The people always discard what they don't need. I have struggled long and hard and have deeds to my credit. These deeds have cost my family and me a great deal. It has cost many other brave warriors a great deal in blood, prison, tears, sweat, danger, and the humiliation of their wives and children. And despite the fact that I carry scars and marks on my body and in my mind as a result of the movement and struggle, these book authors, paid with Anglo salaries, criticize me and create falsehoods. I won't mention their names because they will bother me more, just like flies.

At the Land and Culture conference, a resolution was passed demanding that Nixon return the one hundred million acres of land to our people. We sent Nixon the resolution with a letter. We never got a response. And Nixon was reelected.

While I agonized over being hampered in my activities, some approached me insisting that I do more. What bothered me the most is that these people that wanted me to do more were cowards. They never stood by me in the making of the Alianza. They never helped me find Salazar's murderers.

The Albuquerque Journal was founded the year I was born, 1926. Since then, it has fooled and poisoned people's minds in New Mexico.

Fortunately, a former reporter, Rees Lloyd, broke with the *Journal* and published in *The New Mexico Review* an article entitled "Inside the *Albuquerque Journal*." Lloyd described the hypocrisy, discrimination, and injustice within the *Journal*. He clearly stated that the newspaper purposely and intentionally distorted my words and supressed information that corroborated many allegations I made. I was in prison when the article came out in February.

When I was still in prison, the U.S. Commission on Civil Rights investigated the taking of the courthouse in Tierra Amarilla and concluded that the police in New Mexico had committed acts of racism and assaults, among other misdeeds. The commission also accused the police of hampering the people's pursuit of justice. The words of the commission supported the Alianza.

The Police

The guns of the police protect Anglo power. And the voice of the *Journal* defends police conduct. When the Anglo police kill one of our people, the press takes the police version as truth. You never read the victim's version. When the Anglo illegally came into our lands, he came as a pirate. This criminal mind has been passed down, generation to generation, to the present time. The Anglo is incapable of understanding our people. The truth is that the Anglo is afraid of the Indohispano and knows that one day he must face the law and our rights.

I don't hate the police. They carry guns, and it is not in my interest to make enemies of them. They are but the puppets of the rich and of the politicians that steal from our people. A local policeman shot and killed an eighteen-year-old named Valles here in Albuquerque. The policeman was outside his jurisdiction but nevertheless entered the young man's home and shot him. Another policeman killed an Indohispano because the young man reached into his pocket. The policeman said he thought he was reaching for a weapon, and it was his handkerchief. These types of cases happen throughout the Southwest, thousands every year. And no one speaks for the victims.

On March 29, 1973, I received a telephone call informing me that my son Noé had been kidnapped and was being treated at a local hospital. I went immediately and found that some men had attempted to rape my son. The perpetrator was a police officer, Albert Vega. He and Frank Tenorio had been the two officers assigned to assist my wife during my trials. At first, Vega pled not guilty before Judge Gerald Fowlie and then changed his plea to guilty before Judge Roger Sánchez. At the urging of my son David, I wrote to Judge Sánchez and recommended clemency for Vega. Vega had a wife and six children. I know how the wife and children suffer when the father is in jail.

The Chicano police are another matter. They are not like the Anglo police. In fact, the Chicanos have organized themselves into the Albuquerque Chicano Police Association. The Anglos did not like this at all. I believe that police corruption and bad attitude stem from the moral and spiritual condition of the government they work for. If the government is corrupt, then the police are ten times as corrupt.

When all of these allegations against the police came to light, people started calling me with their stories of abuse. They told me that they had informed the news media about these atrocities, but they were never reported. During this time, the revelations about Watergate had been fully made. Nixon was losing control of the coverup.

The Land Titles Are Returned

I had been accusing the Anglo government of having stolen, burned, and destroyed the title records to our land in New Mexico and the Southwest. The Anglo always denied my allegations. When I was released from prison, the *Tribune* surprised everyone by stating that the land had been stolen. Howard Bryan, the reporter, published an article that confirmed the role of William A. Pile, with the complicity of the White House, in the theft of our land. All my enemies must have been red-faced: Bratton, Burks, Payne, McManus, Maloney, and Myra Ellen Jenkins. I made copies of the article and gave it wide circulation among our members. And, on April 10, 1972, the *Journal* reported that the White House had returned some documents that had been stolen from Santa Fe nearly 102 years earlier. Included in these recovered documents was the declaration that Don Diego de Vargas made in 1692. The *Journal* wrote, "These documents are invaluable in ascertaining the boundaries for land claims and who are the rightful heirs to the land."

With these admissions, many other organizations, such as the League of United Latin American Citizens (LULAC), began supporting the Alianza. Lupe Juárez, of LULAC Council 8002 in Albuquerque, made such an announcement on January 18, 1972. Antonio Mondragón, Ray Otero from Colorado, and I went to visit the Mexican president in November. Dr. Jorge A. Bustamante had invited me to Mexico after having attended my conference on Land and Culture. Dr. Bustamante was the principal instrument for the development of Mexican relations with the Chicano Movement. When the White House learned that I was going to meet with the Mexican president, it began to cause me problems. I could not get a visa. President Echeverría had to intervene personally and order that a visa be extended to me. They called by telephone to assure me that my visa was approved and available. I happened to be at the office of Mario Chacón, Mexican consul in Albuquerque, when the call came. The doors to our Mexico had been opened even more to me.

During 1972, I spoke at more colleges and universities and before more groups than ever before. The good treatment I received more than made up for the years of suffering at the hands of politicians. Both old and young people would thank me for all I had done. They thanked me for removing the fear from their minds. They thanked me for giving them the courage that had been taken from them by the Anglo. They thanked me for liberating their minds from Anglo colonization and control for more than 126 years. According to them, no one had told them of the Laws of the Indies or the Treaty of Guadalupe Hidalgo. I would often give the students copies of our birth certificate as a Mestizo people, dated October 19, 1514. Once, at New Mexico Highlands University, I offered the one hundred fifty birth certificates I had, but there were more than one thousand students who mobbed me. They grabbed for the birth certificates as if they were passports to eternal life. I had never seen such hunger for our identity and culture.

The Land

My mother raised us with ties close to the land. During hard times, she fed us plants growing on the land. My father earned fifty cents a day. It was not enough money to feed the family, so my mother would gather plants such as cactus and cactus fruit, mesquite fruit, and wild chile peppers. She would hunt animals, such as squirrels, rabbits, doves, quail, field mice, and even snakes. We always lived near rivers and streams and would bathe there. My mother taught us a lot about the land. It is not strange that I have this appreciation for the land and passion for its relationship to man.

I lost sight of this principle for ten years while I searched for the Just Judge of Judges. But that search ultimately brought me back to the land. During my ten-year fight with the church, I didn't stray far from the land because I picked cotton. I picked cotton from childhood until I was thirty-five years old. My last year was 1960.

I began to learn of the complaints people had about stolen land. I listened to their stories and became convinced that our people were right and had a just cause. I also realized this was a labor of a lifetime. I had to study property rights. I began with Jewish law and the Treaty of Tordecillas, signed on July 7, 1494. These studies took me into international law. The more I studied, the stronger I felt about the righteousness of our claim to the land. I became convinced that the land, like a mother, depends on her offspring. She loves her children, and her children love her because she cares for them. The land is not an ideology. But it does have all that a people need to make them happy and strong. And if our leaders were closer to the land than to foreign ideologies, there would be less war. My advice is to seek leaders who are children of the land, knowledgeable of property rights and the value of land, powerful in the knowledge of the land. Ultimately, ideology and politics are superfluous.

My appeal was decided by three judges, two Anglos and one Mexican (Ben Hernández). The latter voted against me. The Anglo thought I would blame Hernández, but I know the Anglo is behind him.

The Monument to Justice

The word *justice* that I saw in my first Bible caught my attention. I was only fourteen years old, but I remember being very interested in the concept of justice. My father taught me what was related to justice. I sought out more information. Soon, I not only looked for the word in print but also looked for it within people. Justice had undergone many changes, like the Bible. To some people it means one thing and to others something else. They all give it an interpretation. I quickly learned while I fought with the church for more than ten years that Anglo justice means something else. The more I studied the Anglo, the more I learned he was the enemy of justice. I became convinced that the pursuit of justice was my mission in life. I promised to erect a monument to justice and chose as my motto, "Justice is our creed, and the land is our inheritance."

I want to erect a pyramid in the name of justice. I am a witness to the power of justice. All those who raised their hands against my people and me have fallen. And, on April 10, the government returned documents affecting thirty million acres of land that belong to our people.

Celia Saenz Montes visited me from Victoria, Texas. She is the heir to the land El Pedernal, which is occupied by Lyndon B. Johnson. I could not believe my eyes when she showed me her documents and maps. She told me she had seen the Texas Rangers kill her family. She said, "In front of my own eyes they murdered my parents and uncles. I repeat, I saw it."

In November, I visited Elena López de León in Mexico. She is the descendant of Martín de León, the founder of Victoria, Texas. I wrote to Patricia de Leon in Victoria about my visit with her relative, and she sent me a copy of the book by A. B. J. Hammett about Don Martín de León. Hammett discusses how the Anglos murdered the Mexicans in Texas to take their land. He describes how Martín de León's son, Fernando, at gunpoint was made to sign over title to his land.

The Land in Texas

With Mrs. Saenz Montes' visit, I discovered a history I was unaware of. Doña Celia was sixty-nine years of age when she came to visit me, and she had spent the last thirty-five years doing research on land records in Austin, Texas. She gave me copies of significant documents. Among these documents was the list of claims presented to the government of Mexico between 1923 and 1941. The documents also contained the amount of money Mexico claimed as value for these lands: $400 million.

The land claims in Texas had the same fate as those in New Mexico and California. Commissioner James B. Miller reported to the Texas governor on November 28, 1850, that he had lost the "original titles" to the Mexican lands. Supposedly, Miller had received these titles in Brownsville, boarded a steamer, the *Anson,* and proceeded up the coast. The boat sank near Brazos Santiago some fifteen miles from Matagorda Bay.

Mexico and the United States met to discuss reparations. The Mexicans wanted reparations for claims dealing with the war in 1848, and the U.S. wanted reparations for claims dealing with the Mexican Revolution of 1910. President Harding created a commission, and they began discussions on May 14 through August 15, 1923. They reached an accord, which was signed on September 8, 1923, by the United States, and on September 1, 1923, by Mexico. The agreement to pay Mexico $400 million for the Texas land was signed on November 19, 1941. To this day, Mexico has not paid the 433 land claimants in Texas for their loss. Between 1941 and 1955, several lawyers representing the Texas claimants have sought to collect on this money unsuccessfully. Mexico claims to this day to be "studying the matter."

The Rock of Fraternal Harmony: April 7, 1973

At the Second Annual Conference on Fraternal Harmony, I had a reunion with leaders of the Native American, Black, white, and Hispanic communities. The keynote speaker was Tomas Banyacya, spiritual leader of the Hopis. He lives in Oraibe, Arizona, and is held in great respect by the other tribes. He was the first to sign the rock of Fraternal Harmony. This rock is a monument to the Alianza. It is testimony to the harmony that exists among peoples that truly love peace, justice, and fraternal harmony. The rock itself weighs 430 pounds and comes from Chilili. Adelecio Moya brought the rock from there. The Cosmic Board of Directors dedicated this rock to the spirit of harmony. Jesse Jackson from Chicago also signed the rock.

Some of my followers resented the fact that at the conference I was talking with Anglos. They did not understand my motives. Because of the nature of this conference, only the good Anglos would attend. We could begin to separate the few good Anglos from the bad. But, more importantly, the nineteen Native American Pueblos and my Indohispano community could begin to dialogue and communicate.

Toward the end of 1973, media representatives visited me from Spain. I told them of our struggle for the land and of my trips to Spain. I showed them the documents that prove our right to the land. They were impressed. They did not know the Spanish role in our story. They promised to help me spread the word throughout Spain the next time I went.

I tried to have Judge Payne allow me to visit Blas Chávez in prison, but was denied. Chávez was sentenced to fifty years for a crime he did not commit. At this same time, the congressional hearings on Watergate began. Montoya was on the committee. How could a criminal judge another criminal?

On June 25, another daughter was born: Danitha. I named her that because in Hebrew it means "God is My Judge." Every one of my children has brought me joy and has been a blessing.

The year 1973 ended. My people were not the timid and cowardly ones I had met in 1956. The majority of people respected the Alianza. My family and I had good health. The politicians were appalled at the Watergate hearings and what was happening to Nixon and the White House. Mexico was beginning to open its arms to us. U.S. influence was rapidly deteriorating around the world. The corporations that handle the economy of the world were eating one another up. My people's interest in the land recovery movement had grown by two hundred percent since 1856. Now, more young people than old visited our offices. All said, 1973 had been a profitable year for our people and a losing year for our oppressors.

Chapter 4

1974

From the first day of the year I began to keep a diary. I do this because of the events in my life and the weight of my deeds. I now feel them as a load on my back. I am convinced that this corrupt government will soon fall, and I must orient my brothers in the direction of the road to justice and judgment. My people should prepare themselves to control their destiny. They must rescue themselves from the condition and mentality the Anglo has imposed on them: not just politics but morality, customs, education, democracy, sex, religion, and psychopathy.

January 1

The year began with lots of snow. I felt full of happiness, security, and joy. The principal news story dealt with the global energy crisis and elections in Israel. I had a call from Abraham Sánchez, Alianza representative in El Tecolote, to go speak there on the January 12. I accepted.

Today I met with Jerry Densiger, Max Sklower, heads of Channel 4 and 7, respectively, and Antonio Mondragón and Tobías Durán, heads of the Chicano Studies Department at the University of New Mexico, to discuss the latest information on the death of Salazar. I had new information from Blas Chávez and someone named Lucero, a former state police officer.

January 2

Eulogio Salazar has been dead for six years now.

I had several meetings today, but the most important was with David Norvell, the state attorney general, and Roger Beimers. Beimers was with Channel 7, and I wanted him present when I asked Norvell to provide protection for Blas Chávez because he was a most important witness in the Salazar murder. I also called Ray Davenport, chair of the Prison Commission, and asked him to relay to Feliz Rodriguez, the prison warden, the request for additional protection for Blas Chávez while he remained in prison. Davenport called me back the same day and reported that Rodriguez had gotten the message and Chávez would get plenty of protection.

January 3

My lawyer was able to get a court order from Judge Payne allowing me to visit Blas Chávez and get sworn testimony from him. We visited with him at 11:05 a.m. Representatives from the state also showed up, but I was accusing them of the coverup of the Salazar murder. Jerry Densiger called me and told me to be careful because he knew for sure that a state police officer was involved in Salazar's death.

January 4

I met Blas Chávez for the first time today. We visited with him from 2 to 3 p.m. I was accompanied by Wilfredo Sedillo; Armando Rendón, author of *The Chicano Manifesto;* and Harold Parker, my lawyer. Blas mentioned Max Sánchez and Senator Montoya in his sworn testimony. He said that while he remained in prison, he was in danger, and that was why he would only testify before a grand jury. When my lawyer asked him if he knew about the murder of Salazar, he did not deny it. When Chávez gave us his limited sworn statement, there were four lawyers present representing the state. Present also was Freddie Martínez, the state police officer that headed the investigation into Salazar's death. He now worked for the district attorney for Rio Arriba and Santa Fe counties.

From there we went to visit a friend of Edward Schwartz's, a man named Devereux, who told us that four Anglos had murdered Salazar with the indirect help of a Chicano. He said Edward Schwartz had all the names and details of the assassination. I knew that because I had copies of the letter Schwartz had sent to the *Albuquerque Journal.*

January 5

Margarito invited me to eat at his home. I took lawyer Harold Parker so he could hear what Margarito had to say. Parker learned of all that Blas had told Margarito while both were in prison. Parker went back to visit Blas Chávez, alone to verify what Margarito had said. Wilfredo, Bennie Chávez, and I went back to talk to Devereux. We all returned to Albuquerque about 7 p.m. and met. Parker was more convinced than ever that Blas Chávez knew more details about the murder. Because he had been able to visit with Parker alone, Blas opened up more and told him there was more to say, but only to a grand jury.

January 6

The Cosmic Board of Directors met. The members are Wilfredo Sedillo, Eduardo Chávez, Juan Roybal, Ambrosio González, Antonio Griego, Federico Abeyta, Primitivo Sánchez, Rodolfo Mares, and me. We discussed the need to present a legislative initiative demanding an investigation into the property rights of the Indohispano, given the new evidence of theft of titles. According to the *Albuquerque Tribune* and *Journal,* the government had admitted as much since 1972 regarding the land titles to Santa Fe.

The Cosmic Board voted unanimously to ask the New Mexico legislature to pass a resolution petitioning the U.S. Congress to create a commission to investigate land titles in New Mexico, beginning with Cañón de Chama, also known as the San Joaquín land grant.

The Cosmic Board also approved obtaining a loan from San Ignacio Credit Union to pay Harold Parker for his legal work aimed at getting Judge Payne to order publication of the police investigative report on the murder of Salazar. We also approved purchase of a guard dog for the building. His name is Valiente.

January 7

I visited with Ray Davenport, head of the prison commission, and gave him copies of the documents given to me by Blas Chávez. I did the same with Max Slower, and two reporters from Channel 7. I wanted everyone to know what I knew so there would be no further excuses to coverup the murder. Lt. Governor Roberto Mondragón also wanted to see me about 11 a.m. to discuss the Salazar murder and the information from Blas Chávez.

Moshe Dayan offered to return land to the Arabs. I was very excited by the news because I want to see peace between these two peoples. However, the principal news was about Nixon. The Watergate revelations are drowning him. I was so excited about this turn of events and felt that justice was imminent in New Mexico and throughout the Anglo Nation. I say Anglo Nation because they have never made us feel a part of it, have never invited us to assist in governing it, have never let us write the true history. On the contrary, they have robbed us of our human and civil rights, among other rights.

January 9

I spoke for thirty minutes on Spanish radio, KABQ, a 5,000-watt station on our legislative resolution. I was getting free air time. Some ten years ago, we had to pay for air time. I taped another thirty-minute segment for Channel 7.

I got a letter from James A. Thomson, city attorney, requesting an affidavit on the money, $4,241.75, that the police allegedly stole from me when I was first booked into jail. The police are going to get their bonding company, Ohio Casualty Company, to cover the loss.

January 10

Dan Rather hosted on CBS a special broadcast on Nixon tonight. Nixon was portrayed as the most criminal of politicians. Rather's mistake, however, like that of all other Anglo reporters and media organs, has been to make Nixon an isolated case.

When it comes to reporting on the human rights of minorities, such as the Indohispano, Native Americans, and Blacks, all Anglo media—CBS, NBC, ABC, and all the others—are as bad as Nixon. They have no conscience when it comes to "minorities."

The entire media machinery has been deaf, dumb, and blind to the violence, torture, and kidnapping of my family. If an Anglo had suffered this "hell" as we have, the entire media empire would be interceding on his behalf.

January 11

Channel 4 broadcast a program we had pre-taped while I traveled to Dallas and Oklahoma. In Oklahoma, I spoke to various Native American groups. I had been invited, along with Jerry Wilkerson and Cornell, the leader of Native American groups in New Mexico. I spoke about the Indohispano and the relationships that exist between us and Indian groups in North, Central, and South America. I told them that if Native Americans did not receive justice first, the Indohispano would reject any offer made to us from the Anglo.

At this meeting there were representatives from the World Council of Churches, which is an exact replica of the United Nations in its structure, except that it is more distanced from justice than the U.N. Nathaniel Vanderwerf, vice-president of the World Council of Churches, was present and promised to publish the history and mission of the Indohispano.

I reminded the Indian groups that recent news reports implicated the various Protestant denominations and corporations in the Vietnam War.

January 15

I met with Samuel Vigil, state representative from San Miguel County who has agreed to sponsor our resolution. He told me that Bobby Baca, Senator Montoya's secretary, has said that the senator would present a very similar resolution in the U.S. Congress. This surprised us because Montoya, along with Senator Clinton A. Anderson, had been obstacles to us for years. He has been at the service of the Anglos who have stolen and continue to steal our lands. Now that we have legislative support, he wants to preempt us on the issue. He has had twenty-eight years to do something, but never did. Why now?

January 17

I left for Santa Fe with a group of warriors to finalize our resolution and meet with legislators. I spoke with Samuel F. Vigil, aide to Lt. Governor Roberto Mondragón, State Senator Matías Chacón from Espanola, Ed Barboa, Antonio Lucero, Ray Leger from Las Vegas, Tony Armijo, and many others. I asked them to help clear up the land titles, especially now that the White House had returned documents taken back in 1870. They all promised to help support passage of this resolution in both chambers. I was very pleasantly surprised at the respect afforded us during our visit.

Now we are going to battle for public opinion at the legislature. The Anglo created the Black Legend against Spain. For more than three hundred years, that false propaganda was used until the western world turned against Spain. Using false propaganda, the Anglo has gotten into two world wars to defend the root of its race: England. Later, for the past twenty-nine years, they have used false propaganda in opposition to Communism. They have used the same type of false propaganda against the land recovery movement and me.

I have known that the Anglo does not have any good intentions. Even among the better Anglos, the one I brought back with me from Washington, D.C., after the Poor People's Campaign stole the $30,000 donated to our cause by the Catholic Church.

Because I had conditional liberty at that time, I could not legally hold any office with the Alianza, and could not defend our interests. Understand clearly that I did not have any great hope that the legislative resolution would solve anything. I just want to make it clear so everyone will see that the psychopathic Anglo does not have room in his heart for the Native American people or us. There is no room in his heart for Blacks either.

January 22

César Chávez called me at three this afternoon. With broken hope, he told me that Corky Gonzales had not accepted José Angel Gutiérrez's invitation to meet in Los Angeles. He thought it was best not to meet on this occasion. That ended José Angel Gutierréz's plan. I was now convinced that we were in a crisis of disharmony. Meanwhile, I had to continue searching for ways to promote greater unity and harmony among our people. Many of our own, without knowing, are the product and victim of Anglo mentality.

February 1

Warriors from all corners of the state gathered in Santa Fe to witness our resolution being presented to the legislature. The politicians realized the people were all united behind this initiative. The House of Representatives passed our resolution 56 to 0. Next, it had to go to the Senate, but we were confident it would pass. The people were happy and jubilant over the victory. We returned to celebrate.

February 2

More than two thousand persons gathered at the Alianza building to celebrate the eleventh anniversary of the organization. More than fifty thousand listened on KABQ radio to the activities broadcast by remote control from our hall. Many of the warriors spoke on the radio. We had bought six hours of radio time on KABQ. My wife Patricia and other women served food all day. Many people came to congratulate us. Many who were against us in the early years were now present among us. The triumph in Santa Fe helped make this a special celebration.

February 4

Some of Nixon's people began serving their prison terms today. They are tasting the fruit of justice.

I went to meet with state senators in Santa Fe. I met with Jerry Apodaca and Ray García. They continue to assure me of their support for the resolution. I also discussed with them a new plan of education for 1975. I want New Mexico to teach Spanish as an official language, required under Article 6, Section 2, of the United States Constitution and Articles 2 and 12, Sections 5 and 8, respectively, of the New Mexico Constitution.

The U. S. Commission on Civil Rights has published its report on the education of Indohispanos. It confirmed our allegations and blames the system for discrimination against our children. The report suggests our children be educated in their own language.

I got a call from Gloria Peterson, president of the Veterans Administration Hospital Workers Union, complaining of discrimination and inviting me to a meeting. I have been discussing with my membership the need to join with other groups in order to enhance our position. The government does not listen to an individual anymore, only to organized groups. I remind our people that the major groups, unions, churches, banks, lawyers, police, politicians, and others are all organized and united. We also must join with others to increase strength and promote fraternal harmony in order to be respected.

February 6

Henry Kissinger and Nixon accused the Arabs of blackmail, and I think this is wrong. The United States has no right to tell Arab nations how to manage their affairs. Traditionally, the United States has treated its neighbors with blackmail and violence.

I went to Santa Fe again to observe the Senate deliberation of House Joint Resolution No. 15. Anglo Senator Aubrey L. Dunn, a favorite of the rich in New Mexico, opposed the measure and asked for a one-day delay to study the matter. Everyone in the state is focused on the legislature, and the media is reporting every event related to this resolution.

February 7

Hoping to finalize the resolution, I made my seventh trip to Santa Fe today. I brought warriors from throughout the state: Tierra Amarilla, Canjilon, Coyote, Espanola, Taos, Las Vegas, Tecolote, Chilili, Santa Rosa, Bernalillo, Cuba de Pecos, Belen de Socorro, San Antonito, San Miguel del Vado, Santa Fe, and Albuquerque. At 11:50 a.m., the resolution was passed by a vote of 35 to 0. Senator Aubrey Dunn, who had opposed it, left the chamber just before the vote. We were very happy. Now the state of New Mexico is asking the U.S. Congress to create a commission to investigate our land claims. The resolution was presented to the 31st Legislature, Second Session, by Samuel K.

Vigil, Luis Romero, Richard Crabapple, Bobby Durán, Raymond Sánchez, A. Carroll, Luis Back, and others requesting the U.S. Congress to create a Spanish Mexican Land Claims Commission. Resolution No. 15 reads, "Whereas New Mexico has a unique history of the acquisition of ownership of land due to the substantial number of Spanish and Mexican land grants that were an integral part of the colonization and growth of this area of the country and; Whereas various provisions of the treaties agreed upon by the parties concerned under prior sovereigns have not yet been fully implemented in the spirit of Article VI, Section 2, of the Constitution of the United States; and, Whereas Congress did establish an Indian Claims Commission which successfully adjudicated hundreds of disputed land possession questions; and, Whereas there still exists serious questions about prior ownership, particularly about certain public lands; and, Whereas many of these questions involve land in several of the United States; and, Whereas this Legislature has yet to receive a response from Congress on its petition for assistance on the question embodied in House Memorial 32 of the first session of the 31st Legislature; Now therefore be it resolved by the Legislature of the State of New Mexico that the Congress of the United States is respectfully requested and urged to establish by appropriate legislation a Spanish Mexican Land Claims Commission to adjudicate and make conclusive determination, including where possible the restitution of public lands, rights and appurtenances thereto and the awarding of monetary damages for the taking of property, and the subsequent alienation of those equities, by other than honorable means from the various claimants and their heirs whose rights derive from the prior sovereigns of the Southwest; and, be it further resolved that copies of this resolution be sent to the presiding officers of each House of Congress."

While we were celebrating this great victory, the *Albuquerque Journal* was editorializing against our water rights. For the past fifty years, the Anglo judges have illegally controlled the water of the Rio Grande. Finally, the people had organized and backed a legislative resolution to take control of the water. In November, we would see if the Anglos kept control of our people. The water is controlled by the Middle Rio Grande Conservancy District.

February 8

Native American leaders have invited me to join them in supporting their "Cold War" against Anglos who want to eliminate them from the turquoise market. I know this precious stone and what it means to the Indians. Sumbell is the name of the corporation that seeks a city subsidy to establish itself in Albuquerque and manufacture synthetic turquoise. Berny Atencio, leader of the Santo Domingo Pueblo, asked me to speak for them and against Sumbell. We all met at city hall and discussed the Sumbell proposal. I was thanked for my assistance by Ernesto Lovato, secretary general of all the Pueblos.

February 11

Today the *Journal* accused my son David of shooting Douglas S. Arwell, owner of the Alibi Bar. David was arrested and Cristóbal bailed him out. This Anglo tried to assassinate David, and he only acted in self-defense. They never tried David.

The two leaders of the American Indian Movement, Dennis Banks and Russell Means, came to see me. They asked for a copy of the Laws of the Indies, thinking it could help them in their defense for the taking of Wounded Knee.

I also learned that David Cargo, former governor, was leaving the state and moving to Oregon. I asked Harold Parker, my lawyer, to interview Cargo about what he knew of the Salazar investigation before he left the state. My lawyer did not listen to me.

I received an invitation to attend a conference of farmworkers in Mexico from Jesús Orta of the union of farmworkers and laborers.

At 9 p.m., I received a call from Silvia Beltrán from Milwaukee, Wisconsin, asking me for help. She had been raped. I told her my wife and son had gone through the same thing, and I had not been able to get justice for them in this country, the "leader of the free world."

February 25

Ray Vargas of the Mexican American Legal Defense and Education Fund (MALDEF) called to tell me they will assist in my appeal to the U.S. Supreme Court on the second illegal trial brought against me by the New Mexican politicians. Rio Arriba County did not have money to try me a second time, and the legislature had to approve a special budget request.

March 7

I received the surprise of the year when Jerry Crawford, assistant to Bob Brown, called me and said they had reconsidered and would sign on to my letter demanding release of the state police report on the Salazar murder. Wilfredo and I went and met face to face with Bob Brown. He was pale, sickly, and sad-looking. He told us of his cardiac attack that hospitalized him for three months. He took my letter and signed it without comment. He then told me that Ralph Looney of the *Tribune* had also changed his mind and would sign the letter as well. We went over there and he also signed.

The idea of this letter is getting better and better. Many politicians are beginning to feel the heat on their heels.

March 10

I gathered signatures for my letter from many bishops, Protestants, and Catholics. I also asked the police. Lester Hays, sheriff of Bernalillo County, refused to sign, but his deputy Benny Padilla and Santos Baca did. The city police chief, Robert Stover, refused to sign, but not Ray Chávez, the head of the Chicano police.

March 14

Archbishop Davis signed the letter this morning and told me that he planned to retire and was nominating a New Mexico native to the Pope in Rome. I understood this to mean he wanted my opinion, and I expressed it.

March 16

The *Albuquerque Journal* ran the last of seven articles attacking Mexican labor. Although the last article ended with the admission "Anglos are wetbacks having crossed the Atlantic," I didn't like the articles. The articles also said Chicanos turn in ninety-five percent of the "wetbacks."

I demanded time to respond to these attacks. In November 1972, an Anglo had killed five Mexican workers as a result of this type of propaganda.

March 17

The Cosmic Board authorized me to respond to the *Journal's* attack on Mexican laborers from Mexico. Radio KQEO gave me thirty minutes to respond to Bob Brown's *Journal*.

March 18

Governor King set my appointment with him for March 21. I got an hour of time on Channel 5. My son's lawsuit against Vega began today. The case was not filed in an attempt to make money, but to open the investigation into Vega's higher-ups and the state police. We alleged that this crime was part of a larger conspiracy to force us from the state.

March 19

At 3 p.m. a delegation and I went to confront Bob Brown, the *Journal's* editor, but he refused to meet with us. Instead, we met with Frankie McCarty and Jerry Crawford. Frankie was the one who wrote the poorly documented articles on our land rights. Scott Beaven, the author of the recent articles attacking Mexican labor, was not present. As a concession, the *Journal* permitted me to write one article defending our brothers.

March 21

I went to Jose Vargas' funeral. He was a taxi driver and friend, and was murdered by Anglos.

We went to meet with the governor. An Indohispano delegation and Dorothy Orrison were with me. I gave the governor the letter with signatures of these people:

1. Jerry Banziger, Channel 4
2. Max Sklower, Channel 7
3. Bruce Hebenstreil, Channel 13
4. Larry Dickerson, Channel 5
5. Eliseo Casillas, Radio KABQ
6. J. Mark Wilbenson, Radio KABQ
7. Richard McKee, Radio KOB
8. Del Wood, Radio KRKE
9. Chuck Logan, Radio KQGO
10. Daniel J. Evans, Radio KDEF
11. Chuck Anthony, Radio KDAZ
12. Benny F. Herrera, Radio KAMX
13. A.B. Collado, *El Hispano*
14. Ralph Torres, *Revista La Luz*
15. Mary Beth Craeff, *El Independiente*
16. Robert A. Brown, *Albuquerque Journal*
17. Toger Makin, *Daily Lob*
18. Walter Kublins, *Albuquerque News*
19. John R. Bott, *The New Mexican*
20. Larry Collaway, *Associated Press*
21. Brad Smith, UPI
22. Ralph Looney, *Albuquerque Tribune*
23. James P. Davis, Archbishop of Santa Fe
24. Richard M. Trelease, Bishop of Rio Grande
25. Robert M. Allen, United Presbyterian Church
26. Alsie Carlton, Bishop of United Methodist Church
27. Harry Summers, New Mexico Interchurch Agency
28. Edwin M. Yoder, Mennonite Church
29. Robert Price, Christus Victor Lutheran Church
30. John W. Penn, St. Matthew's Episcopal Church
31. George V. Reiffer, Annunciation
32. Robert Sánchez, San Felipe Catholic Church.

Seven more pastors had signed the letter.

Dorothy Orrison told the governor, "Mr. Governor, I am an Anglo and live among Anglos that believe Mr. Tijerina is responsible for the death of Eulogio Salazar. That is why I came to speak with you today. I believe it is very necessary that the investigation into this death be made public and this unjust suspicion be cast aside." The governor said, "By God, let us publish this investigative report so the people will know the truth. They have a right to it."

I felt great happiness and thought that now the people would get the information. Immediately, Wilfredo started calling the press to alert them of the news.

March 22

I held a press conference at 10 a.m. It was good, but the *Journal* and the *Tribune* did not give the governor's commitment the attention it warranted. They are not interested in solving this crime.

March 23

I now live on a ranch in Madera, New Mexico. My wife and I had wanted to leave the corrupt city life behind years ago. I cannot tolerate what the Anglo has done to the cities. The United States is a replica of England. The Anglo has fooled all the other Europeans he has invited to this country. He promised a nation made up of immigrants, where each would have the liberty to live his life, culture, morality, and values. In the final analysis, the Anglo has made everyone accept his culture. If the other groups do not want to save themselves from the corrupt Anglo life, my people and I do, even if we have to fight and die in such a struggle.

I had taken Isabel out of school for our move to Madera at a good time. I had taken her to school daily and noticed strangers following us. My wife told me of threats she had received over the telephone regarding our children. They wanted me to stop investigating the death of Salazar.

Soon my neighbors in La Madera spread the word that I now lived there.

March 27

The governor announced that the investigative report on the Salazar murder would not be released. I decided the governor was implicated in the coverup and obstruction of justice of the murder. I felt rage but did not lose hope.

Radio KABQ and Channel 7 gave me time to respond to this announcement. I was called from all over the state. The people were more convinced than ever before of my innocence now. It was clear now that the Anglos did not want the crime uncovered. They feared that Salazar's blood would end up on Anglo hands.

April 6

We celebrated the Third Annual Conference on Fraternal Harmony. William Anders, the astronaut, was our keynote speaker. The *Tribune* put photos of Anders on the front page. Max Sklower asked me to speak at their national conference. I will gladly do that.

I began to prepare for my trip to Palestine and Israel. I think the city of Jerusalem divides all of us, and because of this city, the nations of the world feel threatened. I want to go there before it is too late.

April 7

The conference endorsed my resolution to the U.S. Congress that it designate a day to commemorate Fraternal Harmony. We prepared to travel to Washington.

April 11

During the past three years, I have paid $100 each year in taxes for a vacant lot. My mother-in-law gave this land to my children. I protested the overtaxation to E.M. Murphy, the county tax-assessor. He adjusted my tax, but continued to bill me. I called the press and complained of this unfair taxation. The media reported the incident and I had my taxes reduced from $100 to $25, but I was denied restitution for past years. I would have to hire an attorney that would charge me $500 for the case. Many people called me with their complaints of similar situations. This is how the crooked politicians work.

April 15

Lawyer Harold Parker gave me a copy of the sworn affidavit taken from Blas Chávez in prison. And, I spoke with Senator Montoya's son about asking his father to support the designation of a Day of Fraternal Harmony and to support the resolution on the land commission. I have never heard from him again.

April 20

Alfonso Chacón brought a 700-pound steer to celebrate the completion of my parole and the return to my leadership role in the Alianza.

April 24

I visited with various community leaders who complained about the "hippies." The hippie women trade sex for friendship. I am saddened by what I see among Anglo youth who turn against their parents and the corruption of their race. Poor children! They carry the bad habits of their parents. Hallucinogenic drugs and free sex are their dangerous offerings.

The neighbors have revived a saying, "Fly away from this land, bird, it is not yours." It is their way of saying to the hippies to move away and take their bad habits with them.

April 30

There has been a series of murders in Farmington. A group of Anglo youths has been murdering Indians without a motive. Apparently, they believe "a good Indian is a dead Indian." I was asked to join the Indians in protesting these murders. Larry Emerson called and led the press conference. This is not the first time I have been asked by Navajos to join them. I attended and spoke in support of the Navajos and against the Anglo murderers. As usual, the media left out my remarks. Their tactic has been to divide us from the Indians. I mentioned this to my people so they would recognize the audacity of Anglo racism.

May 1

My son Daniel died today, a victim of an automobile accident that happened about 175 miles from Albuquerque. He was just twenty-one years of age. His wife, Iván Ramírez, has suffered a great deal over the loss of her husband.

Danielito was a man of great courage. He was with me in the most dangerous moments at Tierra Amarilla, Echo Canyon, Coyote, and in Washington, D.C. Daniel wrote a letter to Nixon that was published in a book, *Letters to the President of the United States from the Youth of America.* In this letter he outlined the travesty committed against our people by the White House. He pointed out that the poverty we find ourselves in now is a result of the land theft by the White House. Daniel gave his copy of the book to his brother David. My daughters have cried a lot over his death. My sons David, Noé, and Carlitos kept their tears in their hearts, as did I.

We have buried Daniel temporarily at Mount Calvary Cemetery in Albuquerque. Many of his friends, seeing his example, have lost their fear of the Anglo and followed him. I hope his son, Daniel II, also follows in his father's footsteps.

We received letters, telegrams, and telephone calls from across the nation from people who love and respect the Tijerina family, including one from the New Mexico governor. More than one thousand people attended the services held at Salazar Mortuary, which conducted a wonderful service. I leave these words here in gratitude for the esteem and affection that the people afforded my son Danielito.

May 5

The *Albuquerque Journal* finally published my letter in response to William A. Magil's article of March 31. I repeated to him what I had said to the officials and their puppets that had raped my wife. All of this is as true as what Officer Vega did to my son. He himself pled guilty to the offense. And this is as true as the theft by the police of the money I left my family. This was proven by the state attorney general while I was in prison. I had answered this letter because I did not want the Anglo to have an excuse to keep fooling my people. I wanted everything to come to light, but it is impossible because the power of the state is in the hands of my enemies. Only the Just Judge of Judges can undo the Anglo's criminal machinery that controls the gears of "justice."

May 15

José Gallegos, a store owner in La Madera, told me that four Anglo homes in La Petaca, New Mexico, had been burned to the ground. The Anglos used this arson to renew a media campaign against the land recovery movement and me. Emilio Naranjo has begun to intimidate the new generation of Alianza members, made up of returning Vietnam veterans who are taking up where their parents left off. They know their ancestral history well and have a mature conscience and disciplined respect for their property rights and culture.

A delegation of Anglos came to see me and reminded me that I was committed to fraternal harmony. They asked that I speak to the youth and urge them not to use violence. I said, "Fraternal harmony already exists among my people and between my people and the Indian nations of the Southwest." The Anglo, with his psychopathic mentality and his bloody and violent history, has to repent and change. Repentance means doing what the Jews are doing, and that is to return to their ancestral lands. Anglos must return to their lands, if they are to contribute to fraternal harmony. Fraternal harmony and land rights are joined. I finally said to the Anglos that I would continue to speak in favor of fraternal harmony, but I would also continue to fight for our property rights.

May 17

More revelations about President Nixon continue to emerge. The tape recordings are like a spider's web that entangles a fly; they threaten not only Nixon but also the entire nation.

The U.S. gave Israel thirty-six jets, and they used them to bomb the cities of Sidon and Maidia in Lebanon. The Arabs have lived there since 1900 and were forced from their lands in 1947. I have not lost sight of the Middle East, where the last battle will take place. Out of the Middle East, will come the maximum edict and next-to-last law requiring each people to return to its lands. Since I fight for our land, I have to be concerned with these developments, for the ultimate authority that will dictate the last word on property rights on this planet.

May 18

I have been in La Madera a week now, and people have begun to visit me. I had a student delegation visit early this morning. One of the young persons told me that Emilio Naranjo was being used to eliminate me. These young persons, each from a different community, told me they could no longer tolerate the Anglo. They were protesting the widespread use of drugs, free sex, and the hippie movement that is perverting the morality of our children. This is a very serious threat and we must defend against it.

I went to Albuquerque today and, on the way, stopped to visit Orlando Ortega in Espanola. He had lent me a 38-caliber German pistol and an M-1 rifle when we had the confrontation in Coyote in June 1969. The weapons were illegally confiscated by the state police and federal agents. That is why I love Orlando so much: he always thought about me and took care of me. Orlando was beaten by Emilio Naranjo once and had scars on his face from that beating. He had joined the Alianza very early.

Upon arrival at the Alianza offices, I read Senator Montoya's letter in which he promised to introduce legislation in support of our resolution to create a land commission. I did not know that Montoya and the White House were continuing to press on with their efforts to return me to prison. Montoya wanted to return me to prison to discredit me and have the people believe nothing I would say. We now had more evidence, more documentation, and were stronger than ever, and Montoya knew this.

May 23

The *Albuquerque Journal* published my response to the article that attacked our brothers that cross the border from Mexico in search of work. We circulated copies of this article. Border conflicts are the most delicate of matters and exist throughout the world. When it is convenient to the Anglo, he will open borders, just like he did for the Vietnamese and the Koreans, whom he has fought against for twenty-five years. He defends England and has committed everyone into two world wars. And now, he agitates us against our brothers (Mestizos) from Mexico and tries to poison our minds with racist lies and arguments in an attempt to get us to hate our own brothers. But he will fail in his efforts. The border issue, like that of the Vietnam War and Watergate, will fail. My people will triumph before the end of the millennium.

June 4

The Pope designated Father Roberto Sánchez as archbishop for the Diocese of Santa Fe. Roberto Sánchez had baptized my daughter Danitha while he was the pastor at San Felipe Church. Once, I didn't have money to pay for my daughter Isabel's school, and Sánchez paid the $90 I owed from his pocket. My daughter Harmony had been baptized by Archbishop Davis with Sánchez assisting him.

Jerry Apodaca won the primary election for governor today, and Tony Anaya won for attorney general. All the Anglo opponents lost. It was a complete Indohispano victory.

June 5

Today is the seventh anniversary of the taking of Tierra Amarilla. We gathered at the Alianza headquarters in La Madera to celebrate. We were all filled with joy and happiness. My soul cried with joy at seeing my people so happy in their new-found freedom of spirit.

José Angel Gutiérrez from Texas telephoned with a congratulatory message, as did others from California and Colorado. While we celebrated, Nixon was going through sour moments. And, the principal news item was that hunger was the greatest danger to four billion inhabitants of our planet. Even so, the rich will not return the stolen lands to the people.

June 8

Our warriors continue to arrive, and the Anglo Forest Service "rangers" keep looking with terror in their eyes that we are celebrating the erection of a great monument dedicated to all Pueblos and the settlers of the Southwest. Each *Pueblo* is bringing a huge rock with its *Pueblo* name inscribed. In this fashion our children will understand and appreciate the necessity of unity and harmony among our people and with the Indian nations.

June 9

Today was the end of my parole conditions. It is a day of great jubilee. The people returned to me what the Anglo had taken away five years ago, the leadership of the Alianza. I assumed the direction of the Alianza today. The people sang the two ballads that had been composed by Roberto Martínez. The first one is about the taking of Tierra Amarilla on June 5, 1967, and the other, called "The Northern Tiger," is about my war against the United States.

Benecio Serrano, our engineer, began the construction of the monument to the *Pueblos*. The children of the Alianza warriors sang and shouted with happiness. The women cooked and served food for everyone.

I suspected, but did not really believe, that the politicians would be stupid enough to try to return me to prison. But it was written that I would be imprisoned again.

June 10

Over the radio I heard that the U.S. Supreme Court had denied my appeal on the second trial over Tierra Amarilla. This is the fifth time I have been denied justice by this court.

June 11

The news media made a big thing over my appeal. Meanwhile, the people are asking Governor King to commute my sentence. Governor

King had asked for public opinion on the matter, and many people had sent telegrams on my behalf. Everyone felt shame for what had been done to my family; now the politicians wanted to imprison me again.

June 12

I flew to Washington, D.C., while Wilfredo, Federico Abeyta, Adelecio Moya, and Arsenio Garduño traveled by car. I spoke with the aides to Senators Montoya and Pete Domenici. Two days later when the others arrived, we spoke to more legislators. But it was all in vain.

I am completely convinced that there is not one drop of respect for our rights in Washington, D.C. I did not expect sweet water from a sour fountain, but I did want to leave proof that the Anglo has no intention of doing justice in our cause. The Anglo before the world seeks justice for all nations—at least, that is the excuse used to interfere in their internal affairs—but treats us like the worst enemy of "his government." Why? Is he afraid of us? Is he afraid of our ancestral rights, afraid because we have documents and laws that support our claims?

June 25 and 26

I returned to La Madera to spend the last few days of freedom with my family. A year earlier I had a dream in which I saw that I would have to return to prison again. Since then, I had begun to prepare my wife and children for this eventuality. My daughter Rosita organized the community and went to see Governor King, but it was futile. The White House and its puppets will not accept that our mission on behalf of the Indohispano people is divine. Blindly, they are thrashing their arms as if drowning. In their desperation, they think this will stop me. In these last few days, I have seen the love my people have for me. Hundreds of letters and telegrams have been sent to the governor asking him to grant me a pardon. The Anglos in the middle do not want to see me in prison again. They are afraid of the reaction by my people. They know that the majority of the people know that I am innocent of Salazar's spilled blood.

June 29

Emilio Naranjo's agents came to take me to Santa Fe to begin my second prison term. This is how the Anglos respond to my people's demand for justice. But they burned their hands with the first prison term because they made me famous. With their hate and unjust prison term, they made me a hero. They learned this soon, and that is why they wanted me freed. In the last three years, there have been many favorable things for me and against the politicians.

June 30 and following

For the first thirty days of my term I was in quarantine. The head of this prison is Gilbert Naranjo, the nephew of Emilio Naranjo, but Gilbert is different from his uncle. He has treated me well and given me special privileges. I was allowed to work, so I would not be confined all day. The public clamored for my freedom, as did my fellow prisoners. An inmate named Frankie organized a prisoners' protest to free me. They circulated a petition, cell by cell, block by block, and gathered more than two hundred signatures before the guards discovered the effort. Félix Rodríguez, a guard conditioned by the Anglo mind-set, hated me and hated every prisoner that was straight and obedient, because that prevented him from using his brutal and savage violence against them.

The state prison is much better for me than the federal one because seventy percent of the inmates are Indohispanos, and they all respect me. After the quarantine, I was placed in a dormitory with Blas Chávez. He was happy to see me. My heart leaped with joy to know I would be near the one who knew the truth about New Mexico politicians. He had begun his political career with Senator Dennis Chávez, who was in Congress for thirty-five years. The senator took under his wing some young people, among them Max Sánchez (the dentist), José Martínez, José Montoya (the senator), and others. He was in World War II, where he learned new tricks to put into service on behalf of his politician friends.

When Blas began to tell me the intimate details of his relationship with Max Sánchez, Joe Martínez, Senator Montoya, William Fellion, and others, I began to get scared. Several times, I told Blas that we both could be eliminated if we were not careful. He knew enough to place us both in great danger. After he finished explaining his relationships with the politicians, he began to tell me the details of the murder of Eulogio Salazar.

Emilio Narajo, Max Sánchez, and William Fellion were at the center of the story of what was a political assassination. I had spent seven years seeking the assassins. I had to discover who they and their accomplices were. Blas began to tell me detail by detail and fragment by fragment the entire story. Now I knew why I was returned to prison a second time. I had repeatedly asked of the Just Judge of All Judges to help me solve this crime.

I was concerned that the politicians would soon discover that Blas and I were in the same dormitory. The guards all assured me they were there to protect me and they did. They even gave me constant information on the happenings in the outside world. The guards were also tired of all the political corruption and wanted a radical change.

Blas was bitter with his former political friends. He was innocent of the crime he was accused of and convicted for. He was serving a fifty-year prison sentence. He had been used by the politicians. Blas told me of more than one hundred burglaries he committed for politicians, breaking into safes. I listened to all Blas had to say.

August 8

Blas felt that he was a victim of politicians, much like those involved with Nixon in Watergate. The politicians use you while they can. Blas told me one day, "My brother José worked at state police headquarters and was able to steal the report Robert Guilliand made on the Salazar murder. William Fellion is an assassin that works for the state police and politicians of New Mexico. Max Sánchez, in my presence, paid $2,000 to William Fellion a few days before the death of Salazar. I was with Fellion in the red jeep, studying the layout in Tierra Amarilla for the assassination of Eulogio Salazar."

I spent three months talking with Blas. I did not have a doubt about the crime now. I interrogated Blas until I was sure I knew who killed Salazar. Blas fingered each accomplice, much like John Dean III implicated Nixon's loyalists. Since then I have referred to Blas as the John Dean of New Mexico.

I was in prison during the November elections, when the Indohispano people in unity with the Indians of New Mexico voted into office all their candidates and booted out the Anglo foreigners. Not a single Anglo candidate won election, except for the lt. governor who ran on the ticket with Jerry Apodaca.

Just before the November elections, Ford gave Nixon a pardon, on September 9. Before the world, Ford pardoned Nixon for crimes he was yet to be tried for and found either guilty or not guilty. Ford is paying a political debt to Nixon for giving him the position. Ford has made a mockery of all that is law and order, and the Constitution of the United States. All my fellow prisoners were shocked that Nixon had been pardoned. I thought the people would not tolerate such a thing, but I was wrong. It had to be like this. This pardon would be, in the final analysis, the greatest proof against the Anglo. It would follow him for all time until he commits suicide. The entire world realized that there was not a drop of shame in the White House. The pardon shamed even the criminals in the streets. Among the Anglos that control and grant parole, the pardon had an effect. Even though I was sentenced to serve ten years, I was released on parole after serving five months and eighteen days. Just eight days before I obtained parole, Blas Chávez was released. He had fought for three years and finally won.

I walked out of prison on December 18, 1974, and went to celebrate with my family and community. And, on January 1, 1975, I attended the inaugural ceremony for the new governor, Jerry Apodaca.

Chapter 5

1975

I began the New Year with a shower at 1:45 in the morning. While my children slept, I reviewed the history of my life and confessed the ills of my people to the Just Judge of All. I promised to fight even stronger for the salvation of our families, to continue the struggle for the land of our parents, and to prepare the Indohispano community for the coming millennium that is approaching. In Santa Fe, they were celebrating the swearing in of Governor Jerry Apodaca. I spoke via radio to all of New Mexico. I said that I was very happy to see one of our community members taking the control of state government and that now we could expect to have more justice for all of the oppressed.

January 4

I went to Santa Fe to meet with the new governor, and from there I went to see José Amador Gallegos, half-brother to Blas Chávez. He confirmed everything that Blas had told me while I was in prison. I began to prepare a big project for the legislature regarding Spanish-language education in New Mexico. On January 5, the Cosmic Board of Directors met. The following day the Congress announced that it would investigate the CIA. This super secret agency depends directly on the White House, and, on top of being the most powerful, it's the most responsible for political crime in the nation. For many years, my supporters and I have studied and kept a careful eye on the CIA. In the name of national security, this agency has destroyed many groups and persons whose only crime has consisted of seeking justice. In the case of the Alianza, my community and I have a long history of the CIA as the arm of the White House working against us. The Anglo thought that with Nixon's pardon, the global demand for justice would end, but this is not going to happen. I knew that the pursuit of justice would eventually come even to New Mexico and to the last corners where the Anglos have established their illegal power. Ford and Kissinger threaten the Arab nations over oil, and eight million people are unemployed in the United States. The illegal war by the United States against Vietnam is not going well. The nations of the world are lining up with the Arabs or with the Jews. Without knowing, they are probably lining up for the last world war in which the Anglo race may kill the whole world.

January 8

Blas Chávez came to see me. He told me he was ready. From the beginning, Blas had told me that he would only tell his story to a grand jury and not to reporters. He did not want to be killed beforehand.

January 11

Wendell Chino, president of the Indian Nations, invited me to their national convention. I accepted and spoke about fraternity and harmony between the Indians and the Indohispanos. Father Thomas Steele from Denver, Colorado, just published his book *Santos and Saints,* in which he presents me as a great defender of property rights. Unknowingly, Senator Montoya wrote the introduction for this book. The book details my struggle for the land from a Catholic priest's point of view. Representatives from the pueblos of Chilili, Tecolote, and San Miguel del Vado have come to tell me that some legal aid attorneys have received a $100,000 grant to represent them in land claims. These attorneys are trying to divide the community and embroil the land claim in more litigation. They want to appease some claimants with small victories in order to destroy the Alianza. It's the old, eternal plan used by the Anglos to divide and conquer. I advised the community people to reject such offers because, in the long run, they do us more harm than good.

February 4

I told Jerry McKinney, reporter for the *Albuquerque Tribune,* what Blas Chávez had told me about the death of Salazar. Today we had another victory: Ted Martínez and Loraine Gutiérrez got elected to the Board of Education in Albuquerque. All the Anglo candidates lost. The Anglos have sent a spacecraft, the Viking, to Mars. This name reveals the pride the Anglo feels in considering themselves descendants of the ancient Vikings. They are going to try to land this craft on Mars on the 4th of July, 1976, to celebrate their 200th anniversary as a nation. This is how they will demonstrate to the world that the United States does not consider any other race to have any right or heritage. They only reserve that for themselves.

February 24

I told Reverend Harry Summers of the Council of Churches what Blas Chávez had said to me. I wanted them to know who the assassins of Eulogio Salazar were. That's the only way they could help me bring justice to New Mexico. Previously, on February 11, I had given all this information to Ralph Looney, head of the *Tribune,* but he didn't do anything. He preferred, like others, to cover up the crime with his silence. I was going to all these different people because I didn't want the grand jury to be in the hands of our enemies. For example, José Castianos was the Rio Arriba district attorney who disliked me immensely. He was a good friend of Senator Montoya. Similarly, the district attorney for the county of Bernalillio, Brandenburg, is also very committed to the local politicians. I did not know what to do. I had the truth in my hands, but the powerful men in the state would not allow me to give it to the public.

February 25

The world was shocked at the news of the death of my friend Elija Mohammed, head of the Nation of Islam. I felt sorrow because he was a good and loyal friend, a brother in the pursuit of justice for our oppressed people.

February 27

A delegation of twenty-four of us went to see Governor Apodaca. We presented him with a list of five points we wanted to discuss. One, the family. Two, an invitation to speak at our conference on April 5th. Three, prison reform and removal of Félix Rodríguez as warden. Four, evidence about the death of Salazar and a request to publish the police report. Five, an investigation over the land titles of San Joaquín. He accepted the agenda and promised to do what he could.

February 29

Doubleday offered to publish my memoirs. I began to write in English but stopped. English is not the language of my heart, and I cannot express myself as spontaneously and sincerely as I can in Castilian.

March 20

The Bureau of Land Management made public today its intent to take the city hall in the county of Sandoval for a historical site. This site is where Coronado and his soldiers stayed in 1540. This decision has shaken the heart of my people in New Mexico. I asked the governor about this and another taking of a small community named Apodaca. I asked him, "Mr. Governor, how do you feel about the land issues?" He answered, "I feel the same as you do." On this same day, the *Tribune* stated that the United States government was willing to sell some lands in the county of Sandoval for $50 an acre. The idea was to give clear title to the property of the ancient city of Bernalillo. Isn't this the craziest thing you ever heard?

April 5

We held on Indian land the Fourth Annual Fraternity and Harmony Conference. The main speakers were Governor Apodaca and Wendell Chino, a Mescalero Apache. He was elected president of the Indian nations. Before he gave his speech, he signed his name to the Rock of Fraternity and Harmony. Governor Apodaca also signed the rock. Paul Bernal, the Indian representative from the Pueblo of Taos, was also in attendance. This was the first pueblo to get its land back, which had been stolen in 1906. He also had the participation of the secretary general of the Indian Pueblo Council. This last conference brought closer together the branches of the tree of the Indohispano and the Indians.

April 23

Today some of the valiant and courageous people from San Luis, Colorado, came to see me: Ray Otero, Eugenio Sánchez, Rocky and Adolfo Lobato. They told me they were desperate and could not tolerate Jack Taylor anymore. This is the Anglo that stole their land, the Sangre de Cristo land grant. They wanted my support to begin a fight without quarter against this foreign Anglo. I told them to get ready and to be strong.

June 25

Joe L. Martínez was elected judge of the New Mexico Supreme Court, but he has shamed our people. I did not know who Martínez was when I recommended him. Blas, during the time that we were in prison together, told me the history about Martínez that made me hate him. Martínez in effect belonged to the gang surrounding Senator Montoya. When Blas fled on April 23, 1970, Martínez hid him on his ranch in Mexico. Blas did not know that Senator Montoya was the one who wanted him sentenced to fifty years in prison. Martínez, now on the highest judicial throne in 1973, reviewed my appeal and affirmed my fifteen-year sentence. Joe L. Martínez could have rejected this sentence imposed by Judge Burks in 1970. This was something within his power. And Martínez knew full well that I was innocent. Martínez resigned on June 5th of this year from the Supreme Court, knowing that the Ethics Commission of the state would embarrass him.

June 28

U.S. Representative Paul McClosky from Washington met with us today at the Hotel Marina. Blas gave him all the information he needed. I told him what I knew. And Bob Gaugelet presented his information.

June 29

My neighbors told me that they have impeded strange people from harming me on several occasions. Mr. and Mrs. Lark live behind me and have a nightlight on. This nightlight has been destroyed several times, and the Larks keep replacing it; perhaps, they have helped me avoid death. They have told me how they have discovered shell casings, cigarette butts, and lots of footprints in their yard, next to a large tree facing my apartment. Surely these assassins have waited for an opportunity to commit their criminal act.

July 31

Rosita, Raquel, and Lita, my older daughters, accompanied me to Juárez, Chihuahua. I went there for a series of interviews with Bruno Rey, a Mexican actor. He informed me that Jaime Casillas had written a script about several episodes in my life. He also told me that Jaime Hernández would play me in the movie. The movie would be called "Chicano." I didn't like the name much, but I didn't protest. A lot of my people don't want to identify themselves with that name. They feel distant or are made to feel distant from Mexico. But I don't believe that these differences will last more than ten years. Mexico and the Mexican people have recognized our rebellion against the White House through the Anglo press. Soon, our brothers in Mexico will know that our dreams are their dreams. We are the bones and Mexico is the spirit. And this is the hour for the bones and the spirit to join. My daughters and I returned to Albuquerque very happily. We were going to be the bridge to unite true Mexico with the abandoned Mexico.

August 3

The New York Times reveals that the CIA has a secret list of 1,500 organizations that it consider enemies of the United States. Frank Church ordered the CIA to destroy that list. But the CIA defied Congress and still maintains it. Reies Tijerina and the Alianza are included in the list.

August 4

I left with my family for Crystal City, Texas, to speak with José Angel Gutiérrez about the movie they were planning to make in Mexico called "Chicano." From there I left to Mexico and met with Jaime Fernández, Jaime Casillas, and Gregorio Casal. Later, I met with Rodolfo Echeverría, brother to the president of Mexico. At all of these stops, my children, wife, and I were received with great affection. For more than two weeks we discussed and elaborated on this film project, "Chicano." Even though my family, the Alianza, and I would never get one cent from the movie, I was convinced that this film would probably help relations between the people in Mexico and those Mexicans abandoned in the United States. Later, they would make a movie based on my personal biography. This I had decided, and this I will do. The trip left me very happy. I saw a new attitude in Mexico, different from the one in 1964, when I was deported because of the White House reports sent to the attorney general in Mexico. I felt that the hour had arrived where the bones and spirit of Mexico would unite.

October 4 and days following

Today I left for San Antonio, Texas, the land where I was born. I went because Jaime Casillas, the director of the film "Chicano," had invited me to be present during some of the filming. We spent ten days in San Antonio, and then the film crew went to finish in Mexico. This time Wilfredo Sedillo and Eduardo Chávez accompanied me. Most of the filming in Mexico was done around the city of Texcoco. It was a great experience for us. Rosita, my daughter, came out in the film, but no one else.

October 13 and days following

Today I was surprised to learn that Robert Gilliland died. "Gavilán," the name that he had used in court, had said under oath that he hated me and would like to kill me. Now, at age forty, he was dead.

Supposedly, two men got into a fight at his bar, and he killed them both. And, shortly after, within five minutes of this homicide, he died of a heart attack.

On October 17, I gave copies of Gavilán's report on William Fellion to the general managers of television channels 4 and 7, but they were not interested. I also passed out copies to some people, including the state police.

The worst of it was that the FBI knew about Fellion and his criminal activities against the Alianza and me. The FBI had given all this information to Gilliland. Gilliland even provided the FBI file number on Fellion, 3447790, in his report. Yet, the FBI never moved a finger to stop Fellion's criminal activity. The FBI probably remained above the fray until October 23, 1966, when we took Echo Amphitheater Park. The three local FBI heads of Santa Fe, Albuquerque, and Los Alamos met with Martín Vigil, then commander of District 11, New Mexico State Police, and began to confer and report on the events.

During these days, Wilfredo and Eduardo took charge of more duties of the organization. People began to complain that I was ignoring them. But I was preoccupied with the capture of Salazar's assassins.

On October 21, I traveled to Mexico with Wilfredo and Eduardo to consult with the makers of the film "Chicano." Rosita had been in Mexico since October 10. I took advantage of this invitation to go and also meet with the Mexican president about another automobile caravan from the United States into Mexico. While at the filming, I made time to prepare a memorandum for the president of Mexico. He received us on October 28.

We were with him from 7 p.m. to 1 a.m. This reception was unlike any we had received in 130 years. That night I felt we had the support, affection, and warmth of the Mexican people. We were not alone as we had been for 130 years. A new era was born for the abandoned people.

I asked the president for three things: 1) To establish at the executive level an Office on Chicano or Indohispano Affairs, 2) To commission a study on the land grants and their titles and give us a legal opinion about our rights as claimants, and 3) To tell us if our proposed automobile caravan from the United States into Mexico would affect U.S.-Mexico relations. The president told us that night all three items were viable.

That night, Dr. Jorge Bustamante told me that the Mexican presidential candidate would be in Juarez, Chihuahua, on November 15, and he would meet with Chicano delegations.

On November 15, José Angel Gutiérrez and I and other Indohispano leaders met with José López Portillo. I told him briefly about our people's condition in the United States and asked him if he would continue President Echeverría's politics toward us. I was very gratified with his answer.

I returned home on the October 16 and called Richard Bowman the next day. He told me that Fellion had said that powerful politicians had asked him to bomb my home and office. That bombing took place on April 25, 1968, and he blew off his hand in doing so.

I wrote to President Ford again on November 24 and got my return receipt for delivery on the 28th. I never got a reply. I wanted to see if after Watergate, the arrogant "Vikings" of the White House had changed. Ford was the same as Nixon.

December 26

I received Mexico's report on the land titles. Dr. Sergio García Ramírez, assistant secretary to the attorney general, did the study and he personally sent it to me. The report is favorable to our claims. The Mexican report has lifted the spirit of our people. The year, 1975, has ended on a favorable note.

Chapter 6
1976

I closed 1975 by writing an outline of the conditions in which the world found itself. Then, I made a general outline of my struggle and the condition of our movement, particularly the conditions of our property, our family, our homes, and our true liberty that the Anglo took away from us since the day he signed the Treaty of Guadalupe Hidalgo. After I reviewed this outline, I felt we were in an excellent position. I felt great pride in realizing that not only our elders, but also our first-graders, had a new consciousness, a consciousness that did not exist in 1956 when I began my struggle. My community had the courage and honor it had not had in twenty years. Our oppressors had lost their prestige and we had gained it. Our cause of land recovery was ready to be litigated in court or in the street. We had great influence and we were ready. There was only one stickpin in our body politic that had to be removed. That needle was finding the assassins of Eulogio Salazar. Before the end of 1975, I had decided to start 1976 with a thirty-day fast.

While millions of whistles and horns sounded in Albuquerque, I dedicated my fast to the Just Judge of Judges. My life had enjoyed great honor, that of representing and struggling for the legitimate rights of our people. I only asked for one thing of the Judge of Judges: to help me find Salazar's assassins. Doing justice in this regard, my community would be free of any blood tinge of Salazar. And the guilty would be punished, as the law demands.

January 1

I began writing my history of struggle against the White House today. Richard Bowman called and said that the *El Paso Times,* in a series of articles, would cover the history of Eulogio Salazar. I decided to write about twenty years of my struggle, from 1956 to 1976. I would limit myself to talking about the struggle for the land, the land that belonged to my people since the signing of Treaty of Tordecillas on June 7, 1494. If I wrote about my struggle against the church, I wouldn't finish by 1976. I'd have to add ten more years, and I wanted to finish this work by 1976. I will reach the age fifty in September 1976.

January 4

My father died today at the age of eighty-four years and four months. He died in Wichita Falls, Texas.

January 20–31

In this month of fasting, my mind and spirit helped me reflect and meditate on the justice and true liberty that I seek for my brothers. During this time I reviewed the history of my people, the injustice and the theft of our land; the clash of our cultures; the Anglos' mentality; the destructive direction that the U.S. is taking, its sexual liberties and use of drugs; and family disintegration. The Anglos, through the various corporations they control, had put the entire nation in danger. Given the conditions we find ourselves in, we must choose the road most convenient to us so that we do not perish along with the Anglos. We must think about ourselves. This is a very critical hour. We should not pay for the crimes of the Anglos in the United States. It is time for us to chart our own course and mark our own time. We must totally repudiate the mentality and lifestyle of our oppressors. The Anglo has used his best tactics and secret agents to destroy the spirit of our people's movement. He tries to take our courage away and make us forget the significance of our victories in New Mexico: June 5, October 2, and June 8. He made a maximum effort to break up my family, to make me pay for Salazar's blood, to poison the blood of my brothers so that they would hate me, but he failed in all of that. The spirit of courage and justice is still firmly growing in my community.

I offered my fast of thirty days for this great victory against the government and its agents. During the fast, I lost forty pounds, but my health is in good condition. Every day, during the fast, many of my supporters came to see me from the north, south, east, and west. I had fasted up to eleven days before, but I never had done thirty. During my fast, I only drank water. Just before I finished my fast, Felipe Santianes suggested we all gather and celebrate the last day of my fast. And on January 31, in front of all my supporters, I had my first meal, chicken soup.

February 4

I got a call from Kingsville, Texas. Dr. José Reyna invited me to go speak at the university. I accepted because I wanted to know this place. This was land that Richard King stole from my grandparents on my mother's side through violence and terror.

February 6

Today, Blas Chávez authorized me to write in my autobiography everything he had told me regarding the death of Salazar and his assassins. I thanked him.

February 12

David Salmón called me to tell me that he had changed his mind about investigating Salazar's death. I understood that to mean that he had been intimidated. On the eleventh, I again went to the legislature and this time met with Senator D. J. Michaelson, who seemed very enthused about the idea. He made me great promises in front of others that were with me. The next day he called me and said, "I can't, because there is a lot of opposition." Now my supporters and I realize that the conspiracy to cover up this death has grown much larger.

February 16

Today, my sister Josefa got a phone call telling her that if I did not stop my probing into Salazar's death, I would be eliminated. My sister called Margarito, my brother. She thought that I would not believe her, but I do believe them. That's why I had my daughter Isabel taken out of school.

I began to think about taking my family to Mexico to educate them there, but I didn't have any money to live in Mexico. Patricia, recognizing how the people and government of Mexico now appreciated me, said, "Why don't you speak to the president of Mexico and tell him our situation? Maybe it's possible that they could give us a home and some money to live while this danger passes."

February 21

My family and I left for Mexico under the cover of darkness so none of my enemies would detain us. We got as far as San Juan del Río, where I have good friends. One of them, Don Pepe Trejo, had an empty house available. He offered it to me for my family without accepting a penny for rent. I stayed there with my family for two months. Here in San Juan del Río, Querétaro, I feel very secure and safe with my family, except from the CIA.

I've gone to Mexico City by myself after putting Isabel and Carlitos in the public schools of San Juan del Río. In Mexico City, with the assistance of Gregorio Casal and José Antonio Alvarez and his wife Verónica, I was able to get the Fondo de Cultura Económica interested in the history of my twenty years of struggle. Now, I really felt hopeful of being able to put my family out of danger. But this was my true desire: to educate my kids in Mexico and at the same time, take them out of danger.

March 8

I met with the president of Mexico at Los Pinos to confirm the last details of the international caravan scheduled for June 5. Armonía, my daughter, was four today. The president took her in his arms and gave her a kiss. The next day, we returned to San Juan del Río and then returned to the United States. We were making final preparations for the caravan.

The White House has ignored us for more than twenty years. I've sent letters to five presidents, and none of them has ever answered me. I've written to Eisenhower, Kennedy, Johnson, Nixon, and Ford, and not one of them has given me the attention that a citizen of the United States deserves. During these twenty years, we have also knocked on the doors of Congress in the United States and on their courts and at the White House, without getting a single response. And what we asked for is little: that the White House investigate the title to the land of San Joaquín. By ignoring us, they made me think of knocking at the door of Mexico. It is our last hope before we lose patience. We know it is a delicate situation, but the United States has not left any other door open to us. The arrogance of the White House obligates us to ask Mexico for the justice that the United States owes us since 1848.

New Mexico and Texas have the most interest for our caravan. In Texas, Conrado González and Cecilio García are representing those who will join the caravan delegation. From Denver, Colorado, Jesús Gonzales and I are coordinating the general plan for this caravan.

March 22

I spoke at Texas A & I in Kingsville. The audience was very attentive to what I had to say about Texas. They were very interested in my analysis of property rights. There were people there from Corpus Christi, Brownsville, San Antonio, Laredo, and many smaller communities. While in Kingsville, I was asked to speak on the radio. The radio station was owned by "Pirate" King or one of his heirs. In San Antonio, I stopped and spoke to the committee making final plans for the caravan. I also spoke to the Mexican consulate about the purpose of this caravan, and he treated us very well.

March 24

In Albuquerque, the CIA and the FBI are beside themselves, given the rumors surrounding the caravan. An FBI official, Sam Jones, called me to ask for details about the caravan. I got very irritated. I reminded him that he had detained me once in 1964 and that they would not be able to do this again. He lied to me. When I asked him where he was from, he gave me the name of another state. But his Anglo friends told me he was from here. In other words, he was educated in New Mexico. The FBI knows a lot about the death of Salazar. When I had gone to the legislature on February 2, I stopped at the state parole board to talk to the director, Santos Quintana. I told him what I had heard and what I had gone to do at Santa Fe. He told me that another FBI agent named Wirt Jones had already told him and Frank García that, "In those days we cleared up the cause of Salazar's death." But Santos said, "We kept waiting for more explanation, but there was none." To this day, agent Wirt Jones has not explained anything about what he said to Santos Quintana. I firmly believe that the CIA and the FBI have assisted in covering up those responsible for the death of Salazar.

May 8

We celebrated the fifth annual conference of Fraternity and Harmony. As in the past, it was televised live by Channel 4. Everyone could see the events on television (Channel 4 covers the whole state) and could see that the politicians were not present. I wasn't involved in the preparation of this conference because I was very busy getting the support necessary from Mexico for our caravan. I had a surprise planned for this fifth conference: a resolution demanding that Governor Apodaca release the police report on the death of Salazar. This was my last hope at committing the governor to going public with the report. I did not think that Richard Bowman's reporting on this issue would be published by the *El Paso Times*. Every year I was given fifteen minutes at the beginning of this conference to explain the purpose of Fraternity and Harmony. It was during these fifteen minutes that I dropped this surprise bomb. The press and politicians were not expecting it. After I talked about the customary and usual things, I declared that I was still being blamed for Salazar's death and many people doubted my sincerity. The *Albuquerque Journal* had affirmed on its editorial page on January 6, 1968, that there was no doubt that I was involved directly or indirectly in his death. I thought this conference had the solemn obligation to remove the tinge that blocks the progress of harmony between all individuals. So, I proposed that the conference ask the governor of New Mexico to release the police report on the death of Salazar. In lieu of that, it should convene a grand jury to listen to the evidence the people had about this death. Immediately, Don Schrader, a friend of the oppressed, seconded my resolution, or rather, he repeated my resolution saying that he proposed that the assembly adopt this resolution. Randy Baca, a courageous woman, seconded the motion. Everyone, except four people, voted for the resolution. Later that afternoon, Jerry Dansinger, general manager of Channel 4, gave me a copy of this televised moment for my archives. I still keep this tape and save it carefully as evidence against my implication in this death and to discover the assassins used by the CIA.

The powerful Anglos in the state were perplexed about what to do now that I had committed them in this fashion. The *Albuquerque Journal* editorialized, "The *Journal* believes that the police report ought to be made public and also that a grand jury should be impaneled to investigate this death." But the *Journal* did not think our conference was the place to demand such an investigation. What the *Journal* did not say was that Tijerina had been fighting for eight years to break open this conspiracy protecting Salazar's assassin. The *Journal* also did not mention that Edward Schwartz, editor of *The New Mexico Review,* had revealed the names of those assassins in October 31, 1969. The *Journal,* instead of cooperating or informing the public, suppressed the information revealed by *The New Mexico Review,* keeping all of us ignorant. I also have asked the *Journal* for an apology to the false accusation it made against the Alianza and me on January 6, 1968.

May 11

I sent Governor Apodaca the resolution passed regarding Salazar's death at the conference on Fraternity and Harmony. The entire community was anxiously waiting to see what Apodaca would do. The *Journal* published three editorials asking for an investigation into this death.

May 24

The principal news these days is about the tactics used by the FBI and the CIA to destroy Black, Native American, and Indohispano leadership. The many confessions of the agents were publicized. The great

Judge of Judges is opening up the secret criminal books of the government agencies. I am learning a lot.

May 25

Today I sent an open letter to President Ford about our caravan that leaves on June 5 and why we are doing it. As usual, we did not expect the White House to respond, but we did want the whole world to know why we were going to Mexico.

June 1

The New York Times called, asking for information about the caravan. Ed Berry sent a registered letter to Max Sánchez urging him to confess his criminal participation in the death of Eulogio Salazar. He also asked him to tell how much money was paid to William Fellion to kill Eulogio. This letter filled Max Sánchez with terror. I have a copy of this letter.

June 5

Today, our caravan left for Juárez. We crossed the border at five in the afternoon. We presented Arturo Castellanos Lira, a municipal leader, with a gift as a gesture of our love toward our Mexican brothers. The gift was a mural painted by Manual Martínez of Taos, New Mexico, approximately twenty meters by two and a half. The mural represents the Mestizo people. The central figure in the mural has his arms outstretched, reaching for harmony and fraternity between the east and the west. This painting is more than a gift. It captures the tears, blood, and sweat we have shed since February 2, 1848, under the yoke of the "Viking" Anglos who took everything away from us. It was our hope that this mural would be a living reminder of the Mexicanos that are living north of the Rio Grande (Indohispanos, Chicanos, and Mestizos).

June 12

The president of Mexico received our eighty-six delegates at the presidential residence, Los Pinos. The attorney general, Pedro Ojeda Paullada, was with the president. During our presentation, we talked about the protections we felt we deserved under the Treaty of Guadalupe Hidalgo. The president ordered the attorney general to conduct a study on the issues presented. In summary, what my brothers and I asked the president was for Mexico to take our complaints to the United Nations. This treaty was an international one, between the United States and Mexico, and jurisdiction applied in that forum. In 130 years since the United States signed the treaty, it has not done justice and has violated our human rights. That's why it was natural that we would come to Mexico and ask this country to present our case before the United Nations and to form a special international commission to investigate our complaints. Attorney General Ojeda Paullada made an appointment with me that very night. We gave the president another mural, also painted by Manual Martínez. This one had a Mestizo with his arms held high. In one hand was the Mexican flag and in the other, the United States flag. "This painting," I told the president, "speaks eloquently about the condition in which we find ourselves in the United States." That same night the mural we had presented in Juárez arrived at Los Pinos. I explained the significance and meaning of that mural.

June 27

The *El Paso Times,* twice the size of *The Albuquerque Journal,* began publishing Richard Bowman's articles, seven of them, on the death of Eulogio Salazar. I wanted to be in Albuquerque, but found myself assisting several Mexican officials with the presidential investigation into our cause.

July 9

We met with the president again at Los Pinos. Pedro Ojeda Paullada explained why the land in Texas was off limits to Mexico. Supposedly, Mexico and the United States had signed a treaty on September 8, 1923, covering the land grants in that state, 433 of them. Because of this, Mexico could not open new discussions about these properties. Upon listening to this explanation, the president interrupted and said, "I plan to discuss this with the president of the United States, because taking it to the United Nations could result in delay and possibly even losing the request." He began talking about trying to solve our problem by tying it to discussions that were coming in the near future about the salinity of the Colorado River. He asked me to stay another week to work with the attorney general on the content of these negotiations and to prepare a textual narrative about the issues. I accepted. But in light of pressing demands in New Mexico, I came back to the United States. Frederico Abeyta and Wilfredo Sedillo stayed on at the Hotel Guadalupe.

I called a press conference to praise the seven articles published in the *El Paso Times* between June 27 and July 3. I asked the reporters to help me by continuing to publicize the demand made to Governor Apodaca to convene a grand jury and investigate the death of Salazar. I liked the *El Paso Times* reports. They mentioned the names of the most suspicious people: Emilio Naranjo, Max Sánchez, William Fellion, Senator José Montoya, Robert Gilliland, Carlos Jaramillo, and Freddie Martínez, among others. At the end of the series on July 11, the *El Paso Times* published a cartoon. The cartoon featured a can with worms that were coming out. It was labeled "Salazar's Assassination." A hand was trying to place a lid on the can. Pointing to the hand was a sign that said "State Officials." The problem with this series was that the people in New Mexico were not aware of it. It was published in El Paso and not reproduced in the *Albuquerque Journal,* as had been requested by Richard Bowman. The Associated Press had promised Bowman to send copies of his articles over the teletype to various dailies around the country, including the *Journal,* but none of them picked it up. The press, the supposed defender of free speech, suppressed this information.

July 12

Nine of our major supporters and I went to confront Bob Brown of the *Journal* about why it had not published the series from the *El Paso Times*. Brown did not show his face. Instead, we met with Jerry Crofard, his assistant, who told us they would not publish anything they personally did not know. They were admitting that they already knew what the *El Paso Times* series said. They did not want the people to know. This is the reason they covered up this information and would never bring it out. In October 1969, the editor of *The New Mexico Review,* Edward Schwartz, had left all this information about the death of Salazar with the *Journal.* The Anglos continue to cover up Salazar's assassination. It is not convenient for them that I am free and clean of this murder. Because of this mutual reciprocity agreement between the Anglos, the CIA, the FBI, and the White House, they operate freely in New Mexico against me. They consider me the most dangerous man because I am establishing the relationship of the U. S. Southwest with Mexico and all of Latin America.

July 15

I returned to Mexico to meet with the president and finalize what we had started to work on. I stayed there till July 24. I got a call from radio KOB in New Mexico telling me that Governor Apodaca had just ordered Attorney General Toney Anaya to investigate the death of Eulogio Salazar and to convene a grand jury. The news made me jump with joy. For eight years I had been pressing for this investigation, and now we were beginning to get first fruit. I felt that my thirty-day fast had been heard by the Just Judge of Judges. I returned to New Mexico as fast as I could. Now, my preoccupation was with making sure that the investigation did not go off in the wrong direction. That's why I left Mexico somewhat carelessly, but I had left our business in good hands with Wilfredo Sedillo.

A delegation of twelve of us went and met with Toney Anaya, the attorney general. We discussed the history of the death of Salazar for an hour and fifteen minutes. I was most satisfied to see boxes of information regarding the death of Salazar there. Toney Anaya, after asking me my opinion, permitted the press to come into his office. He assured everyone that he would conduct this investigation with my cooperation and that I would be a central figure in this investigation. I had told Toney that I had many items of evidence that pointed to those to be accused. All of my information would be of vital importance to prove the case to the grand jury. This grand jury would not be influenced by the land interests or by politicians. Toney accepted and said that was reasonable.

July 30

Ed Berry called me to tell me he had received threats because he had helped me with the Salazar matter. He asked the governor for protection and obtained it.

August 4

Today, I was in the Santo Domingo Pueblo, the principal Pueblo of nineteen Native American groups. Valentino García, the governor, invited me to break bread. The governor and I concluded that we had to fight together for our lands and to recapture the honor that the Anglo had taken from us.

Chapter 7
The CIA

The White House holds the land that I seek for my people. The power that sent me to prison was the CIA, acting as intermediary for the White House. I did not fully understand the words that U.S. Senator Joseph Montoya had uttered on December 29, 1967 (four days prior to Eulogio Salazar's murder). I did not know that the CIA was involved.

I went to Texas to visit with people about the 433 land grants that demand justice. Our people in Texas were victims of deals between the United States and Mexico made in 1941. Today, we expect Mexico to help us obtain the justice we have sought for 130 years.

José Angel Gutiérrez called me to invite me to San Antonio and meet with the Mexican president. I met with Texas claimants to discuss the substance of our talks with the Mexican president over the U.S.-Mexico treaty of September 8, 1923. This treaty has prohibited our people from having their cases heard by courts in the United States. We met with the Mexican president at the San Antonio Hilton on September 8, 1976. I showed President Echeverría the terms of the treaty of 1923. He assigned José Gallastegui to meet with me and find a solution to the problem that I posed. He asked me to come to Mexico, but I could not. I had other commitments in New Mexico, and I was going to turn fifty years of age. I wanted to celebrate my birthday with my warriors who had been in the struggle with me for years.

During the trip to San Antonio, I took my family to Laredo. I searched archival records on my family. I found out that my grandfather, Santiago Tijerina, was tried seventeen times in eighteen years, and he won fifteen of those cases. His first trial was had in 1886 and the last one in 1903. I brought back photocopies of the seventeen trials. We went from there to Candela in the state of Coahuila, Mexico. My great-grandfather was born in this community. My father's cousin, Andrea Tijerina Cantú, told me the family history. She claimed, along with professor Israel Cavazos Garza, director of the state archive in Nuevo León, Mexico, that my great-great-grandparents came from Portugal in 1583 to Monterrey and then moved to Candela in 1690, when the city was founded.

On September 17, the U.S. Congress established commissions to investigate the assassinations of Dr. Martin Luther King and President John F. Kennedy. The CIA and the FBI (I have no doubt) ordered these assassinations. People never believed the Warren Commission's report on Kennedy. I don't doubt that the same forces that killed King and Kennedy also killed Eulogio Salazar. The CIA and FBI have strong contacts in New Mexico, and they are owed a lot of debts. These debts have been paid with Salazar's blood. People would not have believed this twenty years ago, but now with Senator Church's committee investigating the CIA and FBI, the truth about these agencies has been revealed.

The people must stay informed on these revelations and maintain vigilance on the criminal activity of these agencies. They represent Anglo interests and nothing else. The CIA does not represent the Indohispano and is not concerned with the theft of our lands. The CIA is more powerful than the president, Congress, and the Supreme Court. Their annual budget is $10 billion. And they are not accountable to anyone. As criminal as the CIA is, the church and the Anglo press approve of all the CIA has done. That is why the press, local and national, have never been just or legal toward our movement. They have never quoted me accurately, always twisted and changed my words to make me appear like a psychopath before my people and the world.

This law of the jungle we have endured for 130 years will be the same one they will be subjected to shortly. And they should not complain. They planted the seed: "The only good Indian is a dead Indian." They continue to this day with the making of atomic bombs to impose their will on the world. "Accept our rule or we will destroy the world." Normal people should prepare, work with one another in fraternal harmony to dispose of this psychopathic giant, and place him where he can never harm humanity. I have come to know this giant up close. I know his evil ways and crimes. I have struggled against him and his army, judges, bankers, politicians, senators, police, super-secret agencies, presidents, and Supreme Court chief justice. In short, I have fought against the entire power of the White House.

The giant is now alone. His children have left him. Women have taken his place. Sex and drugs have him unbalanced. He doesn't look out for himself, how can he look out for humanity?

The White House has had me tied down for eight years. Since June 1969, I have been in prison, I have not been freed completely. I am only free on parole, but they watch my every move, hoping I make a mistake. Now that Governor Apodaca has ordered an investigation into the death of Salazar, my enemies are breathing fire. For the past twenty years, Anglo power has sought to paralyze me, but it has failed. As I finish this work of reflection on my life of struggle for twenty years, I feel strong and sure. My people are ready. They are not the same timid and cowardly people I met when I first met them. There are few brave ones, but the few are the ones that make the struggle. The majority just follows the brave ones. The movement is on from Texas to California, with New Mexico as the axis.

As you read this book, do not forget that I never had an education. I was not educated in any Anglo school or college. I learned at home. My greatest education came in the struggle against injustice that the Anglo perpetrated against my people. The Anglo tried to destroy me at first, but I prevailed because the Supreme Just Judge aided me. I am not a friend to those who profess a false Anglo God; they are the enemy of justice.

The land is my cause and justice is my ideology. The universal direction is toward justice and the Anglo knows this. That is why the White House is now defending Blacks in Africa against whites in Rhodesia and South Africa. Nixon began to change the public face of the White House not because he respected justice, but to save his skin from the apocalyptic judgment burning on the White House.

I dedicate part of this story to my warriors in New Mexico, Texas, California, Arizona, Colorado, Utah, and Nevada. Also to the warriors in Mexico who helped me when I first began in 1956 and later when I was a fugitive. A person who helped me a great deal was Lolita Ortiz de Rebeles from Tacuba, Mexico. Another was Santana Vergara, who is deceased, but his children live, and one of them, Francisca Vegara, accompanied me to Los Pinos when my family and I met with the president on April 8, 1976. My family has been a source of pride and inspiration. Because of them and my love for them, I began to comprehend the value of the family in society. My children honor me by following me and suffering on the road I chose to take. In the most difficult and dangerous of times, they have been at my side. In my twenty years of struggle, my daughters have been with me. I leave them this manuscript that I have written with my own hand.

These pages do not signify the end of my struggle; they are just a few chapters. I wrote them because our people and the world need to have the truth about the Indohispano. The Anglo has always hidden this truth for many years. After this book, I plan to go on with another chapter in my life. I plan to unite all my brothers under a fraternal agenda to survive the fall of the Anglo. Since the Anglo has never included us in his "America," we should come together so he will not use us for his ambitious plans, as he has in the past.

In my struggle I have discovered many enemies. I want my brothers to watch out for these enemies. In order of importance they are:

1. The White House
2. The press and publicity organs in the United States dominated by Anglos and their allies
3. The judges and the judicial process in the United States
4. The educational system
5. The film industry
6. Local and national police and the secret government agencies
7. Anglo religion and its politics
8. Corporations and the bank industry and labor

The press, in particular, has done me wrong. It has lied and fooled my people about their rights. It has never told my people the truth about their property rights.

When another group oppresses a people, the oppressor recruits a member of the oppressed group to help perpetrate its wrongdoing. In the Southwest, against my people and me, the White House has used U.S. Senator Joseph Montoya. The Anglos hide behind Montoya. He told the press, "Tijerina is fooling and stealing from the people. And I came to Washington and stopped him." (*Albuquerque Journal,* October 6, 1976). And I responded, "Despite the bombings of my home, the National Guard troops, the five fake trials, the terror used for intimidation, and the abuse of my family, I have not been stopped."

On the contrary, textbooks have been written about our history of struggle. More than thirty-five books written by Anglos tell about our land recovery movement. The first film on our struggle, produced in Mexico, was premiered in San Antonio, Texas, on September 6. My family, a few warriors, and I went to see it.

The White House, with Montoya's assistance, is negotiating our land claims on behalf of a few traitors to our cause. For twenty years they have pretended I do not exist, and now they want to negotiate with those that do not know their rights. Those people will settle for crumbs. That will neither satisfy the letter of the law nor the spirit of justice. My people should not sell their rights to the White House.

Senator Montoya was interviewed on October 4 by Jim Wilkerson on Channel 4 television. He asked Montoya, "Why are you against the land recovery movement?" Montoya said, "I am not against the land recovery movement. I am against Reies López Tijerina because he is a racist and wants to pit the Anglo against my people. Reies is not from here . . . he is not one of us. He is stealing money from the people to enrich himself, and I came to Washington and stopped him." This is where Montoya tripped up. He said, "I . . . stopped him." Everyone realized he was involved in the crimes to have me "stopped."

Montoya was running for reelection after serving twelve years in the U.S. Senate. I was quiet during his campaign until I heard his words. I gathered my warriors and decided to call a press conference to announce our support for his opponent, Jack Harrison Schmitt. We did what I had always warned my people not to do, and that is to help an Anglo over an Indohispano.

I left for Mexico City on October 15 to meet with Mexican Deputy Secretary of State José Gallastegui on the lands lost in Texas. A ten-person delegation accompanied me, and we presented our claims for land in Texas to him. I felt good about this meeting. It was the first time we had actually made a claim and been listened to.

On the return trip, I stopped in Monterrey and visited professor Israel Cavazos Garza. He introduced me to the archival records for the state of Nuevo León and the municipal records. He showed me a document that indicated that José Gregorio Fernández de Tijerina, a relative of mine, was mayor of Monterrey in 1771.

From there I came to the University of Texas at Austin, and Glen Garvin with the *Austin American Statesman* asked me why I was supporting an Anglo over Montoya. I told him that Montoya was working to destroy our movement. I made mention of all the crimes committed against us and how Montoya never spoke up about these atrocities. On the contrary, he was part of the coverup. I mentioned the assassination of Eulogio Salazar, committed to destroy my reputation. Alvino Mendoza, a warrior that had been with me for twenty-six years, said, "Reies, you are still courageous and have not lost your spirit. It does not appear that they have dampened your spirits."

Upon my return to Albuquerque, I read the headline in the *Journal:* "Schmitt praises Tijerina's support." I told my supporters of a dream I had while in Mexico. I always have superdreams that foretell events to come. I dreamt that Governor Apodaca was hugging people and crying. He had red, bloodshot eyes and said to me, "Has Montoya called you? He is broken into pieces. He is in complete shock." I had written the details of this dream in my diary on October 22. I never imagined that this dream forecast Montoya's electoral defeat on November 2.

Schmitt called me before the election. I told him we did not want anything from him except for him to respect the Constitutions of the United States and New Mexico in reference to the Treaty of Guadalupe Hidalgo, our property and culture. I told him that the White House had ignored us for twenty years and that Montoya had resisted our efforts for the last twelve years. I also told him we had never broken the law. On the contrary, the White House, Montoya, and the press had accused us falsely. He told me he would do all he could.

By telephone we organized our campaign against Montoya. We called each of the pueblos in New Mexico, Las Cruces, Socorro, Belen,

Cuesta, Taos, Santa Fe, Tucumcari, Santa Rosa, Chilili, San Mateo, Seboyeta, and Atrisco. In Albuquerque, we called the 1,500 members and asked that they contact their relatives and friends to oppose Montoya. In the last days of the election, Ford and Carter, like Montoya and Schmitt, promised the impossible. They talked about power, money, jobs, and education. Not one of them talked about the family or values. Nobody talked about justice and human rights.

On November 2, Ford lost the election but won in New Mexico by 8,000 votes. I was not surprised. I was surprised, however, that Montoya lost by 58,000 votes to Schmitt. I was perplexed but happy in my heart. KOB radio, with 50,000 watts of power, called me for an interview. People called me from everywhere with congratulations. The Indohispano Judas had fallen. My dream of ten days past had come true. The people of the Southwest shall overcome.

Radio KOB commented, " Montoya claimed to have stopped Tijerina, but it looks like Tijerina has stopped Montoya."

೨ ೨ ೨

I am not happy with the state and condition of our people. In northern New Mexico, about eighty percent of the population is Indohispano and forty percent are unemployed. My people are given food stamps to survive on. Preference to immigrate to the United States is given to Europeans. My people are upset at this cold and unjust treatment. Things are worse now than when Alonzo S. Perales wrote his book *Are We Good Neighbors?* in 1948. Perales humbled himself before the Anglos, and how did they repay him? If he wrote what he did in his book, who can blame me for what I write in this one?

Racism and discrimination have been the object of international conferences seeking to end the practices. President Miguel Alemán of Mexico presided over one conference in 1943. Then, conferences on the subject were held in Chapultepec, San Francisco, and finally, at the United Nations. Mexico's *Tiempo* magazine published the statements of the Mexican attorney general, Héctor Pérez Martínez, denouncing the atrocities committed against Mexicans in the United States. When the U.S. Congress investigated these allegations, New Mexican U.S. Senator Dennis Chávez said, "In time of war we are all called 'Americans.' On election day, we are called Mexican Americans, but when we look for work, we are simply called Mexicans, and in an offensive tone."

At the conclusion of the U.S. defeat in Vietnam, Ford said, "We are a nation of immigrants." He said that because he was going to allow immigration from Southeast Asia, even though twenty percent unemployment was the reality in the U.S. at the time. An immigrant is like a dog without a home. The dog will be grateful for anything it receives. An immigrant does not criticize the government. The immigrant does not have the values and moral conviction an indigenous person has. The U.S. is a nation of immigrants, European immigrants. The Anglo claims we are all immigrants because the Native Americans migrated to the U.S from the East and the Spanish came from Europe. The truth is we are the products of that union, of that meeting of east and west, here in the Americas. We are from here. We are native and indigenous to the Americas. The native people should have more rights than the foreigners.

My advice is that if the Anglo continues to disrespect our rights and demands we respect his, then we should choose between two options:

1. Continue to live as slaves under the Anglo or
2. Fight to gain independence from him.

For more than 130 years, our parents have sacrificed to live in peace with the Anglo. But the Anglo is ungrateful. We have fought in his wars, have accepted his culture (in violation of the Treaty of Guadalupe Hidalgo) and have endured his injustices covered up by his history. And still he treats us as his enemy. I have tried to reason with the White House and be peaceful in our protests. But we have been ignored. An innocent person was murdered so that they could ruin my reputation.

Our oppressors know full well that the power of the Native American and the Indohispano lies in the land. That is why the White House and CIA targeted the Alianza and me for destruction. I have had to defend myself against their raw and crude hatred with my own ire and rage. They have converted me into a giant seeking justice with ire and vengeance. I will not cease until I finish my mission. They have made a mockery of the law, my people, and my family, but they will regret this.